BRIDGING THE GENDER GAP
Seven Principles for Achieving Gender Balance

LYNN ROSEBERRY AND JOHAN ROOS

OXFORD
UNIVERSITY PRESS

2014

UNIVERSITY PRESS

Great Clarendon Street, Oxford, OX2 6DP,
United Kingdom

Oxford University Press is a department of the University of Oxford.
It furthers the University's objective of excellence in research, scholarship,
and education by publishing worldwide. Oxford is a registered trade mark of
Oxford University Press in the UK and in certain other countries

© Lynn Roseberry and Johan Roos 2014

The moral rights of the authors have been asserted

First Edition published in 2014

Impression: 1

Published in the United States of America by Oxford University Press
198 Madison Avenue, New York, NY 10016, United States of America

British Library Cataloguing in Publication Data
Data available

Library of Congress Control Number: 2014931558

ISBN 978-0-19-871711-9

Printed and bound by
CPI Group (UK) Ltd, Croydon, CR0 4YY

We dedicate this book to our children,
Caroline and Christina & August and Quintus,
our most important contributions to a gender-balanced future.

PREFACE

In this book we describe and illustrate how the continuing gap between men and women in leadership and persistent occupational segregation are due in large part to a number of assumptions that people in their different roles as parents, educators, and leaders hold on to. We explain how these assumptions have developed and why it is time to challenge them as well as outline principles that will help all of us develop new perspectives and act differently. The book is structured around seven stories commonly told about men, women, and work, and each ends with a corresponding guiding principle to encourage action.

We generated the seven stories and principles from many interviews, conversations, and engagement in debates at conferences and in executive education. We served as participant observers in dialogues with a few individuals and discussions among many people in both our own and other organizations. We conducted many semi-structured interviews with corporate executives, middle managers, HR managers, and diversity and inclusion managers at ten different organizations. We kept notes of the countless informal conversations we had with colleagues and acquaintances in our own and other institutions about the subjects in this book during the year and a half in which we worked on it. The seven main stories and corresponding guiding principles emerged from so-called first- and second-order interpretations of these data.

We related the stories we developed to literature in relevant academic disciplines as well as to practitioners in executive education and to consultants. In turn, this helped us develop the seven principles that we propose can be used by individuals to determine what might be preventing progress towards gender balance in their own organizations and what kinds of effective action might be taken to bring about change.

We have referred to some of the interviews in the chapters that follow, but have anonymized many of them by using pseudonyms for both the people and the organizations and changing some identifying details. Most of the interviews we conducted do not appear in the text but simply served to provide the data we needed to arrive at our conclusions.

We wish to express our sincere thanks to the many people in private and public organizations who generously shared their experience, views, frustrations, insights, and suggestions about how to close the gender gaps in leadership and occupations. Without their voluntary and generous participation, we could not have written this book.

We wish to acknowledge a number of other people who provided invaluable support in various forms during the process of writing this book. We wish to thank our respective institutions, Copenhagen Business School and Jönköping International Business School, for material and organizational support provided for this project, and Birgitte Moltke, Robyn Remke, Jette Steen Knudsen, and Andreas Philippopoulos-Mihalopoulos for their valuable feedback on portions of the draft manuscript.

We also wish to acknowledge Bonnie Casten and Charlotte Petersen who generously shared their experiences as consultants working to promote women in leadership and to Helene Ahl who let us try out some of the early ideas in her diverse class of HR students. They inspired us to keep our eyes on the practical problems.

Finally, we wish to extend special thanks to Rick Benzel, without whose help we would still be writing this book.

Despite all the help and support received in the course of writing this book, we have undoubtedly made some mistakes. For those we take full responsibility.

CONTENTS

NOTE ON ILLUSTRATIONS

Illustrations for Chapters 2 to 8 by the artist, Oscar van Stapelmohr, copyright © 2013 Lynn Roseberry and Johan Roos.

Introduction

This book is about why we see only a few token women in a sea of men in positions of power and leadership. When we were in the midst of writing this book, that question exploded into an international debate in the wake of an article in *The Atlantic*[1] by Princeton Professor Anne-Marie Slaughter. Under the title, 'Why Women Still Can't Have It All', Slaughter wrote about how difficult it still is for highly qualified women like herself to pursue their career dreams all the way to the top because of anachronistic work arrangements based on the centuries-old male-breadwinner model of the family. Facebook Chief Operating Officer Sheryl Sandberg's book *Lean In*[2] added more fuel to the fire by pointing out how women too often succumb to limiting beliefs about their own abilities and their 'right' to claim top jobs for themselves, and how they should rather and can internalize the revolution started by our feminist foremothers by 'leaning in'.

This book enters that debate with some answers to a slightly different question: *What do all of us—not just women pursuing high-powered careers, not just employers, and not just political leaders—need to do in order to bring about a more equal distribution of men and women in leadership and across occupations?*

We arrived at this question based on our own experiences as university academics and managers who have worked on bringing about a more

[1] Slaughter (2012).
[2] Sandberg (2013).

equal distribution of men and women in our own organizational hierarchies. During the course of our experience working in this area, we discovered that although many people say they are committed to sex equality and believe that men and women should be treated equally, when pressed to answer the question 'Why do we still see so few women in leadership positions if everyone endorses the concept of sex equality?', they offered explanations based on well-known gender stereotypes or the 'invisible hand' of the market. We were shocked to discover how little people knew about where their ideas about masculinity and femininity came from or why families continued to follow the male-breadwinner model even when both parents worked. We decided we needed to write a book to help us—and hopefully others—understand how to respond to these excuses for gender imbalances.

Where we started

Lynn is a female American academic lawyer, and Johan is a male Swedish business strategist and educator, with professional backgrounds in both the USA and Europe. The story about how we came to write this book together is an important part of the background for the chapters that follow. We'll each tell our own stories from our own perspectives. Lynn first.

I am an associate professor of law and politics at Copenhagen Business School (CBS), one of the largest business-oriented universities in Europe with 20,000 undergraduate and graduate students and a faculty and staff numbering over 1,200. I have taught a wide range of courses in employment law, legal theory, diversity management, and the relationship between business and human rights. Johan and I began working together when he became President of CBS and I became Head of CBS' Department of Law—both on 1 August 2009.

At that time, only 14% of the professors at CBS were women, the top leadership team consisted of four middle-aged white men (the President, two Deans, and the University Director), while at the next level down, only three of the 17 department heads were women, including me. The administrative staff were, and still are, overwhelmingly female, while most of their managers were men. The other universities in Denmark had about the same gender composition in their management teams and administrative staff.

I was surprised by the pronounced gender imbalance on the university faculties in Denmark given the fact that Denmark was supposed to be one of the most gender-equal countries in the world. The university faculties and top management teams are far less gender-integrated than in the USA where approximately 25% of university and college professors are female. Most women in Denmark work full time—even when they have children. New parents in Denmark get a total of about a year's leave from work with at least some pay. Mothers get 18 weeks of legally mandated maternity leave, fathers get two weeks, and then they can split 32 weeks. There is affordable public daycare for all children from the ages of about 12 months through pre-school and after-school programmes for children through grade 9.

By the time I became Head of the Department of Law and Johan arrived on the scene, I had long ago concluded that the reasons for gender imbalance in Danish universities were largely beyond the reach of employment discrimination law and traditional concepts of equal treatment. I had written my Ph.D. thesis about the limitations of sex discrimination law as a tool for achieving sex equality in employment in the European Union and the USA. I had read hundreds of court cases and scholarly articles on the subject and knew how difficult it is for judges, lawyers, managers, and employees to agree on what equal treatment of men and women is, and how little progress had been made since the first big influx of women into the European and North American labour markets in the 1970s and 1980s. Neither CBS nor other Danish universities are any exception to that discouraging fact. Since I came to CBS as a research assistant in 1994, the numbers of women in the top echelons of university faculties and administration had hardly changed in 20 years.

Having studied the difficulties of using anti-discrimination law to rectify gender inequality, I became convinced that the way forward requires getting managers in organizations to see gender as an issue worthy of their attention and to reconsider many of their most fundamental assumptions about differences between the sexes.

I began to hope that gender might finally come into focus at CBS when the Dean of Research formed a task force in the spring of 2009 to talk about what kinds of initiatives might help accelerate women's progress into the top ranks of the academic hierarchy. I soon discovered that the new President of CBS, Johan Roos, was more than ready to engage with this agenda at CBS.

Here is Johan's story in his own words.

I am currently professor of strategy as well as CEO and Dean of Jönköping International Business School, a young, private, business school, with a gender-balanced leadership team and student body in Sweden focusing on entrepreneurship, renewal, and ownership. Prior to this, I was President at CBS, as Lynn described. Before taking the Presidency at CBS, I had been a professor of business strategy at the best business schools in Norway, Switzerland, and Sweden, and also spent a few years at a top US business school. In those years, I observed first-hand how more and more young women fill the classrooms in higher education and now make up a majority of university graduates in the developed world. I saw how the number of female faculty grew much slower and how difficult it seemed for women to make careers in the highly competitive business of business schools.

As a business professor I've consulted for CEOs and executives of large corporations in Europe, the USA, Asia, South Africa, and Australia. I've engaged with top leaders, middle managers, and board members of private companies in industries as diverse as newspapers, cable TV, enterprise storage, telecommunications, banking, insurance, information systems, consumer packaging, distribution of consumer electronics, toys, pharmaceuticals, earth moving machinery, automotive, house construction, fine chemicals, transportation machinery, agro business, power generation, re-insurance, yellow pages, and telecom. I have also worked with ministers, including prime ministers, and with civil servants in the public sector, and I have interacted with a range of people in the volunteer sector.

Throughout my personal and professional journey of discovery over the last 25 years, I have met extraordinary brilliance, but I have also encountered a great deal of ignorance among the entrepreneurs, civil servants, and leaders I have taught and advised. I experienced the prevalence and effects of sexism and misogyny of the kind that former Prime Minister Julia Gillard accused opposition leader Tony Abbott during a speech in the country's parliament in 2012, which went viral on YouTube.[3]

I have been impressed with several female academic colleagues and executives that I encountered in my capacities as professor and consultant. I was often far more impressed with their intellectual and management abilities than those of their more numerous male counterparts. As a result, I often couldn't help but think that there must be many, many more women out there who would be better professors, business leaders, and civil servants than many of the men I'd met in those sectors, and I wondered where in the world they were. I included some of them in my academic writing, as anonymous cases and examples, but I wondered what I could do to help bring more women like the ones I admired into the top echelons of organizational hierarchies.

This became an increasingly pressing issue for me when I took on the leadership of CBS, a prominent business school which displayed painfully obvious gender imbalances in its management teams, administrative staff, and faculty.

Lynn and I had many discussions with each other and with colleagues at CBS about gender imbalances at CBS and what to do about it. I eventually appointed Lynn to be CBS' first Equal Opportunities Officer, and in that capacity since then, she has continued to work on developing CBS' policies, spearheading a number of initiatives at CBS. As part of our efforts to educate ourselves about what others are doing in this area, we began speaking with colleagues at other universities and corporate executives and diversity managers in Europe and the USA who have worked on achieving a better gender balance in their own organizations.

This book is a result of all those conversations. It is a record of our journey of discovery as we listened to what people had to say about why

---

[3] ABC News (2012).

men and women are not represented in roughly equal numbers in leadership or in the different occupations represented in their organizations and what should be done about it.

What we heard

As we spoke to managers and employees in all kinds of organizations about gender balance or the lack of it, we noticed that they tended to repeat certain excuses for the status quo, even though no one ever came right out and said that men and women are not equally capable or should not be treated equally.

A surprising number of people we talked to did not see any need to work on promoting more women into leadership positions or eliminating occupational gender segregation. They either believed that the passage of time should be enough to solve the problem or that it is simply not a problem—that it reflects individual preferences no one should interfere with or judge. Some of these people were concerned that working on gender balance would inevitably result in sacrificing excellence for equality. We also talked to a lot of people who agreed that gender imbalance is a problem to worry about, but they didn't believe that much could be done about it.

When we dug a little deeper into the background of all these beliefs, people gave one or more of the following reasons for having them:

1. There is no reliable business case proving the need to achieve gender balance. Because no one can show gender balance creates a measurable positive impact on the bottom line, it is not worth investing effort or resources.
2. Gender imbalances simply reflect the facts of life: women have babies, which means they cannot work as much as men. People who are able and willing to work full time without interruption during the course of their working lives are just more valuable to businesses and other organizations.
3. Gender imbalances reflect biological facts. Women are genetically programmed to prioritize personal relationships and caring while

men are genetically programmed to seek material wealth and leadership to ensure their desirability as mates and to affirm their masculinity. These biological facts make men better equipped to lead large organizations.

4. Whether they're genetically or socially programmed, men and women have very different priorities, and we should just accept it. Rather than worrying about perceptions of sex differences in abilities and interests, we should celebrate, and even capitalize on them.

5. Women are just not ambitious enough. Sheryl Sandberg is right— women need to 'lean in' more. The women's movement was successful: everyone now agrees that men and women are equal, so the gender imbalances we talk about are not due to sex discrimination. So this means that women alone are responsible for their underrepresentation in positions of leadership.

6. Suggesting that organizations should do something to ensure that their leadership teams include equal numbers of men and women tends to promote discrimination against men. It pits men and women against each other in the race to the top and fosters discord and bad feelings between the sexes, and neither men nor women want that.

7. Not all women want to pursue careers or leadership positions. Promoting gender balance implies disrespect for the women who are not interested in those things.

8. We have laws against sex discrimination in employment. Women just need to exercise their legal rights to equal treatment. If they can't prove there's sex discrimination, there's no problem.

We also heard from a substantial number of executives who believed it is very important to ensure that men and women are represented in equal numbers in positions of leadership and that occupational segregation is a serious economic issue, but who also thought it was a far more complex issue than they could analyse and understand themselves. They were aware of the wide variety of approaches that different organizations have adopted to address the problem, but could not identify any they could be sure would work in their own organizations. They felt unable to judge the quality of advice peddled by gender and diversity consultants. They didn't know where to start or what to watch out for.

Then there were those who did not believe they could do anything as individuals to address the problem. In their view, it requires collective concerted efforts rather than the actions of scattered individuals. Instead of focusing our efforts on organizations, we should focus our attention on the political process and get our political representatives to take action.

When we began having these conversations with people, we did not know ourselves exactly what motivated our commitment to working towards a balanced gender composition at all levels of our organizations other than our steadfast belief in sex equality. We also believe that the world is failing to make good use of all the intelligence and creativity out there so long as well under half of the world's leaders in politics, business, and education are women, and men and women are clustered into single-sex occupational ghettos. We found ourselves groping for answers to the questions and concerns we heard, and we shared the confusion of the executives who were uncertain about what strategy is best for achieving a better gender balance. Johan appointed Lynn Equal Opportunities Officer and Lynn accepted, not because either of us really knew what we should do. We were just committed to the belief that some action was better than inaction and that we would learn as we went along.

Our response

This book is our response to all the objections and concerns and confusion we encountered—or experienced ourselves—as we spoke with people about the need for a better gender balance in leadership and across occupations and how to go about achieving it. We decided that in order to communicate effectively about why businesses and other organizations need to take action to promote gender balance, we needed to address each of the eight main reasons people gave us for not investing time, effort, or resources in working for it. To address each of these eight reasons, we embarked upon a review of gender-related scholarship published in the last 60 years by evolutionary biologists and anthropologists, neuroscientists, sociologists, psychologists, historians, political scientists, and legal scholars. Together we arrived at a greater understanding of the 'state of the art' in gender research, which informs the basis for the chapters you will read.

Johan is an expert in strategy—the art and science of engaging people to think and prepare for the future. As a strategy professor with tenures in six business schools in five countries, he has become an expert in using systems thinking, complexity models, and creative arts techniques to challenge and support how executives strategize. He analyses the strengths and weaknesses of organizations, seeks to understand the threats and challenges that lie in front of them, and then helps leaders prepare for both the expected and the unexpected, and to make adjustments in strategy, structure, and governance as necessary. As a scholar and a practising leader, Johan has learned to pay attention to the dynamics of change and emerging trends and technologies and shifting market sentiments, to question his own and others' assumptions, and to uncover his own and others' blind spots.

If there was ever an issue that needed deep analysis and strategic thinking, it is certainly how to plan for and achieve gender balance on a large scale in the future. We have thus applied our skills as academics and organizational leaders, as researchers and educators, and as parents and ordinary citizens to fashion this book.

In addition, we drew on the experiences and insights of the company and political leaders, students, and colleagues, with whom we spoke during the course of our research. We talked with many leaders in multinational corporations and smaller firms as well as public corporations to listen to their experiences with addressing (or ignoring) gender gaps in their organizations. We engaged them, extracted their frustrations and insights, and learned from their successes and failures. We also challenged our own colleagues, students, friends, and families. These conversations fuelled our journey of discovery with a combination of hope and increasing irritation. We have been deeply disturbed by shocking examples of gender bias observed in the course of our investigations, but we have also been inspired by the enthusiasm of the many people we spoke with who want to engage in the work necessary to close remaining gender gaps. As a result of these conversations and our work in writing this book, we are more convinced than ever that we can reduce or even eliminate occupational segregation and get much closer to gender-balanced leadership of our societies' institutions and governments, that everyone can find a way of contributing to achieving these goals, and that we'll all be better off for having made the effort.

What is 'gender balance' anyway?

In our view, gender balance is reached when we fulfil three main objectives. First, it requires that the majority of men and women work in gender-integrated workplaces regardless of what type of job, be it an engineer, politician, CEO, teacher, or nurse. There is no logical or biological reason that these jobs need to be thought of as gender-specific, as we will show in the book.

Second, gender balance requires rethinking the way we work and raise our children so that both men and women are able and willing to participate equally in both arenas. As long as we continue to believe that mothers only are best suited to care for their babies and young children, we will *not* achieve gender balance. We will show in this book why it is crucial for the well-being of mums, dads, children—and society in general—that we recognize that the gender or family relationship of the caregiver does not determine the quality of the care young children receive.

Third, gender balance means that men and women must share relatively equally—at a *minimum* ratio of 60:40—the positions of power and decision-making in business, education, and national and local governments. It is simply poor governance when women in most Western nations hold, on average, only 10–20% of such positions. We will show in this book why 60:40 should be the minimum ratio between the sexes.

These are the three benchmark conditions we must achieve to gain a meaningful degree of gender balance. However, we are quick to add that we do not believe quotas are the best way to make progress towards any of these three conditions. Legislating quotas may be an effective way to force gender balance, and in a limited number of specific situations—such as on company boards—quotas may even be the best way, but as this book shows, the processes that create gender gaps are so far-reaching and their effects so widespread throughout society that we would have to adopt quotas everywhere to close gender gaps once and for all. This is clearly unfeasible and irreconcilable with our commitment to democratic government and individual rights and freedoms. So, as you will see in this book, our proposals for solutions are focused on changing thinking and mind-sets in order to change behaviour.

A note on our statistics and examples
Our emphasis in this book is strictly on how to achieve gender balance, as we define it, in pluralist, secular societies—such as the USA, Canada, Mexico, most of Europe, Australia and the Pacific, and a handful of rapidly developing nations in South America, Africa, and Asia where a vast middle class is emerging and the demand for gender balance is growing. The reason for this is that in these societies, many of the basic building blocks of gender equality are in place and they are ready—or will soon be—to take the next big step towards gender balance. Countries like Saudi Arabia and Afghanistan, where women do not have equal rights before the law, are at a completely different place in their journeys towards gender balance, and the recommendations we make in this book are probably not particularly relevant or helpful to them.

Our overall belief and message is that much of the world is poised for action to seize the advantages of a more gender-balanced way of life, and that the more we expand the footprint of gender balance—making it bigger and deeper—the better the world will be. For this reason, although we cite facts and statistics primarily from the USA and Europe, we believe that our analysis and recommendations may be useful in other parts of the world.

Join us in change
As you read each chapter in this book, we hope that you will begin to see that deep changes in our attitudes and beliefs about gender are necessary in order to change the behaviours that create gender imbalances in

leadership and in the way we employ people to work. To help this process, the last chapter in the book provides a set of principles to guide you on the journey towards gender balance. Every individual's action counts. We invite you to take this journey with us to explore how we can help each other look beyond accepted perceptions of gender differences and recognize that the very qualities that make men and women human bind us much closer together than any real or imagined gender differences can separate us.

1

Making the Case for Gender Balance

In a classroom at the University of Western Ontario in Canada, Professor Alison Konrad is teaching a mandatory class on corporate social responsibility to a class of undergraduate honours students in business administration. Professor Konrad uses the first half of the semester to teach the students about the concept of corporate social responsibility—where it comes from, what it consists of. The rest of the course is devoted to the subject of gender in organizations—more specifically the question of why so few women end up in top management positions. She has taught this course since 2010, and every year someone has asked, 'Why are we talking about gender in this class?' or simply 'Why do we have to study this subject?'[1]

These questions tell us a lot about what young people think is important to business. Gender does not seem to be one of them. They are not alone in thinking that. We have also encountered that belief when talking to business school professors and students and hear it expressed regularly in debates about the gender composition of corporate boards.

What kind of answer can we give to people who raise that question?

A look at the distribution of wealth and power around the globe could help.

Despite decades of consciousness-raising and legislation about gender equality, the majority of women throughout the world still live as second-class citizens—or worse. Considering that women make up nearly half the world's population, and now comprise the majority of college graduates

---

[1] E-mail correspondence between Lynn Roseberry and Alison Konrad, August 20, 2013.

in Europe and North America, we should all be concerned about that.[2] Neither our Western democratic institutions nor the proliferation of educated women with advanced degrees nor economic progress throughout vast swaths of the globe has radically altered the fact that women wield less political power, hold far fewer corporate and government leadership positions, and have less control over their own destinies than most men.

In some nations, women have almost no rights or freedom to choose the way they live their lives. They are forbidden an education, the right to choose their marriage partner, the age at which they marry, the right to say yes or no to sexual intercourse, and the choice of how many children they will be required to bear. A glaring example of gender discrimination thriving among such nations is the shocking statistic that women account for two-thirds of the world's 774 million adult illiterates—a figure that has remained unchanged for the past 20 years.[3]

Those of us in democratic, pluralist societies see ourselves as progressives, given that the living conditions of women in our societies are far better compared to women's living conditions in those 'backward' nations. Women in our societies go to school, study and become highly literate, have careers, drive cars, decide who to marry and divorce, juggle work and family life, and are able to vote and own property. But such evidence of gender equality belies an enormous imbalance in all our political, economic, and educational institutions. Consider just a few statistics that reveal glaring gender imbalances despite widespread commitment to the idea of gender equality:

[2] Contrary to popular belief, women do not make up more than 50% of the world's population. However, statistically speaking, they should, given the fact that when males and females receive the same care, females tend to have better survival rates than males. So where are all the statistically predicted 'missing' women? The horrifying truth is that female foetuses are aborted and babies left to die or even killed in a number of cultures. The Nobel prize-winning economist Amartya Sen has famously estimated that in China alone, the number of missing women was 50 million in 1990. When added to the missing women in South Asia, West Asia, and North Africa, a great many more than 100 million women were missing from the planet. Sen (1990).

[3] United Nations (2010).

Gender imbalances in politics

- In 2010, only seven of 150 elected heads of state in the world were women, and only 11 of 192 heads of government.[4]
- Among national legislatures and parliaments, the ratio of women to men does not reflect the populations they are supposed to represent. Women hold only 18% of the 435 seats in the 2013 US House of Representatives and only 20% of the seats in the 2013 US Senate.[5] In Europe, the average percentage of women in national parliaments is 22.7%. The numbers are only slightly better in Australia and Canada, where women hold about 25% of the seats in the national parliaments.[6] These statistics are surprising given the fact that in all of these named countries, females are 50% or more of their entire populations and sex discrimination in most areas of life has been prohibited for decades.

Gender imbalances in our workplaces

- Although women make up the majority of the US workforce, they hold only 4.2% of Fortune 500 CEO positions and only 4.5% of Fortune 1000 CEO positions.[7]
- In the USA and most Western European countries, the percentage of women on corporate boards and on senior executive teams is a severely disproportionate 15%.[8]
- Women's participation in the global labour market has hovered at 52% of adult women since 1990. Men's participation rate, on the other hand, was 81% in 1990 and 77% in 2010. The participation rate

---

[4] United Nations (2010).

[5] Center for American Women and Politics (2013).

[6] Inter-Parliamentary Union (2013). However, in the Nordic countries (Denmark, Norway, Sweden, Finland, and Iceland) women hold, on average, 42% of the seats in national parliaments.

[7] Catalyst (2013a).

[8] Barsh and Yee (2011a).

of women in the labour force is at its lowest, at 30%, in Northern Africa and Western Asia, and next lowest, at 40%, in southern Asia.[9]

- In the USA, women earn far less than men, despite the fact that they now comprise 47.6% of the workforce, as compared to 33% in the 1950s. In a 2011 report from the Martin Prosperity Institute entitled *The Rise of Women in the Creative Class*, noted business professor and researcher Richard Florida and his colleagues wrote,

> While women have increased their role in the overall economy and in the Creative Class in particular, there is a substantial gender gap in earnings. Overall, men are paid 50 per cent more than women; Creative Class men earn a staggering 70 per cent more than their female counterparts. The gap shrinks somewhat when we control for hours worked, education, and skills, but women still earn $10,600 less than men overall and $23,700 less than men in Creative Class jobs.[10]

- All around the world, most men and women work in sex-segregated occupations and workplaces. In Europe, over 60% of working women are employed in female-dominated occupations (such as teaching, nursing, and childcare), while 60% of working men are employed in male-dominated occupations.[11] In each of the 34 member countries of the OECD, half of all women work in just 11 or fewer of the major occupation groups, while half of all men work in more than 20 of these occupations.[12]
- The male:female gap in the choice of occupations is especially pronounced in the USA, Italy, Ireland, Greece, and the UK compared to other OECD countries.[13]

[9] United Nations (2010).

[10] Florida et al. (2011). Creative Class jobs are those that Florida characterizes as highly skilled, including jobs in computers and maths; architecture and engineering; life, physical, and social sciences; arts, design, media, entertainment, and sports; management; law; finance; business; management; education; and healthcare occupations.

[11] Biletta (2012a).

[12] Catalyst (2013b).

[13] Catalyst (2013b).

Gender imbalances in our educational institutions

- Among full professors at all institutions of higher education (both undergraduate colleges and universities offering graduate education) in the USA nationwide in 2005–6, women held only 24% of the positions while men held 76%.[14]
- In most European universities, the percentage of women faculty is in the range of only 15–20%.[15]
- In the OECD countries in 2010, on average, only 27% of graduates in engineering, manufacturing, and construction were women, compared to more than 74% of graduates in health and welfare.[16]
- Women make up more than four out of five primary teachers in most countries in Central Asia, Central and Eastern Europe, and North America and Western Europe. In several countries in Central and Eastern Europe, including Belarus, the Czech Republic, Lithuania, the Republic of Moldova, the Russian Federation, Slovenia, and Ukraine, almost the entire primary teaching force (97% or more) is female. The same applies to Armenia, Kazakhstan, and Kyrgyzstan in Central Asia.[17] Among 22 middle- and high-income countries with data, women hold the majority of teaching positions in 17 countries, but when it comes to management at the school level, they hold the majority of positions in only slightly more than half (12) of these countries.[18]

Do such statistics about gender imbalances matter? So what if women are so far behind in holding government and corporate leadership positions? What does it matter that women work in only a few professions? Does women's role in the labour force actually make a difference to the

---

[14] West and Curtis (2006).

[15] League of European Research Universities (2012).

[16] OECD (2012).

[17] UNESCO (2010).

[18] UNESCO (2010). On the other hand, women make up the highest proportions of teachers and school-level management personnel in various countries of Central and Eastern Europe, including Bulgaria, Lithuania, and Slovakia.

prosperity of a nation? And why can't we just continue along the path we are on, allowing women to catch up with men slowly, whenever it happens?

The moral and economic arguments for gender balance Answers to these questions are usually framed as either moral or economic arguments. The moral case appeals to our sense of justice and fairness. Most of us agree it's simply not fair to treat men or women worse than the opposite sex. The moral case generated the necessary political support for adopting legislation requiring equal treatment for men and women in the 1960s and 1970s. It is also the main reason why most people today would feel offended if accused of sex discrimination. Most people see sex discrimination as a moral failure—something to be ashamed of. But despite the broad impact of the moral case, business leaders still often argue that their responsibility for addressing gender imbalances only goes as far as what the laws dictate. The business of business is to make a profit, they say, and so they don't need to do anything more than any law requires—unless it pays off at the bottom line. Similarly, many political leaders want proof that investing resources in closing gender gaps will pay off in terms of economic results such as lower unemployment, increased GDP, and other measures of prosperity.

In response to the reluctance of businesses and governments to engage more proactively with the process of achieving gender balance, a number of scholars and consultants have constructed an economic case for gender balance based on a wide array of statistics indicating that bringing more women into leadership positions, ensuring gender-balanced teams, and resolving conflicts between parental and work obligations are all good for business and the economy. Noted consulting firm McKinsey's reports called *Women Matter*[19] and Avivah Wittenberg-Cox's book *Why Women Mean Business*[20] are iconic examples of the business case for gender balance. These publications seek to persuade business and political leaders that investing resources in achieving gender balance will pay off in concrete advances.

[19] Desveau et al. (2007, 2008, 2010).
[20] Wittenberg-Cox (2008).

Here are just a few examples of the studies supporting the economic case for gender equality:

- Since the 1990s, research by leading economists and development scholars has shown that just educating girls and young women—without doing more—leads to significant economic development. In 1991, the chief economist at the World Bank, Lawrence Summers, wrote, 'Investment in girls' education may well be the highest-return investment available in the developing world. The question is not whether countries can afford this investment, but whether countries can afford not to educate more girls.'[21]
- In 2001 a World Bank study[22] argued that promoting gender equality is crucial to combat global poverty.
- In a 2008 research report, the multinational investment bank Goldman Sachs emphasized how much developing countries can improve their economic performance by educating girls, and they donated $100 million to a campaign to give 10,000 women a business education.[23]

All national economies, regardless of their stage of economic development, seem to benefit from investing in gender equality in education and employment. The labour and intellectual contributions that women make to a national economy add to national GDPs as well as the tax base, which in turn provides the resources to help stabilize national economies.

In the USA, for example, we know that the movement for gender equality in the 1960s and 1970s had a direct positive impact on the American economy. In that era, laws prohibiting sex discrimination encouraged millions of young women to get college educations and aspire to a broader range of careers than nurse, teacher, secretary, or flight attendant. The resulting surge of educated women who joined the workforce had a significant positive effect on US growth. Economists say that 65% of American GDP growth in the 1970s can be attributed to the workforce

[21] Summers (1992).
[22] Mason and King (2001).
[23] Lawson (2008).

expansion created by women.[24] A McKinsey report asserts that 'between 1970 and 2009, women went from holding 37% of all jobs to nearly 48%. Without those women, the U.S. economy would be 25% smaller today.'[25]

The McKinsey Global Institute asserts that today, in order to sustain a rate of GDP growth at around 3%, the USA needs even more workforce expansion along with higher productivity from innovation and operational improvements. Where will that expansion come from? McKinsey economists say the answer is, by and large, from women who have yet to join the workforce. In 2011, the average national rate of workforce participation for American women aged 25–54 was about 76%, but the top ten states had participation rates at 84%. McKinsey estimates that just getting all states up to an 84% participation rate would add 5.1 million women to the workforce, which would be equivalent to GDP growth of 3–4%.[26]

The same economic benefits hold true for getting more women into the workforce in other parts of the world, too. In Europe, many countries have only 60% women in employment,[27] and the percentages are even lower in Africa and most of Asia. Adding the large numbers of women outside formal employment in these regions into the workforce represents a gigantic potential for world economic growth.

Here are some examples of the research results showing that gender equality within individual businesses has positive effects on productivity and the bottom line:

- A study by Professor Lynda Gratton and her colleagues at the London School of Business, based on data collected from 400 members of more than 100 corporate teams operating in 17 countries, shows that a team's experimentation and efficiency is optimal with 50:50 proportions of men and women. When either men or women are in the minority, the team's innovative potential is reduced, apparently

---

[24] Barsh and Yee (2011b).
[25] Barsh and Yee (2011b).
[26] Barsh and Yee (2011b).
[27] Biletta (2012b).

because both men and women experience lower life satisfaction, higher negative moods, and less commitment to the organization when they are in the minority.[28]

- These results were also duplicated in the European Working Conditions Survey 2010, produced by Eurofound.[29] In that study, male and female respondents who were working mainly with members of the same sex reported less satisfaction than the respondents working with more equal proportions of men and women.

- Studies looking at companies' financial performance and the number of women on their boards of directors and corporate performance show a correlation between the two.[30] Some data show that companies with the most women board directors outperform those with the fewest women in regard to return on sales by 16%. Companies with three or more women board directors over a period of at least four to five years significantly outperformed those with sustained low representation by 84% in return on sales, by 60% in return on invested capital, and by 46% in return on equity.

- Based on data from the top 1,500 American companies in terms of financial performance between 1992 and 2006, researchers at Columbia Business School and the University of Maryland found that the best performing companies had women in top management positions.[31]

In our view, all of these are important statistics to keep in mind when considering the future of humanity's prosperity and security. Taken together, they suggest that closing the gender gap in leadership and eliminating occupational segregation is necessary to maintain the high standards of living we have already achieved in many countries, to raise it in the others, and to protect us from threats to our security, especially economic threats.

---

[28] Lehmann Brothers Centre for Women in Business (2007).
[29] Biletta (2012b).
[30] Desvaux et al. (2007); Desvaux and Devillard (2008); Joy and Wagner (2011).
[31] Rosin (2010).

So why do we need to convince anyone about gender balance? If the moral, economic, and business cases for gender equality are so strong, why, then, do we continue to hear people question the importance of eliminating pronounced gender imbalances in our governments, workplaces, and educational institutions?

Some might argue that it's because the economic case isn't as strong as its proponents would have us believe. Indeed, we agree that no one can provide conclusive proof that gender balance—or any other initiative for that matter—will bring about better corporate performance or increases in GDP. Try as we might, no one can isolate a single factor—like a new marketing strategy or the addition of women to its board, or better implementation of a particular strategy—and say with conviction that that is why one company succeeds while another fails. All the studies supporting the economic case for gender balance—like virtually all other studies in the social sciences—show only positive *correlations*—not *causation*. There are even some studies that show a negative correlation between the number of women on governance boards and financial performance.[32]

But we don't think the lack of conclusive proof of the economic or business case is the real reason for the foot-dragging. Businesses and governments adopt strategies without that kind of conclusive proof all the time. Unequivocal certainty is just not available because it calls for a scientific investigation that is impossible to carry out in the world outside a laboratory. It's just not possible to control the environment in which companies or national economies operate so that you can isolate and test the effect of any one variable, whether it's the pricing structure, the coolness of the product design, or the presence of women executives. Neither business nor society is a laboratory where you can compare what happens if you change just one variable. There are multiple variables, and they are all changing all the time.

Why do leaders in businesses and governments seem to be willing to accept 'mere' correlations as proof that a strategy or initiative might be effective for anything but gender balance? After all, correlations are not the same as causal effects.

[32] Adams and Ferreira (2009); Smith et al. (2006).

We believe it's because popular explanations for existing gender imbalances lead people to believe that more or faster progress simply isn't possible.

The seemingly stronger case for gender imbalance   In our own practical work with promoting gender balance and in interviews with business leaders and human resource professionals, we have heard all kinds of reasons given for persistent gender gaps in democratic pluralist societies that are otherwise committed to gender equality. Most of the reasons we've heard are variations on the following assertions:

1. Under current market conditions, most women are simply unwilling to give up having children or to delegate family care to someone else, so they inevitably fall behind men with regard to both pay and career progression. Businesses need workers committed to full-time uninterrupted careers in order to succeed.
2. There are real neurobiological and genetic differences between the sexes that explain occupational segregation and gender imbalances in leadership.
3. Regardless of whether it's due to nature or nurture, most women are nurturing and empathic, and most men are competitive and aggressive, which means that men are bound to out-compete women when it comes to leadership.
4. Women don't really want to be leaders.
5. Gender balance is for women. Men are not, and do not need to be, interested or engaged in working for gender balance.
6. Gender balance is a special interest, feminist political issue that has no place in the workplace; even a lot of women don't support it.
7. We can't do any more about gender imbalances than ensure proper enforcement of anti-discrimination laws.

The people we have talked to who make assertions like these are well-educated professionals who generally believe that it's wrong to discriminate on the basis of sex. They all have some experience working with gender balance issues, and they were all quite adamant about the truth of these assertions. We decided that we should take a look at what kind of evidence there is to support each of them. This book is a record of our investigation. Chapter by chapter, we will show why each of these assertions is basically just that—an assertion. They are based on nothing more than untested assumptions or worse. Some of them are directly based on bad science that has simply made great headlines.

Worse than that, though, is that these assertions are often combined into moral and economic arguments justifying gender imbalance.

The moral argument for gender imbalance is made on the basis of the second, third, fourth, sixth, and seventh assertions. It goes something like this:

- It is unfair, even uncompassionate, to treat men and women the same, when they're different by nature.
- It's unfair to girls and women to expect them to be leaders when they aren't interested. You just end up making them feel guilty and you devalue the contributions of the many women who prioritize their families and relationships over careers.
- Promoting gender balance is contrary to some people's religious or political opinions, and we should not pressure anyone to do something contrary to their religious or political convictions.
- We have laws that address gender imbalances by requiring equal treatment of men and women. As long as we treat men and women equally, we do not need to pay further attention to gender in the workplace. The law does not require or even allow more.

Meanwhile, the economic argument justifying gender imbalance is often made on the basis of the first, second, third, fourth, and seventh assertions. It goes something like this:

- We can't change the way we organize work and jobs. The way our world is constructed now is the most rational given current market conditions.
- There are real neurobiological and genetic differences between the sexes that explain occupational segregation and gender imbalances

in leadership. It would be a waste of resources to try to change human nature.

- It also makes good business sense to capitalize on men's and women's inherent different preferences. If women are more nurturing and men more competitive, then it will all balance out if we encourage men and women to follow those preferences.
- The business of business is business. Businesses should not do more than avoid being sued. To do more is a waste of resources.

These economic and moral cases for gender *im*balance seem to carry as much weight in the public imagination as the economic and moral cases *for* gender balance. Thus the debate about the gender gap and what to do about it swings back and forth between two poles. For each moral or economic argument for gender balance, there's a counter-argument. It's gender gap ping-pong, and it has got to stop. Not just because it's keeping us from closing the gender gap, but because the specious moral and economic arguments that perpetuate the ping-pong have a direct and negative impact on our society in a fundamental way: how we govern ourselves and our institutions.

The governance case for gender balance   In this book, we construct the elements of an argument for gender balance from a governance perspective. When we use the word 'governance', we mean it in the broadest sense of the word. It is decision-making about which course of action an individual, organization, or nation should pursue. Governance is all about decisions that define expectations, grant power, make choices, and allocate resources. Leaders of all kinds—not just government officials or corporate executives—make those kinds of decisions. Parents, teachers, scout leaders, and entrepreneurs make those kinds of decisions. Individuals make those kinds of decisions on their own behalf.

The governance argument for gender balance asserts that *gender balance is necessary to produce good governance, which is, in turn, necessary for the stability and sustainability of our societies and our planet.*

Good governance produces decisions that are both morally right *and* efficient. The International Monetary Fund asserts that good governance includes 'improving . . . efficiency and accountability'.[33] The United Nations asserts that good governance is equitable, effective, and efficient.[34] When it is equitable, effective and efficient, governance should produce good results. When it isn't equitable, effective, or efficient, it will not produce as good a result, or in the worst case, it simply fails. Wars between nations, depressions, vast economic inequality, massive systems failure in our urban regions—these are all examples of what happens with poor governance. The financial crisis of 2008 is a recent example of governance failures—both within banks and companies and within national governments.

The moral and economic cases for gender imbalance we've outlined above are clearly related to the many gender imbalances listed at the beginning of this chapter showing the paucity of women in positions of leadership and power. Decisions are made every day on the basis of these moral and economic arguments for gender imbalance, yet because these arguments are based on false assertions, the decisions they support are neither efficient nor right. Taken together they contribute to poor decision-making and governance failures in both public and private life.

In this book we will dismantle each of the assertions on which arguments for gender imbalance are based and instead offer counter-assertions in the form of guiding principles, all of which are informed by the latest research on gender and together support the moral, economic, and governance arguments for gender balance.

Chapter by chapter, we will dismantle the assumptions and beliefs that prevent people from taking action to address gender imbalances. In Chapter 2, we will show you that the way we have organized work is an inheritance from the nineteenth century, and that the time has come to disown it. In Chapter 3, we will show you that despite all the neurobiological and genetic differences between the sexes that we hear about all the

[33] International Monetary Fund (2005).
[34] United Nations (2013).

time, men are more different from each other than they are different from women and vice versa. In Chapter 4 we will show you why it is not a good idea to rely on your own experience of boys, girls, men, and women to make decisions about men and women. It may feel like the right thing to do, but chances are, you're relying on stereotypes. In Chapter 5 we will show you how girls want to achieve their dreams and earn recognition just as much as boys, but they too often give up as they grow into young women and mature adults for lack of role models and encouragement. In Chapter 6 we'll show you that while we owe much of our prosperity and well-being to feminism, we need to move beyond its tendency to focus on women to include men and what they, too, gain from gender balance. In Chapter 7 we will tackle the issue of tolerance, and argue that we should not give up working to promote gender balance in the face of political or religious opposition. In Chapter 8, we will show you why the law is not enough to bring about gender balance, and how we can move beyond it without violating it.

At the end of the book, in Chapter 9, we tie all of this together and turn our explanations and descriptions into simple principles that can guide decision-making, action, and behaviours in the family, in schools, organizations, and society at large. We assert that we all need to:

1. Leave the past behind.
2. Bring men and women back to Earth.
3. Beware when it feels right; it might be wrong.
4. Understand that ambition is genderless.
5. Make peace, not war.
6. Oppose intolerance.
7. Recognize that the law is not enough.

Taken together, these guiding principles constitute the basis for creating long-term agendas for profound change for the better in our workplaces, educational institutions, and legislatures.

Let's get started.

2

Stuck in the Past

In 1995 Johan was offered a position on the faculty at IMD, a noted business school in Lausanne, Switzerland. So he, his five-months' pregnant wife Madeleine, and their one and a half–year-old son August moved from Oslo, Norway to Switzerland, where they lived for 13 years. While it was a great leap forward in his career it felt like a big step backwards in time as far as gender roles were concerned. In Switzerland, then as now, school days include a one and a half hour break for lunch, but no lunch is served. *Women* are expected to pick up their children, take them home for lunch and then back to school. An American mother blogging about her experience living in Switzerland wrote in 2010, 'You are kind of a horrible mother if you let somebody not related to you feed your child over lunch time.'[1] Some schools are adopting a 'Tagesschule' (all-day school) schedule, but according to this blogging mum, it's been slow and hit-or-miss, locally controlled, socially controversial, and generally frowned upon. This way of organizing the school day and the social expectations attached to it obviously rule out full-time and even most part-time work for mothers. For women with career ambitions, like Madeleine, who has a medical degree and a Ph.D. and had given up her full-time job as a medical doctor in Norway to move to Switzerland, it can be a frustrating experience.

Switzerland actually ranks quite high—at number ten—on the World Economic Forum's overall gender gap rankings. However, it ranks only

[1] Saunders (2010).

28th with regard to the more specific category of economic participation and opportunity for women. Perhaps the expectation that mothers should take responsibility for childcare outside school hours is a contributing factor to its lower placement on that scale.

If Switzerland is underperforming with regard to gender-balanced economic participation and opportunity, Denmark should be one of the top performers, at least judging from women's participation in the labour market. Consisting of a peninsula jutting out like a thumb from northern Germany and a number of large and small islands, Denmark has the seventh smallest gender gap in the world. In this progressive nation, most women work full time. The government provides publicly financed daycare for children from the age of six months, as well as paid maternity and paternity leaves.

But even with these great benefits for women, Denmark ranks only 16th with regard to the gender gap in economic participation and opportunity. One of the reasons for this may be that beneath the surface, there is a Swiss-like dynamic operating in Danish culture that puts pressure on working mums and divides them into two groups. There are the 'good mothers', those who work full time yet put their children first. They pick up their kids an hour or more before daycare closes at 5 p.m., bring home-baked birthday cakes and bread to daycare and school events, and are active members of the daycare parents' councils. The majority of women seem to meet these standards. Then there are the 'bad mothers', whom the Danes refer to as '*ravnemødre*', meaning 'raven mothers'. In the public imagination, these are career women who 'neglect' their children by leaving them in daycare until 5 p.m., seldom baking bread and cakes and failing to show up at daycare and school parents' meetings.[2] Meanwhile, no one expects Danish fathers to be so involved in the lives of their children. There is no special word for an uninvolved father.

Most Western industrial countries fall somewhere on the spectrum between Switzerland and Denmark in regard to what is expected of

---

[2] Erhardtsen (2010).

working mothers. In nearly every nation, women are generally in charge of raising the children and are expected to put their families before their careers. And it certainly seems to have an impact on the gender gap in economic participation and opportunity. The top ten performers on that scale include six countries from outside Europe and North America: Mongolia, Bahamas, Burundi, Norway, and Malawi occupy the top five spots in that order. It doesn't get much better when you look at the top 20. The USA, Canada, and New Zealand are in the top 20, but of the 27 countries that are members of the European Union, only six made it into the top 20 countries with the smallest gender gap in economic participation and opportunity.

Why is this? Why do relatively less industrialized or economically developed countries—like Burundi, one of the poorest countries in the world—have smaller gender gaps in economic participation and opportunity than countries in the industrialized West?

Part of the answer lies in the patterns of work and division of labour developed during hundreds of years of gender inequality in the history of Western culture. Until as recently as 100 years ago, men held all the legal authority, rights to property, and political power because women were viewed as morally and intellectually inferior. Until the twentieth century, women were typically denied access to education and skilled employment. The assignment of primary responsibility for 'breadwinning' to men and the home to women is a special remnant of the industrial revolution's impact on nineteenth-century gender inequality. Prior to this time, work and family were not separated into different spheres. Husbands and wives worked closely together, sharing life on their family farm or running a small enterprise, though even in this partnership, men held the authority. Women's subordinate role in society is so ingrained in Western culture that it is nearly impossible for twenty-first-century humans to step outside of this mind-set and imagine that it could be any other way.

But that is what we need to do. We are hamstringing our ability to adapt to the seismic social transformations wrought by accelerating technological and demographic changes by continuing to live according to antiquated and restrictive gender roles. We are unnecessarily putting a cap on both men's and women's ability to develop and make use of their talent. The number of women earning college degrees now exceeds that of men in Europe and North America. Technologies are transforming the nature of work from manufacturing to service and intellectual work, impacting the requirements of job skills and experience. The Internet and digital technology have practically eliminated the need for people to go to one location for their work; both women and men in a number of occupations can work from home or on the go. It is now possible for many people, especially those working in professional services and creative industries, to blend paid work and the work of running a household in a seamless stream of activity during the course of the day.

These transformations in the way we work are producing sociocultural changes that impact both men and women and present us with a unique opportunity to achieve gender balance in political and economic life. Fewer men and women are able to see the logic in keeping the world of paid work hermetically sealed from the rest of their lives. More and more men want to play stronger roles in their families as husbands and dads. At the same time, more and more women have discovered that it is possible, given the right conditions, to be good mothers *and* pursue satisfying careers and achieve higher levels of success and wealth. Both genders are questioning as never before the incongruity between the way we act as if paid work and unpaid care work in the family must inevitably conflict while social and technological developments suggest otherwise.

The perceived conflict between work and family corresponds to the division of the social world into the public and the private spheres. The public sphere includes the market and politics, where human beings seek to satisfy their appetite for power and wealth. The private sphere includes the home and personal relationships, where human beings pursue their desire for connection and community. That our social world is organized this way, and that women have been and still are identified with the values and interests of the private sphere while men are identified with the values and interests of the public sphere, has deep roots in the history of Western civilization. To understand how we can change the way we work to allow both men and women to participate equally in economic, social, political, and family life, we need to examine the historical background that put us here.

Female inferiority: the organizing principle of Western civilization

Considering that it was quite legal and socially acceptable to discriminate against women in employment and education until the 1960s, the idea that men and women are moral, intellectual, and emotional equals is a very recent, and to some even shocking, development in the history of Western civilization. The roots of this unequal gender paradigm go back millennia.

Ancient Greek and Roman culture established men's superiority to women by granting only men citizenship and property rights. In the fourth century BC, the Greek philosopher Aristotle developed a theory of biology in which he defined the female as a 'mutilated male', and 'female-ness' as the absence of maleness. In his works on natural and political philosophy he declared the mental and biological superiority of free men to both women and natural slaves.[3]

In the pre-Christian Roman Empire, Augustus, the father of the Roman imperial state following the civil war triggered by the assassination of Julius Caesar, introduced legal restrictions on marriage—the Lex Julia—when Rome was plagued by deep social problems. Citizens (men) were not allowed to marry prostitutes and provincial officials were not allowed to marry the local women. Unfaithful wives divorced by their husbands could not remarry.

Augustus also passed a law against adultery that divided women into two categories: wives and prostitutes.[4] There was, tellingly, no third category. According to the same law, a father who discovered his married daughter committing adultery in his own house or in that of his son-in-law had the right to kill his daughter and her lover.

After the fall of the Roman Empire and throughout the medieval period, religious scholars studied both Aristotle's philosophy and Roman

[3] Horowitz (1976).
[4] Edwards (2002: 38).

law. Both had a profound influence on philosophical and theological thinking in the Islamic, Jewish, and Christian traditions throughout the Middle Ages. Indeed, they continue to influence Christian theology, especially the scholastic tradition of the Catholic Church.

The Catholic Church traces its origins to the apostle Peter and his successors, whose writings contained arguments against allowing women to preach Christianity or hold any kind of authority.[5] In the late fourth and early fifth centuries AD, St Augustine, one of the earliest and most influential Christian theologians, provided additional arguments for subjecting women to male authority.[6] He wrote:

> [W]e must believe that Adam transgressed the law of God, not because he was deceived into believing that the lie was true, but because in obedience to a social compulsion he yielded to Eve, as husband to wife, as the only man in the world to the only woman.[7]

According to St Augustine, Adam came to eat the forbidden fruit because of his close relationship to Eve, which he interpreted to mean that men should not yield to a woman's judgement. In his autobiographical *Confessions*, Augustine was more explicit about the importance of female submission to male authority:

> And as in his soul there is one element which deliberates and aspires to domination, and another element which is submissive and obedient, so in the bodily realm woman is made for man. In mental power she has an equal capacity of rational intelligence, but by the sex of her body she is submissive to the masculine sex. This is analogous to the way in which the

---

[5] A verse in the Bible, 1 Timothy 2:11–12, which is traditionally attributed to the apostle Paul, is the main biblical authority for prohibiting women from becoming ordained clergy. It says, 'Let the woman learn in silence with all subjection. But I suffer not a woman to teach, nor to usurp authority over the man, but to be in silence.'

[6] St Augustine's writings exerted enormous influence on the development of Western Christianity and earned him the distinction of being named one of the four Doctors of the Church in 1298.

[7] Augustine (1958: 307).

impulse for action is subordinate to the rational mind's prudent concern that the act is right.[8]

Although in this passage he acknowledges that women are men's intellectual equals, he endorses women's submission to male authority because it appears to be ordained by their sexual function. It is simply part of the natural order.

After the fall of the Roman Empire in the fifth century, the Catholic Church began consolidating its influence on Western European culture. By the ninth century, and continuing through at least the fifteenth century, the Church was more than a spiritual institution. It was a powerful political actor with enormous influence. In place of the Roman Empire's military, political, legal, and financial institutions, feudal economies developed based largely on Catholic doctrine and canon law, which, in the ninth century, included the teachings of Augustine and by the thirteenth century also those of Aquinas.

The lawyers of the medieval Church—the canonists—constructed an elaborate system of law to regulate human activities as they touched upon the moral, business, and social interests of the Church in Europe.[9] The canon lawyers represented the most powerful minds of their era. Among the subjects to which they applied their formidable minds was sexuality. They taught that the only legitimate outlet for sexual desire was in marriage and for the procreation of children. Sexual relations for pleasure—even within marriage—were sinful. Building on St Augustine's views on the necessity of women's submission to men, they held that women were always ready for sexual intercourse as they were more susceptible to sexual temptations than men, and their sexual activities had to be confined within a properly structured marriage relationship.[10] In the thirteenth century, Thomas Aquinas, who was considered to be the Catholic Church's greatest theologian, expounded upon women's natural inferiority to men in his *Summa Theologica*:

[8] Augustine (2008: 302).
[9] Brundage (1976).
[10] Brundage (1976: 832–3).

It was necessary for woman to be made, as the Scripture says, as a 'helper' to man; not, indeed, as a helpmate in other works, as some say, since man can be more efficiently helped by another man in other works; but as a helper in the work of generation. . . . Among perfect animals the active power of generation belongs to the male sex, and the passive power to the female. . . . But man is yet further ordered to a still nobler vital action, and that is intellectual operation. Therefore there was greater reason for the distinction of these two forces in man; so that the female should be produced separately from the male; although they are carnally united for generation. Therefore directly after the formation of woman, it was said: 'And they shall be two in one flesh'.

As regards the individual nature, woman is defective and misbegotten, for the active force in the male seed tends to the production of a perfect likeness in the masculine sex; while the production of woman comes from defect in the active force or from some material indisposition, or even from some external influence; such as that of a south wind, which is moist . . .[11]

Given women's moral and intellectual weakness, the canonists held them to a higher sexual standard. Thus, a woman who expressed her sexual desires and enjoyed sex without embarrassment—even in marriage—was 'at heart a whore'; the adulteress was even worse, and sexual promiscuity was considered more detestable in women than in men.[12]

Given the strict controls applied to them, it should be no surprise that women found themselves firmly placed at the bottom of political, economic, and social hierarchies. These hierarchies were quite well defined.[13] There were no market economies as we know them today. Society was structured around the relationships between male lords and their vassals. The lords owned the land while the vassals provided labour and military service in exchange for the lords' protection. The wealth of the nobility

[11] Aquinas (1947: question 42, articles 4, 5).
[12] Brundage (1976: 834).
[13] Folbre (2009).

was derived from agriculture. Production was not organized according to market forces but rather solely on the basis of the labour vassals provided to their lords. Western European society was clearly patriarchal: men held most of the resources and most of the power. Relationships among men, women, and children, and between lords and vassals were extremely hierarchical. The subordinated classes, consisting of vassals, women, and children, received protection and security in return for working long hours in the service of their superiors—the lords and adult male family members.

The secular hierarchies between lords and vassals were based on the teachings of the Church.[14] Lords and monarchs were thought to receive their power and privilege from God, and God, the heavenly *Father*, gave male heads of households authority over women and children. Since this social hierarchy was ordained by God, individual choice was not a concept anyone was familiar with. Any attempt to step outside this order met with various forms of punishment or repression. Men—the lords, master craftsmen, and male heads of households—enforced the social hierarchies by the threat or actual use of violence. The lords held political and military power. Master craftsmen held power over their apprentices, and male heads of households held power over the women and children in their households. Feudal lords inherited their land and power from generation to generation. Marriage was for life. Parents were responsible for their children. Vassals could only work the land according to the conditions imposed by lords. Men could learn a craft, but had to find a master to whom they owed the same kind of obedience as a vassal to a lord. Masters owned their own businesses and had a higher social status than vassals, but if they wanted the protection and security that only lords could provide, they were also obliged to provide a service in return. Boys could enter the service of the Church, where they received an education and could aspire to ascend the ranks of the Church hierarchy. But they, too, owed the same kind of obedience to the monks as they would to their parents and lord.

---

[14] Folbre (2009: 9).

Women had few alternatives to marriage or service to an adult male family member. They were excluded from education of any kind, whether as an apprentice or in the service of the Church. Only wealthy families could send their daughters to be educated in convents or nunneries, since only they could afford the necessary donation to the Church and to live without their daughters' labour.[15] Anyone falling outside the prescribed relationship categories—usually because of death of or abandonment by family members—could only survive on the mercy of strangers. Women without the protection of a male family member or the Church risked ending up in prostitution or accused of witchcraft, usually with fatal consequences.

Market economies: creating the public and private spheres
Until the thirteenth century, the Church generally looked down upon commerce—that is, trade for profit—unless it benefited the Church. Economic historian Nancy Folbre suggests that the Church's proscription against commerce inhibited economic growth.[16] It certainly prevented the development of market economies.

The Church's disapproval of commerce grew out of its condemnation of greed as one of the Seven Mortal Sins. Many early Christian theologians believed that the passage in the New Testament asserting, 'It is easier for a camel to go through the eye of a needle than for a rich man to enter into the kingdom of heaven',[17] should be taken literally. If rich people had to give up their property in order to reach the Kingdom of God, then surely it wasn't a good idea to try to profit from trade. However, the Church was dependent on almsgiving, and in order to ensure that there was some wealth from which Christians could give alms, it was necessary to come up with some way of making it acceptable to amass wealth.

[15] The daughters of noble and royal families were sometimes taught to read by Catholic monks living in their households as preparation for marriage. Stoetz (2001).

[16] Folbre (2009: 9).

[17] Matthew 19:24.

St Augustine provided a way.[18] He rejected a literal interpretation of the gospel's warning against wealth. Instead he emphasized the passage in the Bible immediately following the bit about the camel's eye: 'what is not possible with men is easy with God'.[19] For Augustine, Christianity provided the means for everyone—rich and poor alike—to obtain forgiveness. Forgiveness could be achieved—by anyone—by praying daily for forgiveness and giving alms. The Church readily accepted this rationale, as it provided a convenient justification not just for almsgiving but for the practice of selling indulgences—promises of salvation in return for donations. The practice of selling indulgences, among other things, allowed the Church to accumulate phenomenal wealth.

But from justifying the possession of wealth to opening the door to commerce, and thus the development of markets, was a leap that took the Church nearly a thousand years to make. Thomas Aquinas helped justify making that leap in the thirteenth century, when he wrote in his *Summa Theologica* that commerce is not a sin in and of itself. The real problem, as Aquinas saw it, lay in taking a profit disproportionate to the value of the trade. To provide a way to get around this problem, Aquinas developed the concept of a 'just' price. According to Aquinas, selling something for more than its just price was a sin.[20]

Although the Church technically still admonished Christians to refrain from pursuing profit for profit's sake, commerce expanded between the 1200s and the 1500s.[21] Non-Christians living throughout Europe, having no religious restrictions about trade or lending money for interest, were more than happy to engage in trade for profit. Many began accumulating wealth—including the Church, nobility, merchants, and craftsmen—through agriculture and trade. Some of that wealth was used to pay out as wages and rent, allowing markets to take root and flourish.

In the wake of numerous medieval famines and plagues that reduced the number of people available to work the land, peasants and serfs began

---

[18] Brown (2005).
[19] Matthew 19:26.
[20] Folbre (2009: 9).
[21] Folbre (2009: 7–8).

renegotiating relationships with nobility. In return for guarantees of continued access to land, serfs began paying rent with money instead of crops. Meanwhile another socio-cultural habit created a need for employment, especially in England. This was primogeniture—the practice of leaving the family property to the eldest son. This meant younger sons had to find wage employment. France did not practise primogeniture, but with land being divided over and over again, many sons inherited plots of land too small to support themselves beyond subsistence for their families, and they, too, had to begin combining their farm labour with occasional or part-time wage labour in rural areas. It has been estimated that by the sixteenth century over half of all households were receiving at least part of their income in wages.[22]

Early wage employment was modelled on the only opportunities they had—labouring for other families or for craftsmen. Christian teachings about female inferiority remained in place. Young men could either work as servants or apprentice themselves to master craftsmen who were organized into guilds. But the only wage employment available to young women was to work as servants in households in return for board, lodging, and perhaps modest pay. Women's confinement to the private sphere of the household probably began here.

The Reformation: good for men and money, bad for women and lust

The Protestant Reformation in the sixteenth century opened the gates to the development of wider markets by espousing a more nuanced definition of greed.[23] It wasn't wealth that would keep a *man* (since a woman couldn't own anything) from passing through Heaven's gates. John Calvin preached that men simply had to avoid injuring their neighbours or engaging in deceit to obtain wealth. Borrowing and lending money at reasonable rates of interest was perfectly moral. Calvin asserted that merchants could safely lend money to one another at rates no higher than

---

[22] Folbre (2009: 6).
[23] Folbre (2009: 12).

5%. Calvinists believed in redemption through hard work and frugality. Worldly wealth was merely the inevitable result. And since Protestantism had rebelled against the idea of buying one's way to Salvation, Protestants could safely keep their wealth without worry that they should have donated it to the Church.

As trade expanded, Catholic rules on money-lending began to be interpreted more generously. The Church allowed Catholic Christians to charge interest if the client was not a Christian, if the money was needed to fight a Christian war, if the lender was running a risk, or if the borrower's goal was to make a profit.[24]

Meanwhile, as Christian concerns about greed were loosening to accommodate trade, money-lending, and the resulting accumulation of wealth, another one of the Seven Mortal Sins began to preoccupy the early Protestants.

Early Protestants disapproved of sex for any purpose other than procreation, and in their eyes, the Catholic Church's teachings about and enforcement of sexual morality were ridiculously lax.[25] They thought the Catholic Church's toleration of prostitution—which allowed men to satisfy their sexual desires—was particularly scandalous. The early Protestants— led by Martin Luther, Zwingli, Bucer, Bullinger, and others—advanced a far more rigorous sexual morality. The Catholic aspiration to celibacy was rejected as unrealistic and counter-productive. For all men, including priests, marriage was the only appropriate outlet for sexual desire, while all sex outside marriage should be severely punished. The leading Protestant reformers argued that adulterers ought to be put to death.

In response to the Protestant challenge to its moral authority, the Catholic Church began more rigorous sexual policing. Christian propaganda and action against sex outside marriage, adultery, prostitution, and sodomy intensified throughout Europe.[26] The belief that women were particularly culpable, possessed by an insatiable lust that corrupted

[24] Folbre (2009: 12).
[25] Dabhoiwala (2012: 12–13).
[26] Dabhoiwala (2012: 13).

otherwise good men, persisted. Brothels were closed down and prostitutes were expelled from cities. Oliver Cromwell and his Puritan follow-
ers made adultery a capital crime when they gained control of the English
government in the 1640s, but left room for the usual double standard:
men, but not women, could escape execution if they could prove that they
did not know their fellow fornicators were married.[27]

The mortal sins of greed and lust began to take on very pronounced
gender profiles in the cultural imagination of the Reformation.[28] John
Bunyan's popular *Pilgrim's Progress*, published in 1678 and regarded as
one of the most important works of English religious literature, clearly
portrayed the bifurcation of these two sins between the sexes. The main
character of the book, Christian, struggles to avoid 'temptation' on his
journey from his hometown, the City of Destruction, to the Celestial
City. The names of Christian's tempters need no elaboration: Mr Money-
Love, Sir Having Greedily, Mrs Love-the-Flesh, and Madame Wanton.
The message was: men sin by being greedy, while women are consumed
by lust. Men can be led astray by lust as well, but due mainly to women's
special seductive powers.

This was the cultural paradigm that Anglo-Saxon settlers brought to
the American colonies. Among the first colonists were Puritans fleeing
prosecution in England. The first group of them settled in New England
in 1620, and they were followed by many other, mostly Protestant, English
colonists through the remainder of the seventeenth century. In this way,
the cultural understandings of masculinity and femininity were and have
remained very similar on both sides of the Atlantic.

The industrial revolution: transforming work and families

At the end of the seventeenth century, Western Europe had transformed
from a collection of patriarchal feudal economies to a system of sovereign
nation states. The Peace of Westphalia of 1648, consisting of a series of
treaties that ended the Thirty Years War among the fiefdoms of the Holy

---

[27] Folbre (2009: 12–13).
[28] Folbre (2009: 13).

Roman Empire and the Eighty Years War between Spain and Holland, initiated a new system of political order in Central Europe based on the concept of a sovereign territorial state governed by a sovereign. Although Spain and Holland continued to fight each other, the relative peace was beneficial for trade.

Merchant capitalists now provided the impetus for growth. They sought out markets in Asia and North America, supplied capital, and spurred the invention of new methods of production in order to maximize their profits. These efforts brought about the shift away from agricultural home production for family use and local craftsmen's production of custom work for individual customers towards more standardized production on a larger scale for wider markets.[29]

Given the continuing influence of medieval Christian doctrine about female inferiority, this progress was a boon for men. A growing number of occupations in trade, crafts, and services opened up, considerably diversifying the agricultural base of both Western Europe's and the American colonies' economies. Many aspects of guild regulation had also disappeared by this time, making it easier for young men to learn a craft without binding themselves to years of underpaid service to one master.[30]

Women could not take advantage of the loosening regulation of crafts or the expanding market for labour. Explicit rules and strong social norms—remnants of the medieval Christian doctrines—continued to exclude women from access to education, skilled employment, and the right to own property. Women's perceived moral and intellectual inferiority to men legitimized vesting all authority over children's upbringing and education in their fathers. Like children, women's lives were in the hands of male family members. Only when single and over the age of 18, or widowed, could a woman own her own labour power and personal property.

Despite this gendered hierarchy of authority, however, women's labour was crucial to the prosperity of families and households. Until the beginning of the nineteenth century, family-based farms and cottage businesses

---

[29] Cott (1977: 24).
[30] Folbre (2009: 7–8).

formed the backbone of the economies of Western Europe and the American colonies. Families produced goods in their homes, which were then transported around the country by horse or by river. These businesses were operated under the strict authority of the male head of household, who coordinated the household's productive (and reproductive) work. Children were assigned to chores, running errands, and looking after each other at an early age. Teenagers provided substantial services and could be sent out to work for wages. Adult children assumed responsibility for the support of their parents and sick or elderly family members.

Women specialized in putting food on the table and clothes on family members' backs and caring for young children and the elderly. Women living on farms produced cloth and clothing, knitted gloves and stockings, baked, brewed, preserved food, churned butter, tended vegetable gardens, nursed the sick, made candles and soap, washed, ironed, and cleaned. Women who lived in towns and cities, where more goods and services were available for purchase, were relieved of some of these tasks if their husbands or other male members of the household could afford to pay for them instead. Although both men and women contributed to the economy through household production of agricultural and other goods, men still owned the property. Without the right to own property, women remained dependent on men. Socially and politically, they remained inferior to men.[31]

The industrialization of textile production marked the beginning of the industrial revolution and changed men's and women's daily lives more than any other single factor. These changes also brought about a shift in gender roles to something that seems all too familiar to us today.

All the activities of home production were gradually industrialized and integrated into the market economy. A man's work came to define his social identity.[32] Whereas men used to occupy the higher rungs of the social hierarchy based primarily on the authority granted to them by religious principles, by the late 1800s their position came to depend

[31] Cott (1977: 22).
[32] Williams (2000: 25).

on their individual success in the job market. The term 'self-made man' entered the language in the 1840s. Men bore the burden of providing their families with the money required to buy the food and clothing the entire family had formerly produced themselves. The ability to provide for a wife and children became the measure of masculinity.[33]

The appearance of factories that could mass-produce cotton cloth also marked the end of women's home-based participation in the economy. All the operations necessary to turn raw fibre into finished cloth—carding, spinning, and weaving—could now be put under one roof. By the mid-1800s industrial production of cotton cloth had largely replaced home spinning and weaving in both Britain and New England.

The growing number of non-agricultural occupations drew both men and grown children away from the household, leaving mothers and pre-school aged children at home. The growing market economy also removed activities like spinning, weaving, and soap making from the home. Married women were left with the only activities that had not been integrated into the market economy: household upkeep, child rearing, and caring for the sick. Women with children became identified with cleaning, cooking, and care giving in the home, while men became identified with procuring the means of survival through 'breadwinning'.[34] Young girls and women without children worked outside the home at wage rates generally half of men's, reflecting the view that their need for work was largely temporary, and their wages probably only a supplement to the support they received from male family members.

Industrialization also changed the way work was done and the popular understanding of what 'work' is. In the pre-industrial era, men and women had shared similar work patterns that were tied to the land. It was seasonal and task-oriented, attuned to natural rhythms in contrast to industrial work's regulation by the clock. It was not until the period from 1780 to the 1830s that individuals began to form occupational ambitions

---

[33] Williams (2000: 26).
[34] Cott (1977: 43–4).

and organize their time according to the clock rather than the natural rhythms of days and seasons.[35]

In contrast, the pre-industrial habits of alternating between intense work and leisure, and using social occasions for work or vice versa— for example quilting and sewing—persisted in the household.[36] By the end of the nineteenth century the differences between market work and household work were more than obvious. In comparison to men's time-disciplined and specialized occupations, women's work in the household seemed more like 'life' than 'work'—unsystematized, without deadlines or production targets. People had begun calling the home and women's work within it the 'women's sphere' and thought of it as something separate from the market, which was the 'men's sphere'.

Redefining men and women—and creating the gender norms we live by

As industrialization gradually drew men out of the home in the 1820s and 1830s, popular culture began generating a narrative that created a new understanding of male and female characteristics but left women's dependence—and their economic, social, and political inferiority to men—in place. During this period numerous essays, sermons, novels, poems, manuals, and ladies' magazines presenting a new discourse about family life, child rearing, and women's role began appearing on the market. These publications described the home as an 'oasis in the desert', a 'sanctuary' where 'disinterested love is ready to sacrifice everything at the altar of affection' in contrast with the world outside the home, which was heartless and amoral, subjecting the individual to a 'desolation of feeling' as it disregards 'every principle of justice and honour, and even the dictates of common honesty'.[37]

---

[35] Brown (1972: 219–20).

[36] Cott (1977: 60).

[37] Cott (1977: 63–5), quoting various publications published in New England between 1830 and 1840.

The new discourse distinguishing between 'home sweet home' and the hard ways of the industrial world drew upon and echoed the old Christian teachings against commerce and the pursuit of wealth. One of the lasting central messages of Christianity was the contrast between earthly possessions and the eternal blessings of true faith. Cott suggests that this heritage helped promote a strong movement in the 1800s that created a sort of 'cult of domesticity' that treated the home as a sacred place and women as domestic priestesses.[38] Before industrialization, there was no clear distinction between the business of 'the world' and the home. The world was the home, and women were certainly not regarded as priestesses.

So what was the impact of all this? In many ways, women had made progress from sexual temptress to moral guardian. But throughout these changes, female inferiority persisted as an organizing social principle. Women remained cut off from full participation in the new market economies as well as politics.

Still following nineteenth-century role models

With the identification of women with the home and private sphere, the ideal market worker became identified with the habits and social standing of men. This worker had no or few domestic responsibilities, no interruptions due to the birth of children, and full control over his own destiny. The best jobs required an education, which meant only men could have them. The kind of control over one's life circumstances required to live up to this ideal also presumed property ownership and authority to make decisions that affect the lives and fortunes of one's spouse and children. Underlying these rights is the right to full political participation through the right to vote—but only men could vote until the passage of the 19th Amendment in 1920 in the USA (and later in many European countries).

While women have gained many legal rights in the past century, such as the rights to vote and equal treatment at work and in education, the social norms and behaviours needed to make these rights a reality have

---

[38] Cott (1977: 63–74).

lagged behind. Women didn't even gain access to the same educational opportunities as men until the latter half of the twentieth century.

The expectation that women would marry, have children, and rely on a man for support has lingered on through the end of the twentieth and into the twenty-first century in many parts of the USA and in a number of European countries. A 1997 study of dual-earner families in the USA found that even when their wives were employed, most men still felt a special obligation to provide.[39] In 1998 the *Washington Post* ran a series of articles on gender in the workplace based on surveys showing that 'although men and women agreed they should have equal work opportunities, and men said they approved of women working outside the home, large majorities of both said it would be better if women could instead stay home and just take care of the house and children'.[40] In 2012, a survey commissioned by the Commission of the European Union showed that almost one in three Europeans (28%) agree with the statement that 'women are less interested than men in positions of responsibility'.[41] In Denmark, supposedly a shining example of gender equality, 49%—the highest percentage of any European country—agreed with that statement.

But what about the progress we've made?
This is not to deny that women have made progress towards parity in pay, employment, and education in the last 40 years. Thirty-seven per cent of US working wives now out-earn their husbands. Indeed, if we are to believe Liza Mundy, author of *The Richer Sex*, American women's situations have improved measurably just in the past ten years. She points out that the wage gap is decreasing; in 2010, women earned 81.2% of men's earnings, up from 62% in 1979, and that women hold 51% of jobs in management, professional, and related occupations.[42] Mundy also cites a working paper presented at a 2011 conference of the world's leading demographers that showed that in some fields mothers actually earn

[39] Williams (2000: 55).
[40] Morin and Rosenfeld (1998).
[41] European Commission (2012).
[42] Mundy (2012: 55–7).

more than women without children.[43] The researchers found that women with young children earn more in the most elite occupations—particularly in maths and physical science, engineering and computer sciences, life sciences, medicine, law, and business—than women without children when they have the same education, age, and work hours.

But plenty of other studies document an enduring gap between men's and women's earnings and career opportunities and darken the prospects for achieving such a rosy future. In a critical review of Mundy's book, a reporter for *The New York Times* referred to a 2011 report from the US Government Accountability Office finding that women, despite having acquired more education, make up a higher proportion of low-wage workers than men.[44] The report also cited a 2011 study by Richard Florida, senior editor for *The Atlantic* and author of *The Rise of the Creative Class*, who discovered that female writers, healthcare workers, computer engineers, lawyers, and scientists 'earn lower wages across the board, with the biggest disparities in the fields where they make up the largest share of the work force'. In a paper released by the Council on Contemporary Families in February 2012, sociologists David Cotter, Joan Hermsen, and Reeve Vanneman point out that the pace of occupational desegregation by gender has slowed or even reversed since 1990, especially outside middle-class professions.[45] In fact working-class jobs are nearly as segregated as they were in the 1950s. And since 1994, Americans' support for non-traditional marital roles has slipped.

It's probably reasonable to assume that the majority of people in Western industrial democracies believe that men and women should be treated equally. But this does not go very far when they continue to model their behaviour on nineteenth-century (or even medieval) gender roles. Nor do the characteristics of the ideal market worker seem to have changed since the nineteenth century when the majority of people, as well as religions and governments, believed it was perfectly right to discriminate against women.

---

[43] Mundy (2012: 61).

[44] Shteir (2012).

[45] Cotter et al. (2012).

Aren't we ready to change?

More and more women are well educated and prepared to take on leadership positions while more and more men are feeling torn between the demands of home and work. In fact, a 2008 US workforce survey conducted by the Families and Work Institute found that among Millennials (young adults born between 1980 and 2001 approximately), women are just as likely as men to want jobs with greater responsibility while 'fathers in dual-earner couples are now significantly more likely to experience some or a lot of work-life conflict than mothers in dual-earner couples'.[46]

It seems that both men and women need and want meaningful work and meaningful relationships, yet we continue to organize our work and evaluate men's and women's performance on the job as if men and women want different things. Most American employers, for example, have not even embraced the concept of interrupted careers or flexible working hours, despite their obvious advantages. In 2011 only 53% of US companies offered flex time and only 45% offered telecommuting.[47] Only 16% of US companies offered paid maternity—or paternity—leave. And the *average* number of weeks of fully paid maternity leave at the 100 companies on *Working Mother* magazine's 100 Best Companies in 2011 was only seven weeks, while the average of partially paid maternity leave was just five weeks and three weeks for paid paternity leave.

The fact is that most employers lack the will or imagination, or both, to find other ways of organizing their workforce than simply demanding presence—whether in the workplace or travelling on business. Even in Scandinavia, employers regard interruptions in employees' availability for work due to the birth of children as an unwanted nuisance and will do whatever they can to avoid them. Employees know this, and so men simply don't take paternity leave if they don't have to. Norway had introduced voluntary shared parental leave in 1977, but only 2–3% of Norwegian fathers took time off to be with their children. To proactively change that attitude, the government reserved ten weeks of leave just for fathers

---

[46] Galinsky et al. (2011)
[47] *Working Mother* (2011: 7).

in 1993. Given the choice between extending the time their children can be cared for at home by ten weeks and placing their children in daycare, fathers began choosing to take the leave. Now, 90% of Norwegian fathers use their full quota.[48]

A 2008 report by the Centre for Economic Policy Research on the national parental leave policies of 21 high-income economies shows clearly that when countries leave it to the parents to allocate leave between them, mothers will take most of the leave, unless the fathers are able to take their leave with full pay.[49] The pull of traditional gender roles coupled with the typically lower earnings of mothers relative to fathers create strong incentives for women to reduce their employment and take on the majority of childcare responsibilities. The strong forces pushing women towards the home mean that they fall behind in both pay and career development in relation to men and childless women, while men are deprived of the emotional bonding that arises from caring for their own children. In this way, children learn from the beginning that the home is for women and children, while the market is for men.

In the end, the ongoing lack of affordable alternatives to family-provided childcare coupled with employers' stubborn and unimaginative adherence to workplace policies that value presence over performance mean that each individual worker is left to find individual solutions to what is a common, ubiquitous, and by now, nearly 200-year-old problem. Persistent biases against working mothers mean that their contributions are undervalued and therefore underpaid.[50] Most women accordingly do the rational thing and follow in their nineteenth-century forebears' footsteps while men take their usual places on the labour market. This is a ridiculous situation.

[48] Criscione (2011).

[49] Ray et al. (2009: 2).

[50] Studies published between 2000 and 2004 show that employed mothers in the USA suffer a per-child wage penalty of about 5%, on average. See Correll et al. (2007). In an experiment reported in 2004, describing a consultant as a 'mother' led evaluators to rate her as less competent than when she was described as simply 'having children'. Cuddy et al. (2004).

Can we change the way we work?

Of course we can. We have only to look at how popular perceptions of men and women in the West have changed over the past 300 years. Women have been transformed from being insatiable temptresses, unfit to make any decisions about the education and upbringing of their own children, to being the guardians of virtue in the home, and the equals of men—broadly speaking. Men are no longer authoritarian patriarchs, but rather democratic leaders, and empathic fathers and husbands. Hints of more change to come can be found in the attitudes of younger generations. As the Work and Family Institute's 2008 survey of young American Millennials has shown, they appear to be even more eager than their parents to chuck the last remnants of the cult of domesticity out of the window.

We have only to look at Egypt, Saudi Arabia, and Yemen to see how far industrial democracies have come on the journey to gender balance. European, North American, and some Asian countries look like futuristic gender balance utopias in comparison to those nations.

Dramatic changes in production methods and communications brought about by advances in computer technology present opportunities to reorganize the way we work, the way we think about the public and the private sphere, and the way we think about gender roles. Unlike the societies that existed during the previous social transformations—like those brought about by the spread of Christianity, the Protestant Reformation, and industrialization—pluralist democratic societies ostensibly subscribe to the principle of equality between men and women. But in order to seize the opportunities these changes present to reorganize work and rethink gender roles, we have to be alert to the echoes of the past. We cannot hope to achieve gender balance if we forget where we've come from.

Some employers we interviewed and tracked are good examples of companies that have been taking steps to distance themselves from nineteenth-century conceptions of work and the ideal worker. For example, Swiss Re, a multinational insurance company, launched an initiative to change the company's work culture. Called 'Own the Way You Work™: Living Team Spirit', the initiative seeks to give autonomy to Swiss Re employees to decide how, when, and where to work. Managers are trained to practise trust, openness, and respect in their direct reports, recognize that 'one size does not fit all', and focus on working smarter rather than longer hours and on team rather than individual performance.[51]

Microsoft is another company that has been experimenting with different ways of giving their employees more autonomy. In a number of its European branches it eliminated individual offices and instituted a 'no camping here' policy to discourage people from showing up at work and staying just to show they're working. When he was president of Microsoft in Western Europe, Klaus Holse told us that members of the HR department staff are expected to be present four days a week, salespersons one day a week, and the consultants only one day per month. Senior managers and specialists are expected to be present a little more, but work more from home than at the office. In addition all meetings that have a broader audience are to be held in a way where it is possible to use videoconferencing technology to avoid requiring everyone to come to the office. These policies have been very popular with both men and women, and, in Klaus Holse's opinion, are a major factor in winning Microsoft a place in the top five companies in the 'Great Place to Work' competition in every European country where Microsoft operates.[52]

Deloitte & Touche USA has developed a career development policy it calls 'Mass Career Customization' (MCC) which is based on the concept of a corporate lattice rather than a corporate ladder. Instead of the corporate ladder's one-size-fits-all approach to careers, the career lattice is based on the idea that instead of providing only opportunities to move up, stay put, or move down, the employer allows its employees to move in many directions over time. This approach encourages employees and managers to match 'employees' talents, career aspirations, and evolving life circumstances over time' with 'the enterprise's evolving marketplace strategies and commensurate need for talent'.[53] The MCC approach arose out of Deloitte's recognition that both men and women are disinclined to

[51] Interview with Nia Joynson, Diversity and Inclusion Manager, Swiss Re, 2 July 2012.
[52] Interview with Klaus Holse, President of Microsoft, Western Europe, 26 March 2012.
[53] Benko and Weisberg (2007: 2).

compete on the corporate ladder if the cost to their family and personal lives is too high. Both men and women want meaningful work and meaningful personal lives.

While these companies are moving away from anachronistic models for organizing work, many others are still stuck. It's time for them to leave the past behind.

Leaving the past behind is a constant journey
We think it's important to remind ourselves of the history we've outlined in this chapter as we work on gender balance. Even in the most progressive countries—those that rank in the top ten on the World Economic Forum's Global Gender Gap Report—we still have to watch out for echoes of medieval ideas about the nature of men and women. We cannot leave the past behind if we can't even recognize it when we see it. Here's a story to illustrate what we mean.

Amelia is a bright 16-year-old girl who goes to one of the most progressive and high achieving college preparatory schools in one of the Scandinavian countries ranked in the top ten of the WEF's Global Gender Gap Report. At a party with friends from her class, she was sitting with some boys that she knew and liked. They were watching some of the party-goers flirting and kissing. One of the boys remarked about one of the girls, 'She's a real cock-teaser.' Amelia looked at who he was talking about and got mad. 'Wait a minute. That's my friend. I really don't like to hear you talk about her that way.' None of the boys at the table could understand why it bothered her. And Amelia could not find the words to explain it to them.

Amelia talked to her mum about it afterwards. After some discussion, she finally said:

> The boys get to decide if they want to kiss us or not, have sex with us or not, and no one ever calls them 'cunt-teasers' or anything else. They're just boys who are interested in sex. But if we don't want to kiss them or fool around with them, we're prudes. If we act like we want to kiss them, and take the initiative, but don't want to have sex with them, we're cock-teasers. If we do have sex with them we're sluts and whores. They've set the rules. They get to

do whatever they want—have sex with all the girls they want to—and brag about it while they call the girls they slept with sluts.[54]

The boys involved in this episode are white, ethnic Scandinavians raised in the Christian tradition. Muslims are regularly publicly criticized by Scandinavian politicians and feminists for being especially backward when it comes to sex equality. And yet these young men are behaving as if they have internalized the 'female temptress' lessons taught by St Augustine and Aquinas and by some fundamentalist Muslim clerics today.

Some may think we're being a bit harsh on these young men. After all, they're just newcomers to the mating game, and they're bound to be clumsy and insensitive. Besides, their brains are soaked in testosterone. Isn't this just the way nature made them? Maybe these lingering echoes of medieval patriarchy are just part of human nature—and we will never get rid of them because they are ingrained in our genes. Or are they?

Key points and guiding principle

- Women were not regarded as men's equals, with equal rights to political participation and education, until the twentieth century.
- Until the industrial revolution introduced methods of mass production by the 1800s, work and family life were intertwined, not separate spheres, the way they are today.
- The way we organize work now has roots in a time before sex equality and reflects one of the organizing principles of society before that time: the subjection of women to men's authority and their exclusion from public life.

Guiding principle: *Leave the past behind.*

---

[54] Benko and Weisberg (2007: 2).

3

The White Coat Syndrome

Some people think that biological differences between women and men
are reason enough for the lopsided distribution of men and women over
occupations and on the career ladder. In April 2013, hedge-fund billion-
aire Paul Tudor Jones told an audience of students, alumni, and others
during a symposium at University of Virginia, 'As soon as that baby's lips
touch that girl's bosom, forget it. . . . You will never see as many great
women investors or traders as men—period, end of story.'[1] While Jones
believes that women are just as capable as men, he believes they lose that
ability when they become mothers. Jones explained, 'Every single investment idea . . . every desire to understand what is going to make this go
up or go down is going to be overwhelmed by the most beautiful experience . . . which a man will never share, about a mode of connection
between that mother and that baby.'

Others believe that the relative lack of women in leadership positions or
among Nobel Prize-winning scientists results from differences between
male and female brains. A lot of highly educated, respected intellectual
and political leaders share this opinion. It is hard to blame them when
neuroscientists keep announcing discoveries indicating that men's and
women's brains are different. One of the most recent examples of this was
a research paper published in December 2013[2] that inspired headlines in

---

[1] Johnson (2013).
[2] Ingalhalikar et al. (2013).

newspapers as well as on the BBC website. The scientists claimed that males have better motor and spatial abilities, whereas females have superior memory and social cognition skills. But even before that, highly esteemed academics and leaders held similar opinions.

Larry Summers, who as chief economist of the World Bank spoke so fervently in 1991 in favour of investing in education for girls, seems to harbour a belief in innate and immutable sex differences in cognitive abilities. In 2005, when President of Harvard University, Summers mused publicly that innate and immutable sex differences may be one of the reasons why only 20% of professors in science and engineering in the USA are women.[3] Dr Summers is a highly educated, well-read man, and he did not base his remarks simply on his own personal experience. Summers referred repeatedly to the work of University of Michigan sociologist Yu Xie and his University of California–Davis colleague Kimberlee A. Shauman, whose analysis of achievement test results shows a higher degree of variance in scores among men than among women.[4]

Just a year after Dr Summers' remarks, *The Economist*, the respected international periodical read by the world's political and economic elite, reported that 'biological explanations of human behaviour are making a comeback'.[5] It asserted that it 'is now widely accepted' that males and females 'are programmed by evolution to behave differently from one another'. The article described research indicating that behavioural sex differences are 'hardwired' in our brains, and it included a long list of references to studies published in highly respected scientific journals.

The Economist article reported on a complete turnaround in thinking since the 1970s. At that time a lot of people believed that male/female differences in behaviour were the result of upbringing, not brain wiring. The leading theory of the 1970s was that 'nurture' was more influential on behavioural differences between men and women than 'nature'. It was thought that boys and girls are born essentially the same, but parenting

---

[3] Summers (2005).
[4] Hemel (2005).
[5] *The Economist* (2006).

and cultural milieu affect our style of thinking, our preferences, and even our capabilities, interests, and choices of careers. In fact, a lot of people—experts included—believed that if boys and girls were treated the same from birth, inequality between the sexes could even be eliminated. If you were born in that era, you might even recall that giving dolls to baby boys and trucks to baby girls became a fad.

The 'men are from Mars' phenomenon

So what happened to change popular opinion between the 1970s and now? Why did people change their minds and come to believe that nature is more influential than nurture?

You might be tempted to think that scientific discoveries had something to do with it, but you'd be wrong. The shift in thinking actually started with two best-selling self-help books in the early 1990s. The first was Deborah Tannen's *You Just Don't Understand: Men and Women in Conversation*, and the second was John Gray's *Men are from Mars, Women are from Venus*. Neither of these books claimed that men and women were innately different in ways that affect their intellectual and psychological abilities; they simply presented some generalizations about how men and women communicate differently and offered suggestions about what they could do to communicate better with each other.

But following the publication of these two books interest in finding out if there are innate and immutable cognitive and psychological differences between the sexes surged. By the late 1990s and early 2000s, popular science books began appearing claiming that recent studies in neuroscience and psychology had revealed a number of brain-based sex differences to explain why men become scientists, doctors, and leaders, while women become teachers, social workers, and stay-at-home mums.[6] Popular opinion began shifting towards the view that maybe men and women had provable 'brain-based' neurological differences that result in sex differences in cognitive and emotional skills and capabilities.

---

[6] Pinker (2008); Brizendine (2006, 2010); Baron-Cohen (2004).

The 'men are from Mars' meme soon dominated the professional literature. Meanwhile, few people noticed that another flurry of popular science books had appeared, arguing that those earlier books misrepresented the research and misled the public.[7] The newer books argued that the few innate behavioural and psychological sex differences that had been identified in human babies and children were simply not significant enough to account for either the persistently high degree of occupational segregation by sex or the relative absence of women in positions of leadership.

So which books and research should you believe? Can we be truly certain that innate biological sex differences explain more about behavioural and psychological sex differences than the way parents raise their children, how schools educate them, or the influence of the media on boys and girls as they become men and women?

The brain-based explanations of behavioural differences between men and women constitute an area of tremendous confusion caused by conflicting scientific studies and at times even by misrepresentation and misuse of scientific findings. This kind of confusion can lead a lot of people to believe that it's not worth investing more effort in achieving gender balance if nature limits what men and women can do anyway.

Given this state of affairs, we want to give you a tour of the research in this area so you can understand why we argue that it's time to stop focusing on sex differences and recognize the common humanity of both sexes instead.

So what exactly is a sex difference?
The first thing we need to be clear about is what the term 'sex difference' means. A simple question, but nothing in science is simple.

First of all, some scientists say '*gender* difference' when they believe the difference is socially determined, and '*sex* difference' when they believe it is biologically determined. But other scientists prefer to use only the term 'sex difference' because they think it's impossible to make a distinction

---

[7] Eliot (2010); Fine (2010); Cameron (2007); Barnett and Rivers (2004).

between biology and culture. These scientists say all social behaviours are controlled by our brains anyway, so everything we do has some basis in biology. We agree with the latter group, and so we prefer to use the term 'sex difference' for purposes of this discussion. This means that the goal is to find out if science can actually prove that the biological differences between men and women include innate and immutable brain differences that cause them to think, feel, and behave differently. Do their brains really differ enough to explain why more men than women become engineers, scientists, and leaders while more women than men become nurses, social workers, and teachers?

This leads to the question: How much of a difference between men and women is needed before you can say they are innately and immutably different from each other?

The answer turns out to be fairly straightforward. Scientists define a sex *difference* as being a 'characteristic that differs on *the average* for males and females of a given species'.[8] The emphasis here is *on the average*. In other words, when scientists talk about 'sex differences', they are not saying that *all* men have a certain characteristic and that no women have it. That would be an *absolute* difference. An example of an absolute sex difference is the Y chromosome—only males have it.

Instead, a true sex difference simply means that the average for each sex must reflect a difference. For example, if you take height as a sex difference, you get the average height for men by measuring a bunch of men, adding up the measurements and dividing by the number of men you measured. Then you do the same for women. In general, men and women have a height sex difference because women as a group are shorter than men as a group. When you subtract the women's average from the men's average you get the 'average difference'.

When talking about average differences between the sexes, we have to remember that many people fall outside the average. Take a look at the graph shown in Figure 3.1.[9]

---

[8] Hines (2004: 3–4).
[9] Schiebinger et al. (2011–13).

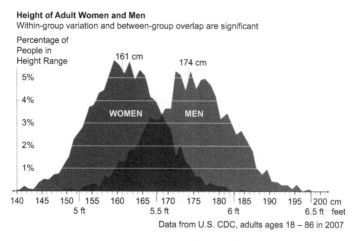

Figure 3.1 Graphic representation of a sex difference where d = 2.0

The points along the horizontal axis correspond to height while the points along the vertical axis correspond to the percentage of American men and women that have a given height. The largest percentage of American women lies between 159 and 163 centimetres. The largest percentage of American men lies between 171 and 175 centimetres. But as you can see from the graphs, there's a huge amount of variation among men as a group and among women as a group. There is also a large area where the heights of men and women overlap.

When researchers want to compare how different the sexes are, they use a statistical measure called *d*. This measure indicates how far apart the averages for men and women are. The larger the number for *d*, the bigger the difference. The difference between men's and women's average height is one of the biggest sex differences, with a *d* value of 2.[10] If this were a psychological difference, this would be considered extremely large.[11] If the difference in average height were smaller, the graphs would overlap more, and the *d* value would be smaller.

---

[10] Hines (2004: 10).
[11] Hines (2004: 10).

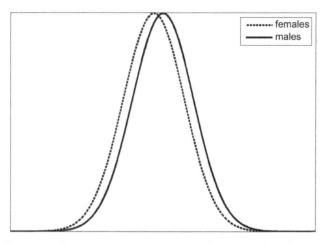

Figure 3.2 Graphic representation of a sex difference where d = 0.21

Figure 3.2 is an example of how a small gender difference with a *d* value of 0.21 looks when plotted out on a graph.[12]

Now that we've explained how sex differences are measured, in the next section we'll look at whether men and women have meaningful psychological sex differences that explain the differences between their educational and career choices that we see in society. When considering the evidence of psychological sex differences, we will refer to the *d* values researchers have assigned to the categories so that you can see how similar or different males and females are in comparison to each other. For psychological sex differences, a *d* value greater than 0.8 is considered large, 0.5 is considered moderate, and 0.2 is considered small. A *d* value below 0.2 is considered negligible.[13]

What scientists know—and what they don't

Scientists have been investigating psychological sex differences since at least the early twentieth century, but the only book on the topic that ever seemed to earn the respect of most scientists in this field was published in 1974. Written by two eminent psychologists, Eleanor Maccoby and

---

[12] Kling et al. (1999).

[13] Hines (2004: 10).

Carol Jacklin, *The Psychology of Sex Differences* is regularly described as a 'watershed'[14] or 'landmark'[15] book on psychological sex differences. Maccoby and Jacklin reviewed more than 2000 studies of a wide variety of psychological sex differences, including cognitive abilities, personality, social behaviour, and memory. The book summarized their findings and concluded that scientists had established the existence of real psychological sex differences in just five areas: physical aggression, children's play behaviour, and in three cognitive abilities—verbal ability, visual-spatial ability, and mathematical ability.

In an article published in 2005, Janet Hyde of the University of Wisconsin–Madison refined some of those earlier conclusions. She reviewed the results of 46 major 'meta-analyses' of studies in sex differences since Maccoby's and Jacklin's book. (A meta-analysis is a statistical method for combining the results of many studies on the same question to arrive at a conclusion based on all the studies.) She grouped the newer results into six categories, based on the subject matter assessed:

- cognitive variables;
- communication;
- social and personality variables, such as aggression or nurturance;
- measures of psychological well-being, such as depression symptoms, coping, and self-esteem;
- motor behaviours, such as throwing distance;
- miscellaneous mental constructs, such as moral reasoning.

She found that 30% of the differences measured were in the close to zero range—that is, they had d values less than 0.10. That is so small as to make it hardly existing. Consider Figure 3.2 again. That shows a d value of 0.21—twice as big as 30% of the differences measured. Another 48% were in the small range, that is, d was between 0.11 and 0.35. Hyde was surprised ____ver that only 22% of the sex differences studied was above the

05).

4: 9).

small range. Think about that for a minute. If Figure 3.2 demonstrates a *d* of 0.21, think about how much overlap there must be for 78% of the sex differences, which measure between 0.10 and 0.35. In fact, as you'll see, none of the differences found in these studies come even close to the difference in average height between the sexes. Remember? The *d* value for differences in average height was *2.0*—not 0.2, but *2.0*. Because so few of the sex differences studied so far rise to the level of moderate or large, Hyde argues that males and females are similar—not different—on most psychological variables.

To understand the significance of Hyde's research, we need to look more closely at some of the studies covered by the meta-analyses she examined. We'll focus on the studies of cognitive abilities, communication, and psychological traits—the first four categories on Hyde's list— since these features would seem to have more influence on sex differences in education, occupation, and career patterns than motor behaviours and moral reasoning.

Let's start with cognitive abilities. Hyde reviewed nine meta-analyses of studies on cognitive sex differences. Each of the nine meta-analyses synthesized the results of hundreds of studies testing thousands of participants on different types of cognitive variables, including a wide range of mathematical abilities, various visual-spatial abilities, and a number of verbal and reasoning abilities. Together, the scientific studies had investigated a total of 39 cognitive variables in human functioning. Of the 39 abilities covered, one-third of them (13) were close to zero. Only seven measured above the small range. Of those seven, only one measured in the large range: mechanical reasoning.

Furthermore, two of the meta-analyses of studies of mental rotation— one of the abilities where males are thought to have a clear advantage— had different results. One showed a moderate sex difference in favour of males (0.56). The other showed a larger difference (0.73) in favour of males. However, according to Melissa Hines, a psychology professor at Cambridge University, these results can be even further refined. She says that the sex difference for performance on mental rotation tests range from small for two-dimensional rotations (0.26 in favour of males) to large (0.94 in favour of males) on a three-dimensional task.[16] Other visual-spatial abilities include spatial perception and spatial visualiza- tion. The sex differences measured in these abilities range from negligible in spatial visualization to moderate in spatial perception.[17]

What does all this add up to? As it turns out, not much. Despite the differences in a few cognitive areas concerned with mental rotation, researchers have essentially *not* found significant evidence of the exist- ence of a clear male or female advantage in visual-spatial or mathematical ability.[18] The fact is, the variations in cognitive abilities among men and women are far greater *within* each sex than *between* the sexes. Harvard psychology professor Elizabeth Spelke puts it this way: 'When you add up all the things that men are good at and all the things that women are good at, there is no overall advantage for men that would put them at the top of the fields of math and science.'[19] The average sex difference in the one cognitive ability where men seem to have a clear advantage—three- dimensional mental rotation—is not enough by itself to explain why no women have yet won the Nobel Prize in mathematics or science and so few become mathematicians, engineers, or scientists.

Now let's look at communication differences between men and women. Hyde also found that there were no large sex differences in this area, either. Her review of the research in this area included five meta- analyses of studies in various aspects of communication. The only type of communication in which a large sex difference was observed was in infants' processing of facial expressions, and the results obtained across the various studies included in these meta-analyses ranged from small to large (0.18 to 0.92) in girls' favour. Such a broad spread of results is normally not considered to be reliable evidence of any conclusion about the magnitude of the sex difference. In order to be reliable, the results of different studies should replicate each other, or at least be more similar.

---

[16] Hines (2004: 12).
[17] Hines (2004: 12–14).
[18] Hines (2004: 14–16).
[19] 'The Science of Gender and Science—Pinker vs. Spelke: A Debate' (16 May 2005).

Furthermore, the sex difference in processing facial expressions even diminished as children got older. By the time children reach adolescence, the studies show men and women process facial expressions with a very small *d* value ranging from only 0.13 to 0.18 in favour of girls. The only documented sex difference in communication that fell into the moderate range was in adolescents' and adults' smiling—and this was only when the people were aware of being observed. When they were unaware of being observed, the sex difference reduced to small (0.19) in favour of girls. All the other measures of sex differences in communication (such as interruptions in conversation, talkativeness, assertive speech, affiliative speech, and self-disclosure to strangers and friends) were in the small to negligible range.

What can we conclude from the research on male and female com-munication behaviours? Oxford University professor Deborah Cameron puts it this way in her book *The Myth of Mars and Venus*: 'The idea that men and women differ fundamentally in the way they use language to communicate is a myth in the everyday sense: a widespread but false belief.'[20] In other words, men and women appear to come from the same planet with regard to communication.

What about sex differences in personality and social traits and meas-ures of psychological well-being?

First, we want to point out that sex differences in personality traits have been documented in many empirical studies. Maccoby and Jacklin con-cluded that men are more assertive and less anxious than women while no differences were found for two other traits they analysed—self-esteem and locus of control (that is, the extent to which individuals believe that they can control events that affect them). In 1994 Feingold confirmed these and other gender differences in a meta-analysis. He concluded that women scored lower than men on assertiveness and higher on extraver-sion, anxiety, trust, and tender-mindedness (or nurturance).

In 2001, Costa, Terracciano, and McCrae published the results of their secondary analysis of data taken from personality inventories

---

[20] Cameron (2007: 3).

administered in 26 different cultures.[21] Their results essentially replicated the sex differences found in the previous studies and added some additional nuances. They show that gender differences are modest in magnitude, consistent with gender stereotypes, and replicable across cultures. The women reported themselves to be higher in neuroticism (a term used to cover a broad domain of negative affect, including predispositions to experience anxiety, anger, depression, shame, and other distressing emotions), agreeableness, warmth, and openness to feelings, whereas men were higher in assertiveness and openness to ideas. However, the authors also point out that their data suggest that sex differences in personality traits are small relative to individual variation within the sexes and that the differences are broadly consistent with gender stereotypes. Finally, they point out the limitations of their and others' studies of sex differences in personality—namely, that personality inventories are tests taken by individuals so that the data are based on self-reports, not observation by others, and that the causes of these differences cannot be deduced from the results of these studies. The authors do, however, suggest that because the magnitude of gender differences varied across cultures, the data do not support evolutionary explanations. That is, the data do not support the belief that women are more agreeable and nurturing because that behaviour promoted the survival of their children and gave such women an evolutionary advantage.

Now let's look at two of the most widely assumed differences between the sexes with regard to personality traits: aggressiveness and empathy.

Aggressiveness—Hyde reviewed five meta-analyses of studies on aggression. No surprise here, as some studies document the sex difference for physical aggression as being moderate to large (0.4–0.8) in favour of males. But while this research documents that males are more prone to physical aggression than women, this trait surely is not the rationale for why males should have an advantage when it comes to rising to positions of leadership, where physical aggression is frowned upon.

---

[21] Costa et al. (2001).

As for verbal or psychological forms of aggression, the research is inconclusive. Hyde notes that a lot of publicity was given to a 1995 study showing moderate gender differences in aggression in relationships, with girls scoring higher, but a 2004 meta-analysis of work in this area showed that the magnitude of gender differences in relational aggression varied: it was 0.13, when based on data from teacher reports, 0.45 when measured by direct observation, and 0.19 based on peer ratings.[22] With such a wide variation in measures, Hyde regards the evidence as inconclusive regarding the magnitude of the gender difference in this form of aggression. Perhaps a reasonable conclusion might be that men and women are roughly equal in terms of aggressiveness—they just express it in different ways.

Caring and empathy—Hyde reviewed various studies on helping behaviour and care-oriented, rather than justice-oriented, moral reasoning. The meta-analysis of studies on helping behaviour showed close to *no sex difference* in contexts where the subjects were *not aware of being observed*, but a large sex difference *in favour of males* when they *were aware of being observed*. (In other words, *men* became more helpful when they were aware of being watched.) But there was only a small sex difference in care-oriented moral reasoning (0.28) in favour of females.

Other studies also indicate that observations about a sex difference in empathy depend on whether participants are aware of what's being measured. Not surprisingly, self-reports—in the form of answers on written questionnaires—tend to result in higher scores for women than men.[23] When other indicators of empathy—such as facial expressions and physiological responses, which cannot be self-reported—are considered, the sex difference practically disappears. What do scientists conclude from this? Men and women seem to differ in how empathetic they would like to appear to others (and perhaps to themselves)—not how empathetic they actually are.[24]

[22] Archer (2004).
[23] For a discussion of the research on this issue, see Ickes et al. (2000).
[24] Klein and Hodges (2001); Ickes et al. (2000).

Much ado about nothing

In the end, the science behind sex differences proves very little, if anything at all. The sex differences many have believed existed are not supported by reliable scientific evidence. The overall research shows:

- no clear male or female advantage in verbal, visual-spatial, or mathematical ability;
- no clear overall difference in communication;
- no difference, or at most a small difference, in verbal aggression in favour of males.

The only reliably documented psychological sex differences appear to be these:

- a moderate to large sex difference in physical aggression in favour of males;
- a moderate sex difference in assertiveness in favour of males;
- a small difference in favour of females in care-oriented moral reasoning;
- a substantial sex difference in caring and empathy in favour of females *when they are aware* that that is what is expected of them; but *virtually none when they are not aware* of that expectation.

Since we are not psychologists, we cannot comment on the quality of Hyde's review of the meta-analyses or on the meta-analyses themselves. There may be flaws or nuances in Hyde's review and the other studies that we have missed. Nevertheless, the sex differences—and far greater similarities—we have summarized here are widely considered to be reliably documented. The data come from peer-reviewed studies by qualified researchers, and the meta-analyses were all published in peer-reviewed journals. That is as professional and credible as any scientific study in any discipline can be in terms of rigorous criteria for judging the quality of the data and the accuracy of the conclusions.

So are these sex differences enough to explain the persistent gender imbalances we observe in society today or not? In our view, and we hope in yours, no. This research merely confirms that a few small sex differences in specific areas have been observed and measured. The fact that scientists have documented significant sex differences in regard to physical aggression and assertion, and, in some situations, also nurturance, does not explain much about why there are far more male than female leaders, or whether male- and female-dominated occupations are the results of natural preferences alone or something else, such as cultural influences.

The 'Variability Thesis': another groundless claim

If there aren't any significant psychological or cognitive sex differences, what about Larry Summers' argument that there may simply be a higher degree of variation among men—more geniuses and more idiots—than among women with regard to cognitive and psychological abilities? Is this what accounts for more men at the top of everything from science to investment banking?

Known as the Variability Thesis, this claim is not new. It originated in the early nineteenth century with Johan Meckel, a German professor of anatomy, surgery, and obstetrics, who believed that most geniuses and most mentally retarded people are men, and that this greater variation among males was evidence of female inferiority.[25] In an article published in *The New Republic*, Harvard psychology professor Steven Pinker defended Larry Summers' with a modern version of the Variability Thesis:

> In many traits, men show greater variance than women, and are disproportionately found at both the low and high ends of the distribution. Boys are more likely to be learning disabled or retarded but also more likely to reach the top percentiles in assessments of mathematical ability, even though boys and girls are similar in the bulk of the bell curve. The pattern is readily explained by evolutionary biology. Since a male can have more offspring than a female—but also has a greater chance of being childless (the victims of other males who impregnate the available females)—natural selection

---

[25] Benjamin (1990).

71

favours a slightly more conservative and reliable baby-building process for females and a slightly more ambitious and error-prone process for males.[26]

Pinker is a smart man—a Harvard professor. And this argument sounds reasonable. But when we took a look at what other experts in this field are saying, we found little scientific support for either the Variability Thesis or Pinker's evolutionary explanation. In fact, there is growing evidence to refute both claims.

You would expect that if greater male variability were innate, you would find evidence of it across cultures. But one cross-cultural study published in 1994 showed that the well-established findings of consistently greater male variability in mathematical and spatial abilities in the USA do not repeat themselves across cultures and nations. Males were more variable than females in some nations and females were more variable than males in other nations.[27] Similar results have also been found in more recent studies.[28] The weight of the evidence is not on Summers' or Pinker's side.

The perennial question: is it our hardware or software?
The research we've summarized above says nothing about what *causes* psychological and behavioural sex differences. Whether there *are* sex differences is a separate issue from the question of what *causes* them. You cannot conclude from the mere *existence* of sex differences that they are innate or learned.

This is an important question, because if it turns out that nurture has a lot to do with behavioural sex differences between men and women—like differences in educational and career choices—then perhaps they can be reduced or eliminated through training and education.

So in addition to looking at whether there *are* measurable psychological and behavioural sex differences, scientists have been investigating

[26] Pinker (2005).
[27] Feingold (1994).
[28] Cited and discussed in Fine (2010: 180–4). See also Professor Elizabeth Spelke's response to Steven Pinker in 'The Science of Gender and Science—Pinker vs. Spelke: A Debate' (16 May 2005).

the *causes* of psychological and behavioural sex differences. Perhaps not surprisingly, a lot of this research has also focused on the brain and hormones. But when evaluating scientific research about biological causes of sex differences, it is important to consider whether the research is investigating an already proven sex difference, or whether the research is simply investigating a biological difference in male and female brains and hormones. Finding a difference between male and female cognitive abilities or psychological traits is not the same as finding a difference in brains or hormones—or vice versa. That is, a study that finds a difference in male and female cognitive abilities or psychological traits tells us nothing about whether nature or nurture causes that difference.

Now let's take a look at one of the leading proponents of the view that behavioural sex differences, including career choices and intellectual achievements, are hardwired: Simon Baron-Cohen, professor of developmental psychopathology at Cambridge University in England. In his book, *The Essential Difference*, he argues that there is 'growing support' for his theory that 'the female brain is predominantly hardwired for empathy' while 'the male brain is predominantly hardwired for understanding and building systems'.[29]

The first clue that maybe you should take what Baron-Cohen says about behavioural sex differences with a grain of salt is that he is an internationally respected expert on autism, not behavioural sex differences. Another clue that assertions like his might not stand close scientific scrutiny is the harsh professional criticism directed at similar assertions by Louann Brizendine, a psychiatrist at University of California in San Francisco, whose book *The Female Brain* hit the best-seller list in 2006. In her book she argued that 'outstanding verbal agility' and 'a nearly psychic capacity to read faces and tone of voice for emotions and state of mind' are 'hardwired into the brains of women'.[30] The highly respected scientific journal *Nature* published a scathing review of her book, pointing out that

[29] Baron-Cohen (2004: 1).
[30] Brizendine (2006: 31).

not only did she lack documentation for many of her assertions, but she misrepresented the scientific research she did cite.[31]

Another clue that these assertions are not to be accepted as facts is that they don't match up with the sex differences that scientists have generally accepted—the ones we described above. Baron-Cohen and Brizendine argue quite simply—without any conditions attached—that women are better at empathy, which as we've seen has only been shown to be true when women think that's what is expected of them. Not only that, but Baron-Cohen claims there's another sex difference—he calls it 'systemizing'—that has not yet even been identified or measured by any other scientists.[32]

Despite these shortcomings, these two authors have enjoyed tremendous popularity, perhaps in part because they are scientists with otherwise respectable credentials who are saying something that makes people feel better about the obvious gender imbalances we see in the world today. These are cases of the tail wagging the dog.

Hidden under the white lab coat of science

We respect science, research, and valid conclusions based on evidence, but science is complicated, and the public can often be misled into accepting assertions that seem true, but shouldn't carry any more weight than an expression of personal opinion. You have undoubtedly heard some of these assertions. And because so many people believe stories told by people clothed in the white lab coat of science, we would like to show you why you can't always believe what someone says just because they're wearing a white lab coat.

Human face vs. mechanical mobile experiment   One of Baron-Cohen's more controversial studies is also one of the most often cited by people

---

[31] Young and Balaba (2006).
[32] Levy (2004).

claiming that women are innately more empathetic.[33] In this study, one-day-old babies were shown both a live human face and a mechanical mobile while they lay in their cribs in the hospital rooms they shared with their mothers. The study claims that girl babies spent more time looking at the human face, while boy babies spent more time looking at the mechanical mobile. This study is cited as evidence that girls innately have superior empathetic skills at birth, before any cultural expectations about women have exerted an influence on them.

But this study has been questioned for a number of reasons, including numerous methodological problems that undermine the reliability of its results.[34] First, no other scientist has been able to replicate its results. That fact alone indicates unreliability. Second, and more importantly, it cannot be ruled out that the girls were responding to something other than the 'human-ness' of the face. It seems especially doubtful given how poorly day-old babies actually see. They could just as easily have been responding to some other contrast between the two presentations. Baron-Cohen himself has cautioned against over-interpreting the results of his own study for those reasons.[35]

Foetal testosterone and eye-contact studies   Proponents of the hardwired theory of sex differences frequently assert that they result from the effects of foetal testosterone on human development. Testosterone is the male hormone, present in both males and females in differing amounts. A study done by Baron-Cohen's team is one of the sources of this popular myth.

The team tracked a group of children whose mothers had undergone amniocentesis during pregnancy and gave birth at Addenbrooke's Hospital in Cambridge, England. The researchers measured the levels of foetal testosterone in the amniotic fluid that had been taken from the mothers.

---

[33] One of the more well-known people who like to tell this story is American author and consultant Leonard Sax (2006). For citations to additional people repeating this story in the media, see Fine (2010: 112–13).

[34] Fine (2010: 113–16).

[35] See Schaffer (2008).

When the children were one year old, they recorded how many times the infants made eye-contact with their parents in the course of 20 minutes. Boys showed decreasing eye-contact frequency with increasing levels of foetal testosterone—but only when the foetal testosterone was in the low range. Boys who had been exposed to high levels of foetal testosterone showed higher eye-contact frequency.[36] Despite these results, Baron-Cohen claimed that 'the higher your levels of pre-natal testosterone, the less eye contact you now make'.[37]

When the children reached four years of age, the researchers asked the parents to fill out a questionnaire on their children's social relationships. The parents' answers indicated that children who had been exposed to higher levels of foetal testosterone tended to have lower 'quality of social relationships'. But the difference between boys and girls on this scale was *not* statistically significant; within each sex no significant relationship between foetal testosterone and quality of social relationships was observed.

The last time the researchers checked in with the same children was when they were between the ages of six and eight. The children were given a questionnaire and a test in which they tried to discern emotions from pictures of eyes. Children who had been exposed to higher levels of foetal testosterone tended to score lower on both tests, especially boys considered alone as a group. However, there was no correlation between different foetal testosterone levels and performance among the girls, and there was no overall difference between boys and girls on the eye-reading test.

This study has become popular to cite as proof that boys' relatively higher exposure to foetal testosterone has an impact on their nurturing or empathic abilities. Yet in reality, the results are either mixed or show no impact from foetal testosterone. Furthermore, this work has not been replicated and the results come from a non-representative sample of children from one geographic area. In short, the findings from this study cannot be treated as having established anything about the role of foetal

[36] Our interpretation of the results of these studies relies heavily on Fine (2010: 108–9) and Schaffer (2008).

[37] Baron-Cohen (2004: 101).

testosterone in hardwiring empathic behaviour in the brain. And remember, unless they are made aware that it is being measured, a significant difference between males and females with regard to empathic behaviour has not been scientifically established by any studies.

Brain scan studies It is well known that the right brain hemisphere is involved in spatial ability, while the left hemisphere is involved in verbal abilities. This specialization of the two hemispheres is called *lateralization*. People who argue that female brains are hardwired for empathy and communication while male brains are hardwired for maths and engineering often point to brain scans showing more lateralization in male brains than in female brains.[38]

As we write these words, the most recent example of this particular claim was a US study mentioned at the beginning of this chapter. Published in the journal *Proceedings of the National Academy of Sciences*,[39] and reported widely in news media,[40] the study involved scanning the brains of nearly 1,000 young people, ranging in age from eight to 22, in order to obtain images of brain connectivity. The images show that male brains appear to be wired front to back, with few connections bridging the two hemispheres, while in females, the pathways criss-crossed between left and right. The researchers concluded that these findings 'might explain why men, in general, tend to be better at learning and performing a single task, like cycling or navigating, whereas women are more equipped for multitasking'.[41] However, the BBC interviewed other experts who pointed out that extrapolating from anatomical differences to explain behavioural differences between the sexes is a 'huge leap' and that brain connections are not fixed, but can change throughout life. The latter phenomenon, called 'neuroplasticity', suggests that our brains become what

---

[38] Baron-Cohen (2004: 103); Brizendine (2006: 169).

[39] Ingalhalikar et al. (2013).

[40] See, for example, BBC News (2013); Connor (2013); and Sample (2013).

[41] BBC News (2013).

we do with them.[42] The BBC's experts also pointed out that neuroscientists are far from understanding how neurotransmitters—the chemicals in our brains—function together with different aspects of brain structure. Before they understand that relationship, they cannot answer a fundamental question like 'how do we think?', let alone whether men and women think differently.

The main problem with claiming that brain scans show that male brains are better at cycling or navigating and female brains are better at multitasking is that brain scans don't measure ability or performance. That requires other kinds of tests. Brain scans only show what areas of the brain are active while the person is performing some kind of task. Claims that brain scans prove that male or female brains are better at anything leap over several unproven intermediate steps. And, as we have already pointed out, decades of studies have *still not* uncovered any significant overall sex difference in mathematical or verbal ability. The fact remains: differences among individuals' abilities and behaviours are far more numerous and larger than differences between the sexes.

Can we ever know?

Discoveries in genetics and neuroscience are casting doubt on whether scientists will ever be able to disentangle the strands of nature and nurture that are woven together in a single human being. Scientists now know that genes by themselves don't determine what our brains become.

Genes start and stop working depending on what else is going on. This phenomenon is called gene expression. Our environment, our behaviour, even our thinking, act as triggers and can change which genes are expressed and to what extent. Our genes, brain, and environment continuously interact to such an extent that no one can determine exactly

---

[42] Over the past four decades, neuroscientists have been discovering that education, training, and experience can actually change both the brain's physical structure and its functional organization. For an explanation of the research in easily understood, non-technical language see Eliot (2010: 6–7).

where the effect of one starts and the other ends—at least not given the current state of the art in neuroscientific research.[43]

We want to emphasize that we are *not* claiming that the potential for brain development in humans is unlimited. We're making two other claims. The first is that evidence of a few psychological sex differences in adults is not proof that those differences are the result of differences in neural hardware, as opposed to software. The second point is that no one is currently able to disentangle the effects of genes, brain, and environment on how any human being develops, let alone their role in defining maleness and femaleness. The science that proponents of immutable, hardwired sex differences rely on is shaky at best. It is definitely not a settled issue, nor is it likely to be in the near—or even distant—future.

Being aware of scientific tomfoolery

The irony about the debate going on about whether psychological sex differences are hardwired or the result of social programming is that there is so little evidence for believing that men and women are fundamentally different to begin with. Scientists have done plenty of looking, but it's not as if a smoking gun has been found to prove significant, innate, and permanent psychological sex differences once and for all. In this chapter, we have only listed *some* of the studies used to support claims of hardwired sex differences. We have left out others because they don't really add anything to the discussion. They are all characterized by similar uncertainties—small sample sizes, lack of replication, small statistical variances, and so on.

So if the science is so shaky, why do we keep seeing popular science books and articles written by scientists who claim that men and women are so fundamentally and immutably different? And just as important, why do their books hit the best-seller lists?

Part of the problem is that scientists underestimate how many studies get published even though they do not pass their own tests for reliability.

---

[43] For an accessible explanation of gene expression and its relationship to neuroplasticity see Fine (2010: 176–7).

Reliability of scientific results depends on the ability to reproduce the same results over and over again. In a recent article, *The Economist* reported that the problem of irreproducibility is much more widespread than most people—even scientists—think.[44] The article listed a number of reasons for this problem. One reason appears to be that statistical mistakes in scientific studies are widespread, in large part because most scientists are not statisticians, and 'professional pressure, competition and ambition push scientists to publish more quickly than would be wise'. Another reason is that the peer reviewers who evaluate papers before journals commit to publishing them are not as good at spotting irreproducibility problems as they think. Finally, the structure of scientific careers emphasizes quantity rather than quality of papers. Brian Nosek, a psychologist at the University of Virginia who studies and points out his own discipline's persistent errors, explained, 'There is no cost to getting things wrong. The cost is not getting them published.'[45]

We have acted as peer reviewers for scholarly journals, as Ph.D. advisers, and as members of committees that assess candidates for positions on university faculties, and we have to agree with Professor Nosek. Our experience has taught us a few things about what motivates scientists to publish the things they publish and why some of it makes it to the top of best-seller lists. It has also taught us what to watch out for when we judge the quality of research. There are five common booby traps in scientific research that not only mislead the media and the public but sometimes also the researchers themselves.

1. *The white coat effect*: The basic problem for people who are not experts in a particular subject is that they tend to believe what experts in that subject—or even only marginally related subjects— say. We call that the 'white coat effect'. That's one of the booby traps that we all need to watch out for. Just because an expert *says* research has proven something is not a reason by itself to believe it has been proven. The next items on our checklist explain why.

---

[44] *The Economist* (2013).
[45] *The Economist* (2013).

2. *U2 science—'I still haven't found what I'm looking for'*: When scientists investigate the hypothesis that males and females differ psychologically in some way, it leads to a phenomenon known as the 'file drawer effect'. The positive results are over-reported because the scientists doing the research tend to publish only studies where they observe a sex difference, not other studies where no sex difference emerges. Meanwhile, the studies where *no* sex difference appears often get filed away under the title of U2's famous song, 'I still haven't found what I'm looking for'. The mere fact that there are lots of studies reporting the existence of psychological sex differences is not conclusive by itself. It depends on whether all those studies replicate the results of a particular study, and if all the studies fulfil all the requirements of good scientific methodology. Only then can the results of those studies be regarded as reliable.

3. *If you have a hammer, you'll find a nail*: When individual scientists study psychological characteristics from a single research perspective, they unfortunately develop a tendency to forget other factors that can contribute to the development of those characteristics. For example, if an endocrinologist is trying to prove the hypothesis that women have better verbal skills, she will explore the role of hormones in producing sex differences in verbal skills. She will probably not investigate why it is that in many non-Western societies, men are believed by both sexes to be more verbally skilled than women.[46] One of the unfortunate consequences of this tendency is that scientists studying biological reasons for psychological sex difference may see stronger limitations on human potential than they would if they considered social influences as well.[47]

4. *Headline science*: This problem concerns the news media's tendency to publish stories about the results from a single study. A single study does not constitute conclusive evidence of anything. Think of how many times you've read a study about the health effects of coffee. One study says it is good for us, and then a year later another

[46] Cameron (2007: 116).

[47] Hines (2004: 227).

study proves it is bad for us. Before scientists accept the results of a single study, the same results have to be replicated in numerous studies with numerous participants.

A good example of this research booby trap was one of the first studies to use functional MRI (fMRI) to investigate sex differences in brain function. The husband-and-wife team Bennet and Sally Shaywitz and their colleagues at Yale University in the USA measured brain activity in 19 men and 19 women as they performed *three* different language tasks. During *one* of the tasks—identifying rhymes—the fMRI images showed strong activation of the *left* frontal lobes of men's brains while the same frontal area on *both* sides of women's brains were activated in *11*—not all—of the 19 women. *The New York Times* science section reported on the study under the headline: 'Men and Women Use Brain Differently, Study Discovers'.[48]

Subsequently, Iris Sommer, a scientist at the University of Utrecht in Holland, and her colleagues reviewed 26 comparable brain-imaging studies of sex differences in language processing that had been completed since the Shaywitz study. These studies provided data from a total of *more than 2000 participants*. After putting all the findings together, Sommer and her colleagues concluded that the studies do *not* prove the existence of any sex difference in language processing.[49] But the results of Sommer's review did not make headlines in the science section of *The New York Times*.

5. *Making a chicken out of a feather*: The best example of this kind of problem is found in the use of brain scans for identifying psychological sex differences. The scientifically most reliable use of fMRI is to measure local brain activity in response to cognitive tasks performed during the brain scan.[50] Data obtained from these kinds of brain scans allow the cognitive neuroscientist to infer something about the role of particular brain regions during a particular

[48] Kolata (1995).
[49] Sommer et al. (2004, 2008).
[50] Poldrack (2011).

cognitive function. This kind of inference is called a forward inference. It could be compared to taking a feather from a chicken as a sample to study chicken feathers.

However, there has been increasing use of data from brain scans to make the opposite inference—that is, to infer particular cognitive functions, like men are better at reading maps—from activation of particular brain structures and regions. This kind of reverse inference is like drawing conclusions about chickens from studying a feather. A Swedish saying calls this kind of thinking 'making a chicken out of a feather'. It skips way too many steps in between; and scientists have been criticizing this tendency. As one of these scientists points out in a recent paper, drawing inferences about cognitive functions from the mere fact that particular brain regions are activated can be a means towards generating interesting hypotheses, which require further testing, but until then they remain interesting hypotheses, not proven claims about how things really are.[51] No matter what someone in a white lab coat says to the contrary, accepting reverse inferences from brain scans as proof of anything would be making a chicken out of a feather.

To avoid falling for any of the five booby traps of sex difference science, commit them to memory and practise applying them to news stories and in conversations with other people. To help you do that, study the examples in Box 3.1.

Men and women are earthlings

Why did we bother reviewing all this science? Because making chickens out of feathers, mistaking headlines for science, and giving too much weight to U2 science has had very unfortunate consequences in the debate about gender balance in our societies. They have clothed numerous sex stereotypes in white coats and persuaded us that men and women are so different that that they must be aliens from two different planets rather than human beings from Earth.

---

[51] Poldrack (2011).

Box 3.1 The five booby traps of sex-difference science and how to avoid them

1. *The white coat effect*

Someone wearing a white coat or carrying a Ph.D. diploma always tells the world about things that have been proven scientifically.

- How to avoid: Remember that individual scientists like to and often need to promote their work, regardless of whether it conclusively proves anything or not.

2. *U2 science*

Some scientists still haven't found what they're looking for.

- How to avoid: Remember that scientists like to find proof for their hypotheses. They keep looking even when their own experiments indicate that they might be wrong.

3. *If you have a hammer, you'll find a nail*

Scientists usually study psychological characteristics from a single research perspective, like neuroscience or endocrinology, and tend to explain what they study in terms of neuroscience or endocrinology, forgetting about what other scientific disciplines studying the same things have discovered.

- How to avoid: Remember that the causes of human behaviour cannot be explained by one discipline alone.

4. *Headline science*

Some science makes great headlines.

- How to avoid: Remember that great headlines do not make great science.

5. *Making a chicken out of a feather*

Observing differences in the appearance of scans of male and female brains while their owners are doing the same task—like reciting poetry or solving maths problems—means men and women think differently or have different abilities.

- How to avoid: Remember that there's more to brain functioning than can be shown on a brain scan, just as there's more to a chicken than its feathers.

The bottom line is that science has not proven that brain-based differences explain why men and women are clustered into different occupations and follow different career paths. It is doubtful that it ever will. In seeking explanations for human behaviour, we are dependent on social sciences like psychology, anthropology, and sociology. Human behaviour is the product of an enormous number of interconnected variables that are extraordinarily difficult—if not impossible—to distinguish and study separately. It is simply too complex for anyone—whether she's a neurobiologist or a psychologist—to make any valid claim about the existence or causes of behavioural differences between the sexes based on a single study of any kind.

We cannot afford to pretend that a feather is a chicken, that a headline tells the whole truth, or that fMRI can unlock the secrets of sex differences for us. On the other hand, we do have substantial evidence that investing in women's education and employment contributes to our common prosperity. Including balanced numbers of women and men in all aspects of our social and economic life will enrich us all.

The most recent and reliable research in neuroscience and sex differences suggests that it is not sex differences in our genes and brains that are the main obstacle preventing us from achieving gender balance. It is the limits of our own imagination.

Key points and guiding principle

- There is no scientific evidence showing that differences between male and female brains account for gender gaps in leadership, intellectual achievement, or occupational preferences.
- Differences among individuals are much larger than they are between men and women.
- Brain plasticity and discoveries showing that genes start and stop working depending on how we behave, how we think, and what we experience make it unlikely that scientists will ever be able to figure out how much nature and how much nurture determines how our brains work.

Guiding principle: *Bring men and women back to Earth.*

4

Slugs & Snails, Sugar & Spice

In April of 2008, two Icelandic businesswomen, Halla Tomasdottir and Kristin Petursdottir, launched a new financial service business, Audur Capital. They had spent the previous 20 years pursuing successful careers in international business and investment banking. Six months later, Iceland was on the brink of economic collapse. Inflation and interest rates were raging upwards. Iceland's currency was in free fall, rated just above those of Zimbabwe and Turkmenistan. Halla and Kristin could hardly have chosen a worse time to start a business of any kind—and certainly not in the financial sector. Nevertheless, they made it. Audur Capital did not take any direct losses to its equity or to the funds of its clients. Meanwhile, Iceland went bankrupt.

The company's success earned Halla an invitation to speak at the famous TED conference in 2011. Giving the reason for her firm's remarkable performance before a receptive, largely female audience, she told them that her firm made it through the Icelandic crisis because the company's investment practices were based on and led by what she called five core values. They are:

- Risk awareness: Audur Capital will not invest in things it doesn't understand.
- Profit with principles: Audur Capital defines profit to include not just economic profit, but also positive social and environmental impact.

- Emotional capital: When Audur Capital invests, it carries out an emotional due diligence—a check on the company—to see whether the corporate culture is an asset or a liability.
- Straight talking: Audur Capital believes the language of finance should be accessible, and not part of the alienating nature of banking culture.
- Independence: Audur Capital aims to give unbiased advice as well as support women's financial independence.

Halla says that these values are *feminine* values, implying that women are more likely to have these values than men. In contrast, Halla told her audience that the financial sector's troubles since 2008 stem from investment practices guided by a different set of values that produced dishonesty, too much risk taking, ignoring the people behind and in front of the investment, and the pursuit of profit for profit's sake without regard for the physical or social environment. Although she did not say that these are masculine values, or that men hold them, her implication was clear: men tend to be greedy and reckless, while women tend to be more prudent and socially responsible.

Halla is not the only one to suggest that men—or at least stereotypically male behaviour and values—were one of the main causes of the disastrous 2008 financial crash. At the 2009 meeting of the World Economic Forum in Davos, a spontaneous discussion broke out about whether Lehman Brothers would have failed if the company had been called Lehman Sisters. *New York Magazine* reported that the conclusion of the discussion at Davos was that Lehman would probably still be in business although it would have made less money during the boom years.[1] The implication here: women would not have taken the big risks to make big money, but they would have not caused the company's demise as its male executives did.

[1] Kolhatkar (2010).

Assigning gender to values: makes as much sense as nursery rhymes

Such gender-based analyses of the reasons for the financial crisis sound a lot like the sentiments expressed in the classic English nursery rhyme 'What are little boys made of?'[2]

> *What are little boys made of?*
> *What are little boys made of?*
> *Slugs and snails*
> *And puppy-dogs' tails,*
> *That's what little boys are made of.*
> *What are little girls made of?*
> *What are little girls made of?*
> *Sugar and spice*
> *And everything nice,*
> *That's what little girls are made of.*

Where do such ideas about the difference between masculine versus feminine values and traits come from? Are they based in reality? As adults, should we really believe the equivalent of a nursery rhyme that goes something like this:

> *Little girls are sugar and spice, and*
> *Female bankers are careful and nice,*
> *While little boys are slugs and snails, and*
> *Male bankers are greedy and unafraid of jails.*

[2] This is one of the classic nursery rhymes attributed to Mother Goose, an imaginary author of a collection of old English nursery rhymes, often published as *Mother Goose Rhymes*. The first compilation of Mother Goose rhymes was probably published in the late 1700s, while perhaps the most famous collection of works attributed to Mother Goose is *The Real Mother Goose*, first published in 1916 by Rand McNally & Co. in Chicago, with cover and illustrations by Blanche Fisher Wright. Various versions of this particular nursery rhyme have circulated. In other versions, boys are made of 'Snaps and snails', 'Snakes and snails', or 'Frogs and snails'.

Quite a few news media outlets have been popularizing this very idea. Many have reported on research claiming that testosterone and other biological sex differences—such as those we covered in Chapter 3—are the reason for the volatility of Wall Street and the irresponsible behaviours of investment bankers. If you Google 'testosterone and financial crisis', you'll get literally thousands of hits, echoing the story reported in *New York Magazine*, 'According to a new breed of researchers from the field of behavioural finance . . . it's the chemicals pulsing through traders' veins that propel them to place insane bets and enable bank executives to make risky decisions.'[3]

We hope you can see by now that these stories are full of the research booby-traps Chapter 3 discussed. They especially single out one or two studies that arrive at results that make punchy headlines, which the journalist or the researcher then uses as a launch pad to proclaim they've found a chicken when they only found a feather.

Indeed, most of this research on testosterone's role in the financial crisis is contrary to decades of research on the effect of testosterone on male behaviour. Evidence from a range of different studies conducted since the 1970s indicates that men's testosterone levels jump in anticipation of some source of competition—it could be any kind of contest, from sports to maths exams. But it rises even higher if they win.[4] This evidence suggests that the largest testosterone increases are a *result*, not a *cause*, of achieving dominance or winning a contest. Furthermore, a parallel rise in testosterone in connection with sports contests or having a high-status job has been measured in women, although their baseline testosterone is just a fraction of men's. Still, none of this research shows that testosterone is the cause of irresponsible investment behaviour.

Besides, losses in the banking sector are not just the result of the pursuit of high-risk ventures that have the potential to make huge profits by

[3] Kolhatkar (2010); Solon (2012), citing research at Cambridge University led by former Wall Street trader now senior research fellow in Neuroscience and Finance John Coates; Adams (2011).

[4] Archer (2006).

a bunch of testosterone-pumped men. In 2012, JP Morgan Chase experienced a $2 billion loss, in large part because the bank's 55-year-old female chief investment officer, Ina Drew, told traders at the bank's chief investment office to execute trades meant to shield the bank from the turmoil in Europe. She believed the trades could protect the bank from losses and maybe earn a profit. But when the market suddenly shifted in April and early May of 2012, and she instructed traders to reduce the exposure, it was too late to avoid a gigantic loss. The full explanation for the loss is not yet known as we write, but the testosterone argument does not seem to fit here.

The testosterone argument also does not hold up when considered from a cultural historical perspective of finance and banking. Not long ago, the entire banking industry was considered to be a highly conservative culture, guided by values like honesty, straight-talk, and responsible risk-taking—before women were even working in that sector. The explanation for today's behaviour points more towards cultural and even political factors. A number of respected economists and commentators agree that there has been a radical shift in corporate, banking, and investment culture, driven by ideological commitments to unhindered corporate governance, and unleashed by the wave of massive deregulation that swept through the financial sector over the past 30 years.[5] We have to ask: Why are some people so willing to conclude, with little scientific proof, that the financial crisis was caused by these so-called *masculine* values instead of looking for a gender-neutral explanation? For example, might a more significant contributing factor have been the uninhibited pursuit of the deregulatory political agenda introduced by President Reagan and Margaret Thatcher when they held power on both sides of the Atlantic? In our view, the greed, risk-taking, and drive for wealth in the financial sector cannot be identified as masculine or feminine; they are simply human traits that are more present in some people, male or female, than others.

[5] Guerrera (2010); Kay (2011); Ghoshal (2005).

Gender boot camp: learning to be male or female

The fact that a woman from Iceland can talk about masculine or feminine values before an international audience at TED and be reasonably sure that she'll be understood—and even applauded—is testimony to the fact that Western cultures share roughly similar understandings about masculinity and femininity. The distinction between male and female is, in fact, one of the basic organizing principles for every human culture. Throughout the world, women and men are clearly viewed as two categories of human beings with different psychological and behavioural propensities linked to their reproductive functions. We distinguish between masculine and feminine behaviour in our mind-sets. We notice when men and women behave in ways that do not match our sense of what we believe to be normal gender behaviour.

How and why does this happen? From where do we get our notions of gender-appropriate behaviour?

In Chapter 3 we argued that the claim that specific cognitive and behavioural sex differences are hardwired in our brains lacks sufficient scientific evidence to be regarded as representing the Truth. Here, on the other hand, we want to argue that humans seem to be hardwired to distinguish between males and females. That claim appears to be rather uncontroversial. A substantial amount of research shows that knowing how to identify the biological sex of other people—without looking at their genitals—and to behave in ways that are consistent with the standards of those gender norms become part of our social repertoire right from infancy.[6]

Babies just three to four months old learn to distinguish between female and male faces as well as same-race and other-race faces. Developmental psychologists have found that a baby's preference for faces of one sex or the other stems from acquired experience with those kinds of faces. Babies who have spent most of their time with female caregivers prefer female faces while babies who have been cared for by men prefer

---

[6] Ruble et al. (2013).

male faces. At just ten months old, babies will look longer—perhaps from surprise—at a picture of a man with an object that had been previously included in pictures with women, and vice versa.[7]

This ability to distinguish between male and female human beings coincides as well with the process of the child's formation of his or her own gender identity. Psychologists do not believe babies are born with a coherent sense of self since their brains are largely unformed at birth. Their neural circuits become organized only through experience. Babies begin to understand themselves as separate beings through their relationships with the adults who care for them. By the time they are two, children learn to use gender labels—he, she, him, and her—and can tell you if a person is a boy or girl.[8] There is also some evidence that by the age of two years children associate things like fire hats, makeup, and dolls with different genders.[9] In effect, learning to recognize and distinguish gender appears to be one of our first social achievements.

As babies grow, not only do they learn to distinguish between male and female, but they also begin to formulate how each gender behaves. At around the age of two, as we leave babyhood, we begin to get messages about the difference between baby behaviour and big girl or big boy behaviour.[10] Being called a baby is an insult when you're no longer a baby. Thus it becomes vitally important for children to find out what it means to be either a big girl or a big boy.

Developmental psychologists Carol Martin and Diane Ruble describe pre-school aged children as 'gender detectives' because they are constantly searching for clues about what actions they should take to be big boys or big girls.[11] Children seem to seize on just about anything as clues to their appropriate gender behaviour. Martin and Ruble report that the clearest evidence that young children are 'actively constructing' gender categories

[7] Levy and Haaf (1994).
[8] Zosuls et al. (2009).
[9] Serbin et al. (2002).
[10] Cahill (1986).
[11] Martin and Ruble (2004).

'as part of a process of finding meaning in the social world' is their habit of drawing faulty conclusions about gender distinctions and ignoring information that is not consistent with their perception of appropriate gender roles. For example, in one study, children were shown equal numbers of pictures of people engaged in gender-stereotypic activities—like a girl sewing—and gender-inconsistent activities—like a boy cooking. The children were three times more likely to misremember the non-stereotypical than the stereotypical pictures. So instead of remembering that they'd seen a picture of a boy cooking, they remembered that they'd seen a picture of a girl cooking. Experimental research also suggests that young children are quick to jump to conclusions about sex differences, even on the basis of only a single instance, making it difficult to find any gender-neutral stimuli to use in psychological experiments. For example, in one study, when three-year-olds were told that a particular boy likes a sofa and a particular girl likes a table, they generalized this information to draw the conclusion that another girl would also like the table.[12]

Trying not to be babies, children focus on imitating the actions, facial expressions, and gestures of the big boys or big girls in their lives. All they can do is assimilate what their parents (nurture) and surroundings (culture) teach them about being a boy or a girl. In fact, children don't get the idea that their boy-ness or girl-ness does not depend on their behaviour but on something more permanent—their anatomy—until the age of about six or seven. Lise Eliot, author of *Pink Brain, Blue Brain*, tells how her four-year-old son knew perfectly well he was a boy, but somehow got the idea that he might get a baby in his tummy when he grew up.[13] He was very excited about it and disappointed to learn that it simply wasn't possible. For children this age, says Eliot, 'You simply *are* male or female based on your choice of clothes, toys, hair length, and favourite colour'.[14]

---

[12] Martin and Ruble (2004).

[13] Eliot (2010: 116).

[14] Eliot (2010: 116).

Little boys and girls are not just gender detectives; they are also their own gender police. Once they've learned behaviour and applied it to themselves as a norm, they often try to enforce adherence to it among their peers—even if the norms they have learned are idiosyncratic compared to other children. One amusing example of this phenomenon comes from a psychologist couple, Sandra and Daryl Bem, who decided to raise their young children Jeremy and Emily in a gender-neutral way 40 years ago. Their child-raising strategy included promoting the idea that the only difference between males and females is their anatomy and reproductive functions. Although their children seemed to understand this, their peers in pre-school, who had learned how to behave like big boys and girls from their own parents, did not grasp it. In a well-known journal article published in 1983, Sandra Bem tells the following story about what happened when their son Jeremy, at the age of four, decided to wear barrettes in his hair to nursery school:

> Several times that day, another little boy told Jeremy that he, Jeremy, must be a girl because 'only girls wear barrettes'. After trying to explain to this child that 'wearing barrettes doesn't matter' and that 'being a boy means having a penis and testicles', Jeremy finally pulled down his pants as a way of making his point more convincingly. The other child was not impressed. He simply said, 'Everybody has a penis; only girls wear barrettes.'[15]

Developmental psychologists observing pre-school age children at play have also found that children are distinctly less friendly towards their peers who play in ways that don't correspond to their notions of what's gender-appropriate. They can be exceedingly judgemental, saying things like, 'That's dumb, boys don't play with dolls.' Or they can simply declare that it's against gender rules. For example, when researcher Cordelia Fine's kindergarten-aged son asked to see a little girl's book, she wouldn't let him, explaining, 'Boys aren't *allowed* to look at books about fairies.'[16]

[15] Bem (1983).
[16] Fine (2010: 218).

Children are acutely aware of what their peers are policing, and they adapt their behaviour accordingly. Psychologists have observed that pre-school children spend more time playing with gender-appropriate toys when an opposite-sex peer is nearby than when they play alone. Other experiments show that four- to six-year-old boys express more interest in playing with boyish toys when they are with peers than when they are on their own.[17]

The parental influence on gender

Parents are obviously not oblivious to the existence and power of these cultural gender norms. Even those who consciously try to raise their children as free from gender stereotypes as possible often find themselves treating their children in conformity with the widely held beliefs of their culture about gender. Gender norms are almost impossible for individuals to shake.

Developmental psychologists recognize that the way adults treat children is actually a major contributing factor in children's adoption of gendered behaviour. Acknowledging that they do not yet know precisely how and when children absorb and adapt their behaviour to gender norms, psychologists are finding evidence indicating that rather than parents responding to the different behaviours of female and male infants, it is more often the other way around—the parents respond differently and model different behaviours based on their own perceptions of gender.

For example, a number of studies have found differences in the way mothers respond to infants and toddlers depending on their gender. In one study that examined mothers' speech and play behaviour with 6-, 9-, and 14-month-old infants, researchers found that the mothers treat baby girls and boys differently, despite the absence of any discernible differences in the babies' behaviour or abilities.[18] For instance, they found that mothers conversed and interacted more with girl babies as young

---

[17] Fine (2010: 218) cites a number of studies from the 1980s, 1990s, and 2000s.

[18] Clearfield and Nelson (2006).

as six months old and young toddlers, even though boys were no less responsive to their mother's speech and were no more likely to leave their mother's side. The authors of the study suggested that this parental behaviour is rooted in training girls in the higher level of social interaction expected of women, while boys are learning the more independent behaviour expected of men.

Another study found that mothers are also more sensitive to happy facial expressions when an unfamiliar six-month-old baby is labelled as a girl rather than a boy, indicating that gender affects a mother's perception of babies' emotions.[19]

Another well-known study showed that beliefs about gender also bias mothers' perceptions of infants' physical abilities.[20] Mothers were shown an adjustable carpeted slope and asked to estimate how steep a slope their eleven-month-old children would attempt to crawl down. The boys and girls did not differ in their crawling ability when it came to testing them on the slope, although girls were found to be willing to crawl down even steeper slopes than the boys. Not being aware that girls were actually more daring than boys on this test, mothers underestimated the girls and overestimated boys with regard to both crawling ability and the steepness of the slope they'd be willing to attempt.

The gender bias in the way mothers relate to children grows more pronounced as children get older. For example, when children reach toddler and pre-school age, researchers find that mothers talk more to girls than to boys, and that they talk about emotions with girls in a way that is consistent with the belief that girls are better at talking about and understanding emotions.[21]

A large meta-analysis in 1991 gathered all the studies that looked at whether parents treat boys and girls differently. Parents seemed to treat boys and girls much the same in many areas, except with regard to

---

[19] Donovan et al. (2007).
[20] Mondschein et al. (2000).
[21] Fine (2010: 199), citing several studies from the late 1990s.

activities and play. Parents encouraged gender-typed activities and play and discouraged cross-gender behaviour.[22]

Today, more than 20 years after that study, it appears that gender norms are changing a bit, at least for some girls. For instance, in a small study of 26 pre-schoolers, almost all the parents agreed that girls should be encouraged to engage in cross-gender play and activities, like playing with building blocks and toy trucks or playing baseball or other competitive sports.[23] However, when the researchers asked the children themselves whether their parents would approve of such behaviour, they got a different story. Only 25% of the three-year-old girls thought that their mother would want them to play with a baseball and mitt or a skateboard, and the girls readily identified both activities as being 'for boys'.

Meanwhile, almost all of these same parents thought it was equally important for boys as it was for girls to have good social skills, which may be interpreted as indicating some support for encouraging non-conformity with gender stereotypes in their sons. However, one-third of them were either uncertain that they would buy their son a doll or they would definitely not do so. And regarding self-perception, just two of the 12 boys in the group, aged three and five years, thought their parents would be happy for them to play with a doll.

The results of this study are consistent with another interview study carried out by psychologist Emily Kane with 42 parents of pre-school children.[24] These parents encouraged gender non-conformity in their young daughters. They also mostly 'accepted, and often even celebrated' activities they thought would promote domestic skills, nurturance, and empathy in their sons—including play with dolls, toy kitchens, and tea sets. However, many of these parents drew the line at playing with Barbie dolls, for example, even though the little boys regularly asked to play with them. Many only grudgingly let their sons participate in activities they regarded as 'feminine'. Just like in the movie *Billy Elliot*, one father said

[22] Fine (2010: 202, endnote 17).

[23] Freeman (2007).

[24] Kane (2006).

that if his son 'really wanted to dance, I'd let him . . . but at the same time, I'd be doing other things to compensate for the fact that I signed him up for dance'.

These examples demonstrate the role of nurture in developing children's gender identity and adherence to gender norms. They confirm in fact how hard it is for parents to raise their children in gender-neutral ways, even when they make a conscious effort to encourage cross-gender activities. Rather than falling back on biology and hardwired theories to explain why young girls and boys seem to prefer sex-stereotyped play and activities, we need to recognize the role of nurture from parents, the surrounding culture, and the fact that children are their own gender detectives and gender police. As long as they see a world with clear divisions between feminine and masculine interests and activities, they will teach themselves and their peers to behave accordingly. Given the continual emphasis on gender stereotypes in the media, in school, in the marketing of toys, and the obvious differences between men's and women's behaviour and life patterns, it is hardly shocking that attempts at gender-neutral parenting don't seem to have much impact.

Looking in the mirror without seeing
What we learn from all the research in the field of gender identity leads to one conclusion. Because gender identity is such an integrated part of our self-concept, it is nearly impossible to imagine that it is something we learn, rather than something we're indelibly born with. Our formation of gender identity and internalization of gender norms seems very similar to language acquisition, wherein researchers believe that biological evolution provided us with 'language-ready brains', which enable us to learn any language our parents and culture teach us while at the same time enabling us to express ourselves in our mother tongue each in our own inimitable way. Perhaps we are similarly provided with 'gender-ready brains'—brains capable of registering sex differences and learning what constitutes gender-appropriate behaviour in the social context into which we are born and where we are raised. Each individual may create his or her own templates for identifying masculine and feminine traits

and behaviour based on inputs from parents, the surrounding culture, and his or her own personal preferences. This means that the traits and behaviours we, as a society, expect men and women to display are perhaps far more fluid than we tend to think.

In our view, this explains why the world is full of such a diversity of human beings. The notion that men are more different than the same as women is belied by reality. We see an enormous spectrum of men living out lives that range from 0 to 100 on the macho scale. We see the same diversity among women on the spectrum of girliness. If the brain is hardwired for specific gender behaviours, the wires are pretty loose.

The big 'why'?

Why do we put so much emphasis on defining our gender identity so concretely, far beyond any need for a basic biological need to distinguish between men and women? Why do we create so many mental boxes to categorize personality traits, behaviours, and activities as either male or female?

It turns out that there are many advantages to our innate ability to recognize and assimilate gender. Chief among them is the ability to automatically simplify what would otherwise seem like a cacophony of social stimuli around us, by sorting people into two categories, which we then use to guide our entry into all manner of social relationships. We are able to do this because our brains have been equipped with two complementary cognitive skills that help us simplify and structure the vast number of sensory stimuli we receive from the world. On one hand, we have the ability to create stable mental pictures of the environments in which we operate. These are what help us learn what to expect of a situation, and to make sense of the world. On the other hand, we are able to recognize new and surprising stimuli in our environment. This capability allows us to override the automated action plans that arise almost unconsciously from our stable mental pictures, so we can respond in adaptive ways. That we possess such flexibility of intelligence is one of the triumphs of human cognition.[25]

---

[25] Macrae and Bodenhausen (2000).

Some psychologists call the cognitive process of structuring incoming information 'schematic processing'. This involves the mobilization of cognitive structures, or schemas, to form a network of associations that organize and guide our perceptions.[26] A schema works like a mental framework that helps us look for and process incoming information in an organized way. Schemas include the ability to recognize social categories and sort people according to them. Each time we meet someone, rather than figuring out how to relate to them by understanding their uniqueness, we instead 'construe them on the basis of the social categories (e.g. gender, race, age) to which they belong'.[27]

Each of us builds up an enormous library of material in our long-term memories that we use, largely unconsciously and automatically, to define these categories. The material necessarily varies from individual to individual, given that we each have our own personal history of experiences. However, to the extent people share a culture, much of the material is the same for all people within a single culture.

Psychologists investigating schematic processing say that we maintain a number of different schemas. Our readiness to invoke one schema rather than another is called 'cognitive availability'. A number of psychologists investigating gender have concluded that we learn to process information about ourselves and other people in terms of an evolving gender schema. We automatically learn what is culturally accepted masculine and feminine behaviour through our relationships with others. Our sense of gender becomes second nature to us, though it changes over time.

But gender schemas have a downside, too. Researchers have been finding out that our innate ability to generate gender schemas tends to limit our ability to see each other as individuals and instead to focus on broad gender stereotypes. Gender schemas are constantly operating in the back of our minds, directing our perception and behaviour.

Data from a wide range of sources have led researchers to conclude that once our gender schemas are activated, they direct and skew our

[26] Bem (1981).
[27] Macrae and Bodenhausen (2000: 95).

perceptions of an individual's traits and abilities, even something as inconsequential as height. In one study, experimenters investigated whether knowing that men are on average taller than women can affect perceptions of men's and women's actual height. They showed photographs of men and women of different heights to college students and asked them to estimate the subjects' height in feet and inches. All the photos contained an object that could be used as a point of reference, like a desk or a doorway, so that the students were not simply guessing. The experimenters did not tell the students that for every photograph of a male of a given height there was a matching photograph of a female student of the same height, meaning the group averages were exactly the same. The students nevertheless judged the women in the photos as shorter than they really were, and the men as taller than they really were. Both male and female student observers were equally likely to misjudge height, demonstrating that both men and women apply non-conscious hypotheses about males and females—or gender schemas—in order to perceive and evaluate others.[28]

Other data show that the gender schemas we share skew our perceptions of competence in such a way that we consistently overrate men's and underrate women's abilities. This fact has been well known to professional orchestras since the 1970s. Among the five highest-ranked orchestras in the USA (known as the 'Big Five')—the Boston Symphony Orchestra (BSO), the Chicago Symphony Orchestra, the Cleveland Symphony Orchestra, the New York Philharmonic, and the Philadelphia Orchestra—none contained more than 12% women until about 1980. The gender gap was so severe that orchestras were obliged to implement 'blind' auditions in which performers played their instrument behind a screen so that the evaluators can hear but not see the gender of the performer.

Not surprisingly, it made a difference. By the late 1990s, the New York Philharmonic had 35% women, the highest percentage among the big

---

[28] Valian (2005).

five. The others followed a similarly dramatic upward trend. According to a study conducted in 1996 by researchers at Harvard and Princeton, the practice of blind auditions increased by 50% the probability that women would advance out of certain preliminary rounds and can explain between 25% and 46% of the increase in the percentage of females in the orchestras from 1970 to 1996. This surge of women in symphony orchestras has occurred despite the fact that the number of positions is highly fixed and turnover is slow.[29]

Gender stereotyping is so ingrained in our cultures that even fake résumés provoke a preference for male candidates for male-dominated jobs and females for female-dominated jobs. A large number of studies using so-called 'paper people' (fictitious job applications created in the lab) have found that, overall, paper men are rated more favourably than identical paper women for masculine jobs, while paper men applying for stereotypically feminine jobs, like secretarial work or teaching 'female' subjects, are rated less favourably than identical paper women.[30] In one study, more than 100 university psychologists were asked to rate the CVs of either Dr Karen Miller or Dr Brian Miller, fictitious applicants for faculty positions at a university. The CVs were identical, apart from the names. Brian was, nevertheless, perceived by both male and female reviewers to have better qualifications than Karen in all categories: research, teaching, and service experience. Overall, about three-quarters of the psychologists thought that Brian was qualified for the job, while only just under half had the same confidence in Karen.[31]

---

[29] Goldin and Rouse (2000).

[30] Davison and Burke (2000).

[31] Steinpreis et al. (1999). In 2012, researchers at Yale University published the results of a study showing the same phenomenon with regard to the way university science faculty evaluate student applications for research jobs. The results showed that pre-existing subtle bias against women played a role in rating male student applicants to a laboratory manager position as significantly more competent and hireable than the (identical) female student applicants. Male and female faculty evaluating the applicants were equally likely to exhibit bias against the female student. Moss-Racusin et al. (2012).

Gender is so powerful, we even stereotype ourselves

Other studies indicate that our inner gender schemas do not just affect our judgements of other people—they also affect our judgements of our own competences. For example, some French psychologists asked a group of French high school students to rate the truth of stereotypes about gender difference in talent in maths and the arts. Next, they were asked to report their scores in maths and the arts on an important national standardized test taken about two years earlier. The researchers found that the more the female students endorsed the belief that men are better at mathematics than women, the more they underestimated their own test scores. The male students produced similar results when asked to report their school marks in the arts after rating the truth of the stereotype of women's greater ability in arts. Both males and females overestimated male students' marks consistently with the strength of their belief in stereotypes about what males and females are good at.[32]

The researchers noted that the results of this study are in line with recent research documenting that even women who perform as well as men on a reasoning test tend to underestimate their performance on that test compared to men. These results suggest that women may be less likely to pursue scientific careers than men in part because gender stereotypes lead them to underestimate their past achievements and abilities.

Researchers have also been studying the negative effects that negative stereotypes have on performance. Psychologists call this phenomenon 'stereotype threat', a sort of self-fulfilling prophecy.[33] It occurs when a person's awareness of her gender in test or evaluation situations causes her to underperform in a manner consistent with a negative stereotype about her gender. Researchers believe the underperformance is caused by increased anxiety, which manifests itself in various ways, including

[32] Chatard et al. (2007).

[33] This term was first used by psychologists Steele and Aronson, who showed in several experiments that black college freshmen and sophomores performed more poorly on standardized tests than white students when their race was emphasized. When race was not emphasized, however, black students performed as well as white students. Steele and Aronson (1995).

distraction and increased body temperature, both of which diminish performance level. Researchers have found that the effect is strongest in individuals who identify strongly with both the relevant stereotyped social group and the intellectual domain in which they have to perform.

Meanwhile, other studies indicate that reducing the level of awareness of the stereotype can have a tangible positive effect on performance.[34] In one test of this hypothesis, psychologist Catherine Good and her colleagues at City University of New York recruited as participants 174 university students enrolled in the final course of the most rigorous calculus course offered by their university.[35] The course satisfied degree requirements for mathematics, engineering, and many of the natural sciences, and the students were already well on their way to obtaining degrees in maths or hard sciences as they had all successfully completed the previous semester's mandatory course.

The experimenters designed a calculus test to be given as a practice test for an upcoming course examination. The practice test used questions from the Graduate Record Examination (GRE) that covered the same content as had been covered in the course. The professors announced the practice test to the students. In order to increase the likelihood that the students would take the test seriously and perhaps experience it the same way as they would a regular course examination, the professors told the students that they would get extra credit on the course examination based on their performance on the practice test. (In reality, though, every student who took the practice test received the same number of extra credit points regardless of their performance.)

To test the effect of stereotype threat, some randomly selected students were given written test instructions that included a statement indicating that the test they were about to take was designed to measure their maths abilities. Statements like this had been shown to elicit stereotype threat

[34] For references to the academic literature and discussion of status of current research, visit the website http://reducingstereotypethreat.org, which is administered by social psychologists Steven Stroessner and Catherine Good.

[35] Good et al. (2008).

effects in previous studies. To compare their performance with students not subject to stereotype threat, the same instructions were given to the other students, but they also included an additional statement indicating that no gender difference had ever been found despite testing on thousands of students. Telling students that a test has never shown any gender differences in the past had been previously shown to reduce stereotype threat for women on general mathematics tasks.

Of the 174 students who took part in the study, 100 were male, 57 were female, and 17 did not report their sex. The experimenters analysed data only for those participants who indicated their sex, leaving a final sample of 157 participants. Two of those failed to answer some general questions about the testing conditions, so the experimenters analysed the test answers of only 155 participants. Not surprisingly, given that men and women in the course had until that point received much the same course grades, the women in the threat condition performed as well as the men on the test. The experimenters were quite surprised, though, to find that the women in the non-threat condition substantially outperformed not just men and women in the stereotype condition, but also the men in the non-threat condition.

The researchers suggest that the reason women outperformed their male counterparts in this situation is likely because women are more apt to self-select out of maths and science fields early in their educational careers. Women in advanced mathematics classes, like those in this sample, are therefore the most motivated and prepared female students taking mathematics classes. The researchers believe that men, on the other hand, may be more likely to pursue maths and science careers even if they are less prepared academically to do so. Accordingly, the female participants in the sample could well have been a more select group of maths students than the male participants. When *not* constrained by stereotype threat, these women were able to perform closer to their actual ability levels, which appear to be higher on average than the males in the course.

The researchers also suggest that the calculus course itself—not just the test—was inherently prone to induce stereotype threat in women. They asked 364 calculus students at the same university whether *they* believed men or women were better at calculus and who they thought *other* people believed was better at calculus. The women believed that men and women have equal abilities, whereas the men believed that men are superior. Both men and women believed that other people thought men were better than women. In other words, the stereotype of male superiority in calculus was present in the minds of the men and women in these calculus courses. As a result, the researchers suggest that since the course grades men and women were getting in calculus were basically the same, which mirrors the lack of sex differences in test performance in the stereotype threat condition, the women are likely capable of substantially higher performance in mathematics than their course grades predict.

This is just one study among many of the effects of stereotype threat on women's performance. Other studies have shown that stereotype threat can occur simply as a result of asking students to record their sex at the beginning of a quantitative test, or when women can see that most of their fellow test-takers are men.[36] It also occurs when women have watched TV commercials portraying women as ditsy airheads, and when they have instructors or peers who display sexist attitudes. Studies have also documented the negative effects of stereotype threat on performance of girls all the way down to middle school (grades 7–9).[37]

Given the prevalence of the stereotype that men are better at maths, among other things, it seems reasonable to suppose that social forces are indeed a contributing factor to women's under-representation in disciplines and occupations stereotyped as particularly male. Additional support for this view can be found in the substantial differences in the size of gender gaps in maths and science across countries. Social psychologist Brian Nosek and his colleagues analysed 500,000 scores from around the world on the gender-science Implicit Association Test (IAT),[38] and

[36] Fine (2010: 31–2).

[37] Good et al (2008: 27).

[38] The gender-science IAT measures how much easier it is for someone to pair masculine words with science words and feminine words with liberal arts words than it is to pair the same words with the opposite sex.

checked the scores against the size of the gender gaps in maths and science in 34 countries. They found that across countries, the more strongly a society associates males with science and females with liberal arts, the bigger the gap between girls' and boys' performance in science and mathematics in the eighth grade.

We want to emphasize that we are not claiming that stereotype threat by itself explains the gender gap in performance and achievement in mathematics and science. It appears to be one among perhaps multiple causes and further research is needed to determine how much of the gap it can explain. Nevertheless, the idea that stereotypes about male and female traits and abilities affect not just the way we evaluate others but how we evaluate ourselves and our own performance is at least as reasonable as the claim that our gender differences are unchangeable and innate.

Time for new lenses: seeing gender differently

Given the fact that we can't be certain about anything, perhaps it's time to at least try to change the things we can change. We know that gender gaps are narrower in some countries than others, that they have narrowed over time, and that more women are breaking into the ranks of elite mathematicians and scientists.[39] We don't know how narrow we can make the gaps by changing the way we see masculinity and femininity until we change the lenses in our gender glasses.

And while we seem to be equipped with 'gender-ready' brains with an uncanny tendency to categorize everything from colours to professions as masculine or feminine, we seriously doubt that most cultures will ever eliminate 'gender' as a social category. However, we do believe that societies can reduce the number of things we put in those categories so that being masculine or feminine no longer has anything to do with whether you're good at maths or art, taking care of children, or trading on the stock market. Research provides us with more than enough evidence to suggest that much of the content of our masculine and feminine

---

[39] Fine (2010: 180–4).

categories is determined by the cultures in which we live, created and acted out in all the social relationships we enter as we go through the education and training that prepares us from infanthood to take our places in the adult world.

Just considering the tremendous variation of personalities and behaviours among men as a group and among women as a group should persuade us that our gender identities are the result of a combination of unconscious and conscious processes. We are each, to a great extent, perfectly able to choose which images, practices, ideas, and role models we want to make our own, and which we do not. The experiences we base our choices on include direct personal contact with individual people, as well as exposure to cultural representations of men and women in nursery rhymes, jokes, gossip, rumours, newspapers accounts, books, movies, marketing, and other media. We may not be able to change our 'gender binary' brains, but we can teach each other to pay greater attention to the things men and women have in common than the things they do not. In doing so, we can learn to put fewer things in our gender boxes and let men and women discover their talents and interests without looking over their shoulders for the gender police.

Key points and guiding principle

- Human beings seem to be equipped with 'gender-ready' brains that learn early in life to distinguish between males and females and tend to categorize everything from colours to professions as masculine or feminine.
- Research shows that parents think and act more in response to their own perceptions of gender than to actual gender differences observed in children.
- As soon as we become aware of another person's gender, everything we've learned about distinguishing between male and female directs and skews our perceptions of an individual's traits and abilities.

Guiding principle: *If it feels right, it might be wrong.*

5

The Roads Not Taken

In the spring of 2011, Lynn had a meeting with the director of an executive education programme at a well-known international business school. The director is an attractive woman in her late thirties, single, no children, and has been quite successful in her own career. When Lynn asked the programme director what she thought about the under-representation of women among the world's corporate executives, she said, 'Everyone knows it's because of women's choices. They choose not to pursue those jobs. There have been a lot of studies about that.'

At about the same time as this conversation, Sheryl Sandberg, Facebook's Chief Operating Officer, made a similar assertion in her widely publicized 2011 commencement speech at Barnard, an elite women's college in New York City. She said, 'Studies show very clearly that in our country, in the college-educated part of the population, men are more ambitious than women. They're more ambitious the day they graduate from college; they remain more ambitious every step along their career path. We will never close the achievement gap until we close the ambition gap.'[1]

We don't know what studies Sheryl Sandberg and the programme director are referring to, but they may be thinking of a spate of reports in popular US news media dating back quite a while. For example, an

---

[1] Sandberg (2011).

article in the *New York Times Magazine* in 2003 was entitled 'Q: Why Don't More Women Get to the Top? A: They Choose Not to—Abandoning the Climb and Heading Home'.[2] In a lead article in *Fortune*'s October 2003 issue, Patricia Sellers asked: 'Power: Do Women Really Want It?', and then answered it using stories about women refusing promotions and avoiding jobs perceived as requiring too much personal sacrifice, especially with regard to having children.[3] A February 2004 article in *Fast Company* under the title 'Where Are the Women?' argued that women do not have the drive to compete as hard as men for leadership and power.[4] Then in March 2004, *Time* ran a cover story with the headline 'The Case for Staying Home: Why More Young Moms Are Opting Out of the Rat Race'.[5] CBS' popular in-depth news programme, *60 Minutes*, joined in the chorus in late 2004 with a segment entitled, 'Staying at home: Career women deciding to stay at home to raise their kids'.[6]

The message could not be clearer. Fewer women than men occupy positions of power because most women 'choose' not to pursue them. It seems that Sheryl Sandberg and the programme director had heard and remembered that message.

The problem with this message is that a very different story emerges from recent scientific research. Citing several large studies, social psychologists Alice Eagli and Linda Carli have reported that both men and women with well-established managerial careers and occupying similar positions in their organizations' hierarchies report similar ambitions to rise to positions of authority.[7] Eagli and Carli noted that studies show women and men are quite similar in their preferences for such traditionally masculine job characteristics as making good money and the

---

[2] Belkin (2003).
[3] Sellers (2003).
[4] Tischler (2004).
[5] Wallis (2004).
[6] CBS News (2004).
[7] Eagli and Carli (2007).

potential for promotions. In the same way, among university students, women and men regard managerial roles as equally attractive. However, the women believe it is less likely that they will attain such positions. This research suggests that the so-called 'ambition gap' may actually be more of a 'belief gap'.

But how can so many smart people like Sheryl Sandberg—a recipient of the prize given to Harvard's top student of economics—be so wrong about this? Once again, it comes down to a difference between media reports and scientific studies. In this case, some researchers have already pointed out that the media reports of an 'ambition gap' are poorly documented. According to them, the media reports are 'based on anecdotal information from small samples of women'.[8] For example, to support the claim that there is an 'ambition gap' the article in *Fortune* referred to a number of quotes from various male and female leaders, the resignations of a few female CEOs, and gender-differentiated statistics on the employee turnover rate at General Electric.[9]

These kinds of sources are a far cry from the statistical surveys social scientists use to arrive at conclusions and support their arguments. Social scientists do not regard statistical surveys as capable of producing reliable results unless they are applied to large numbers of

[8] Merrill-Sands et al. (2005).

[9] The *Fortune* article also misrepresented the only statistics it cited that actually might qualify as resulting from sound research methodology. It described a study by the research firm Catalyst as reporting that 26% of professional women who are not yet in the most senior posts say they don't want those jobs. We checked the study, 'Women and Men in U.S. Corporate Leadership: Same Workplace, Different Realities?' (2004), available on Catalyst's website, www.catalyst.org. First, it wasn't 26% but only 19% of women who were not interested. The 26% was for women who weren't sure. Second, the article neglected to include the interesting statistic showing that 29% of the men in the same category were not sure either, while 14% were definitely not interested. In fact only 5% more women (19%) than men in the same category were definitely not interested in pursuing top jobs. This figure is clearly not large enough to support the assertion that a lack of ambition or interest explains the obvious absence of women from top positions.

randomly selected people within the target group. This precaution helps minimize the risk of biased results. Furthermore, the questions posed must be carefully formulated to ensure that all the respondents are likely to understand them in the same way. Finally, the interpretation of the answers is not always a matter of simply counting the number of yes-es, no's, or other kinds of answers. Social scientists spend a good deal of time determining what it is they can actually conclude from the results obtained.

What then are we to think about women like Anne-Marie Slaughter, whose attention-grabbing article entitled 'Why Women Still Can't Have It All' for *The Atlantic* explained how gender issues triggered her resignation from a prestigious job at the State Department? Slaughter wrote that she was 'finding it difficult' to be away from her 14-year-old son—despite the fact that her husband, a tenured professor at Princeton, fully supported her career and has spent more time with their two sons than she has and was taking care of them—truly taking care of them—on the weekdays when she was working in Washington, DC. In her article Slaughter acknowledges that she could have tried to work out an arrangement allowing her to spend more time at home, but that she 'realized that [she] didn't just *need* to go home. Deep down, [she] *wanted* to go home.' Others might say she actually didn't really *need* to go home, she *chose* to go home.

If prioritizing home over career is lack of ambition, then Slaughter seemed to be lacking ambition. Those who argue that the gender gap in top positions across sectors is due to *women's* choices would claim that ambitious women like Slaughter *choose* careers like academia that offer working conditions that allow for time with family instead of high-powered careers in the C-suites of large companies or in high political office that rule out active participation in family life.

We don't think that's an accurate interpretation of Slaughter's story, though. First of all, Slaughter could hardly be called unambitious. She was a tenured professor at Princeton University—quite an accomplishment in itself—before taking the job at the State Department, which she describes as a 'foreign-policy dream job that traces its origins back to George Kennan'. And she returned to her professorship after she left the State Department.

Second, to describe a woman's decision to stay on the career track to the top, or to stay put in some position along the way, or to get off completely and stay at home with small children as a 'choice' leaves much unsaid. The fact is women's decisions are often made in a context of limited—not unlimited—choices. A combination of external factors over which many women have no control—such as the availability of affordable and trust-worthy childcare, the earning potential of their chosen occupations, the decisions of their spouses and other family members about their own liv-ing and working arrangements, the availability of other jobs, what kind of bosses they have—can exclude some choices for some women that may be available to others. Furthermore, psychological factors that we tend to think we have some control over—such as willingness to ignore social norms and forge our own way, setting priorities regarding work and fam-ily, or even choosing our spouses—are shaped by gender norms gener-ated by the culture we live in and which can seldom be ignored without emotional or material cost.

To understand what role women's 'choices' play in their under-representation in top leadership positions, we need to take a look at what kinds of 'choices' men and women are actually making.

What choices are we making?

Many people believe that the recognition of sex equality in Western industrial democracies means that ambitious men and women truly have the same options—limited only by their own drive, natural abili-ties, and personal preferences. We can probably also agree that pursu-ing high-powered careers requires personal sacrifices of both men and women and that if you aren't willing to make those sacrifices, you can't have the high-powered career. As one of Lynn's friends commented after he read Slaughter's article, 'Why Women Still Can't Have It All': 'Neither can men.'

But that comment seems true only because it is so general. Of course no one can 'have it all', but if 'having it all' just means having top jobs and families at the same time, it does seem like more men than women 'have it all'.

First, as Sheryl Sandberg stated in her commencement speech at Barnard, 'Women are not making it to the top. A hundred and ninety heads of state; nine are women. Of all the people in parliament in the world, 13% are women. In the corporate sector, women at the top—C-level jobs, board seats—tops out at 15 and 16%; numbers which have not moved at all in the past nine years. Nine years. Of full professors around the USA, only 24% are women.'

Second, more men in those positions get to have families too. This is true in both the private and public sector. As for the public sector, Slaughter pointed out in her article that all six male justices on the US Supreme Court have families, while two of the three female justices are single with no children. The female justice with children, Ruth Bader Ginsburg, began her career as a judge only when her younger child was almost grown. Condoleezza Rice, the first and only woman national security adviser, is also the first and so far only, national security adviser since the 1950s not to have a family.

As for the private sector, a large international survey of corporate executives from 2003 showed that 90% of the men as compared with only 65% of the women had children.[10] There is also an interesting gender gap in the survey's results concerning the question of having a spouse who does not have full-time paid work. While 75% of male executives had spouses *who did not have* full-time paid work, 74% of the women had spouses *with* full-time paid employment. There appears to be a correlation between more men in top positions with children and having a spouse *without* full-time paid work. In comparison, fewer women in top positions have children *and* fewer of them have spouses without full-time paid work. In other words, it seems like more male than female executives have families

[10] Galinsky et al. (2003).

because more male than female executives have spouses who are not pursuing careers themselves.

It seems rather logical. Both men and women probably find it easier to combine families with top jobs when their spouses are willing to commit significant amounts of time to childcare. It's just that fewer men seem willing to do that.

A lot of people explain this imbalance between male and female leaders with children and working spouses by saying that men and women simply have different preferences and make different choices. It's just a matter of preference and commitment in the choices men and women make. But what choices do men and women with the potential to rise to the top actually have?

Let's start with high-level government jobs, like Anne-Marie Slaughter's. In her article for *The Atlantic*, Slaughter describes a world built on the assumption that high-level government officials will not be participating in the care of their children because someone else (i.e. the official's wife) assumes full responsibility for childcare—either providing it all themselves or with help. These government careers involve unrelenting travel, inflexible schedules that conflict with school schedules, long hours, and constant pressure to put in those hours at the office. The working conditions Slaughter describes developed long before universities began producing equal numbers of male and female graduates with the qualifications for these jobs in the 1980s. They are the product of a time— basically the entire history of Western democratic government—when women were neither expected nor welcome to participate in politics or government.

Harvard Business School professor Rosabeth Kanter made a similar point in her classic book on organizations, *Men and Women of the Corporation*.[11] She asserted that organizations are not sex-neutral machines. Rather, organizational roles are organized according to the characteristic images of the kinds of people that occupy them.[12] The fact that high-level

---

[11] Kanter (1977).
[12] Kanter (1977: 20–8).

government jobs require lots of travel, long hours in the office, and very limited opportunities to work from home are not the result of entirely gender-neutral considerations of the requirements of the job. Rather, the demands placed on the people in these jobs have been formed around the characteristic images of the men who still hold most of them. Kanter explains:

> A 'masculine ethic' of rationality and reason can be identified in the early image of managers. This 'masculine ethic' elevates the traits assumed to belong to some men to necessities for effective organizations: a tough-minded approach to problems; analytic abilities to abstract and plan; a capacity to set aside personal, emotional considerations in the interests of task accomplishment; and a cognitive superiority in problem-solving and decision-making. These characteristics supposedly belonged to men; but then practically all managers were men to begin with.[13]

The characteristics of the male breadwinner developed in the nineteenth century and erected a wall between the home and the workplace. Personal and emotional considerations like the care and education of children belonged at home, and are still treated that way. In other words, in order to have children and a high-powered job in government service at the same time as Slaughter did, you have to delegate most of the care and upbringing of your children to someone else.

A lot of parents are willing to let other people take care of their children for a number of hours on a daily basis, depending on the age of the child. Most parents can even contemplate the idea of having someone responsible for the *care* of their children on a full-time basis if the caregiver is subject to their direction. But we think it's safe to say that most parents are not willing to entrust the *upbringing* of their children to someone else—especially not someone outside the family. Most people do not have children in order to hand them over to someone else to raise. That responsibility has almost always been held, and, in the vast majority of families, is still held by the mother.

[13] Kanter (1977: 22).

Flexibility from the bottom up: an essential condition for ambitious women—and men who take fatherhood seriously

Recent public statements by two top female executives in the USA indicate that top management jobs in the corporate world are probably a bit more flexible than the high-level government jobs Slaughter described in her *The Atlantic* article, and that this flexibility allows them to pursue both their career and family ambitions. One of these female executives is Sheryl Sandberg, who confesses to trying to hide the fact that she was 'only' arriving at work at 9.00 a.m. and leaving at 5.30 p.m. after she returned from her first maternity leave until 'it began to dawn on [her] that [her] job did not really require that [she] spend twelve full hours a day in the office'.[14] Greater flexibility for women can also be found in Europe. The top manager in an influential Danish non-profit organization we interviewed said that she had no trouble making it a top priority to be home nearly every night in time to put her children in bed, limiting evening engagements to one or two per week.

But despite what appears to be slightly more flexibility for some high-level corporate executives, it still does not translate into a larger percentage of women at the top of the corporate world. Part of the explanation may be that this kind of flexibility is a privilege mostly enjoyed by top managers, not by people on their way *up* the corporate career ladder. As we mentioned in Chapter 2, statistics published by *Working Mothers* magazine in 2011 show that only 53% of US companies offered flex time and only 45% offered telecommuting. We have no reason to believe that companies outside the USA are much different in that respect.

There are undoubtedly many reasons for the persistence of inflexible working conditions in so many workplaces. The case of one large multinational based in Europe suggests it may sometimes simply be due to top management's lack of awareness of the problem. We interviewed the company's Global Diversity and Inclusion Manager, who had recently developed a company-wide initiative to get managers to give their employees

---

[14] Sandberg (2013: 128–9).

more flexibility with regard to when and where they work. She told us that the senior executives in her company are accustomed to the freedom they have to arrange their own schedules. Some of them were so surprised to learn that managers further down the line weren't already allowing their employees the same flexibility that they reacted to her presentation of the initiative by declaring that managers like that should be fired. They were apparently unaware that being present during office hours was a firmly established element of the company's practices and that changing it required nothing less than a change in company culture.

Given how many companies continue to be committed to rigid 'presence' policies, finding a job in an organization that allows enough flexibility to combine work and family care obligations is not something anyone can simply 'choose'. Whether an individual can even find a job with this benefit really doesn't say anything about her level of ambition, but it *is* one of the elements that must fall into place in order to allow anyone—male *or* female—to combine work and family obligations and still make it to the top.

A choice with heavy gender baggage

Even supposing that all career paths included sufficient flexibility to combine work and children, choosing to pursue a career path towards leadership or investing time and energy in raising children is not a gender-neutral choice—and, in fact, sometimes employers make the choice for you based on their own gender prejudices. The experiences of some of the female executives we interviewed for this book illustrate this point.

Meg Tiveus is a tall sporty woman in her sixties whose career has spanned 30 plus years at the top of the Swedish corporate world. She grew up in a family and culture deeply influenced by the idea that women and men are fundamentally equal. She decided when she was a teenager that she would go after a top job in business because she was inspired by the stories an older brother told about his work in a big Swedish company. It never entered her mind that jobs like that were mostly occupied by men. Growing up she never considered her femaleness as something that could determine what subjects she might be good at or whether she could pursue a high-powered career and have children. In fact, she always believed that both men AND women should be able to have careers and children. She thinks of it as a human right rather than a woman's right. At least one employer she encountered early in her career had a different opinion.

When Meg was working in her first job after graduating from Stockholm School of Economics with a degree in business, she had twins. Her husband was a student in law school, and her mother had been recently widowed, so she could rely on both of them to help with the childcare. When the twins were three months old, she saw a job announcement for a management position she thought would be exciting and applied for it. She was called in for an interview. The employer asked if she had children. She said yes. When he asked how old they were, she said, 'They are both 3 months old.' He responded promptly, 'I think you need to go home and take care of your children.' Being the kind of person she is, Meg did not let that stop her. Of course she didn't get that job, but she found another one that eventually led her to the top positions she has held for the past 20 years or so.

Meg's experience of being denied a job because she had two young infants was a long time ago, but things have not changed that much. Most employers are not as direct as the one Meg Tiveus encountered, but many still make hiring decisions based on the perception that women *should* find it difficult to combine top jobs in management with having children. Another anecdote illustrates how this happens.

Anna (a pseudonym), the Chief Financial Officer of a Scandinavian multinational with 7000 employees worldwide, is married with two teenage children. She met her husband about 25 years ago when they were both starting their careers in another large multinational. Early in their relationship, it became clear to them both that Anna was the more ambitious of the two. That was not a problem for Anna's husband; he supported her career 100% while building his own. They managed the childcare logistics by hiring a nanny when their first child was born, and they have relied on a combination of public daycare during working hours and the nanny or each other to fill in the gaps ever since.

In 2005, Anna was offered a promotion to a C-suite level position that involved relocating to London. Her husband, who had a good job in a small international company, decided he would resign from his position and move to London to be with Anna and the family. But when he handed in his resignation, his boss refused to accept it, saying something like, 'You can't just quit your job and tag along with Anna.' Instead, he offered to let him keep his position as long as he could be present at the company's headquarters three days a week, and that's what they agreed to do.

Anna believes that her husband was allowed to keep his job because he is a man. If their situations had been reversed, and she had offered her resignation in order to follow her husband, she doesn't believe anyone would have refused it. It would be regarded as the normal and natural thing for a working mother to do, and her decision would not have been questioned. To support her speculation, she points to her discussions with male managers in her own company about potential female candidates for promotion to senior positions in their company. They have often expressed the belief that women with young children will not be interested or able to take on such positions. It does not occur to them to discuss the issue with the potential female candidates until Anna reminds them that they are merely making an assumption and that they do not make the same assumptions about men with young children.

Organizational and social practices that code childcare as a woman's responsibility do not just affect working women. They affect the rest of society. But because these practices are so embedded in our history and culture, they have come to seem natural to us. For many women, it undoubtedly feels like a force of nature they come up against—and society tends to fall back on 'natural instinct' to explain women's more frequent decisions to sacrifice career for family. Even Slaughter, recognizing that she's stepping on 'treacherous' territory, agrees, saying that she has 'come to believe that men and women respond quite differently when problems at home force them to recognize that their absence is hurting a child, or at least that their presence would likely help. . . . [M]en do seem more likely to choose their job at a cost to their family, while women seem more likely to choose their family at a cost to their job.'

There are exceptional men who do choose their families at a cost to their jobs, though. Slaughter mentions two: James Steinberg, US deputy secretary of state, and William Lynn, deputy secretary of defence, both of whom stepped down—like Slaughter—after two years in the Obama administration so that they could spend more time with their children. 'For real', adds Slaughter in parentheses. And in 2012 the news media were reporting that the number of stay-at-home fathers has doubled in both the USA and the UK over the past ten years. Of course, it was a small number to start with—roughly 75,000 in the USA and 80,000 in the UK.[15]

More importantly, as we stated in earlier chapters, there is very little reliable evidence to support the view that women have a stronger natural instinct for caring and empathy than men do. That is not to say that it doesn't *feel* like a natural instinct. Gender norms exert a very powerful influence on the way we understand the world and ourselves. They are re-enacted in virtually every situation in which men and women are present. We incorporate them in various ways into our identities as men and women, and it can feel uncomfortable when we do things that are atypical for our gender or do not fit our own individual understandings of femininity and masculinity.

In addition to our own psychological barriers, we may meet criticism and hostility among friends, family, and colleagues when we do not conform to widely accepted gender norms. Socially non-conformist behaviour—of any kind, whether it concerns gender norms or some other norms—tends to meet resistance that may exact an emotional or even material price that not everyone is willing or brave enough to pay. The fact that men cannot resign from top government jobs to spend more time with their children without generating a rumour that they were actually forced to resign is an example of the cost of doing something that does not conform to gender expectations.

[15] Alfonsi and Pedersen (2012); Farberov (2012).

This fact is what makes Sheryl Sandberg's advice to ambitious young women to choose their husbands carefully particularly unhelpful. It is a highly individual solution to a problem that springs out of widespread collective behaviours and beliefs. If every woman who ever wanted to have a family AND pursue a top management career like Sheryl Sandberg's could find men willing to marry them and participate equally in childcare, we would have seen many more women doing it, and we would not have felt compelled to write this book. The experiences and insights of a number of the executives and professionals we interviewed for this book suggest that getting this particular element in a working mother's life to fall into place is not such an easy task.

For one thing, as Slaughter's article so compellingly shows us, many people in Western societies, including, it seems, highly educated top government officials, still perceive masculinity as including a substantial element of the 'breadwinner' norm—even in Scandinavian countries, which are supposed to be among the top ten most gender-equal countries in the world. Anna, the Scandinavian CFO, seemed to be reacting to exactly this cultural norm when she told us that she doesn't think men in her home country have the same freedom to choose between career and family as women do. She believes that fathers who choose to stay at home with their children are not respected as much as mothers.

The female CEO of a high-profile foundation in Denmark shared a similar insight with us when she explained why she would give up her job to be with her children if she ever felt they needed a parent at home. We asked if she wouldn't consider having her husband, who has always earned less than she has, stay home with the children instead. She promptly asserted, 'Oh but there's no prestige in having your husband stay at home with the kids.' When we suggested that having a wife at home is a symbol of success and carries a certain amount of prestige for many male executives, she agreed, but asserted that it simply didn't work the other way around.

For every individual woman who finds a partner willing to support her career and family ambitions, there's at least one woman who does not. Caroline's story is just one example. About ten years ago, Caroline was married with two pre-school age children and had been working in her first top management job in a large company when her husband told her that he had not signed up for the role he had come to play in the marriage: secondary breadwinner and equal (if not primary) provider of care for their children. Her husband's announcement was a painful blow to Caroline. That she was ambitious and valued her career should have been obvious from the beginning of their relationship. Her career began with a good position in a highly regarded international consultancy and continued in an upward trajectory. He was running his own small business from an office at home and had sufficiently flexible working conditions to allow him to take up the childcare responsibilities not covered by public daycare, and his wife was earning a much bigger salary than he could or would ever aspire to. Nevertheless, he became more and more uncomfortable as her career developed. They divorced, amicably, and have shared custody of the two children on an equal basis. What he couldn't do as her husband, he was able to do as her ex-husband.

Caroline's husband is not an isolated example. One of Lynn's unmarried male colleagues at Copenhagen Business School, an associate professor, told her a few years ago that he was not interested in marrying a 'career woman'. Several divorced female academics have told Lynn about ex-husbands who would not or could not support their wives' career ambitions. During their marriages, their husbands resisted participating as equal partners in raising their children, which made it difficult for these women to do the research and writing necessary to move further up the academic hierarchy. After they divorced, they shared custody with their husbands, and they suddenly found themselves with substantial amounts of time they could invest in their careers.

These individual examples of male discomfort with women's career ambitions appear to be just the tip of an iceberg that includes men in both Europe and North America. For example, a story by *Forbes* magazine editor Michael Noer that was published a few years ago on Forbes.com on two-career marriages began with the following advice to young men: 'Marry pretty women or ugly ones. Short ones or tall ones.

125

Blondes or brunettes. Just, whatever you do, don't marry a woman with a career'.[16] The story provoked so much criticism that Forbes eventually issued a public apology.[17]

An even more powerful expression of male disdain for women in traditionally male roles and occupations occurred at a conference for 800 people in the IT sector sponsored by Dell's Danish subsidiary in April 2012. Dell hired a popular Danish stand-up comedian, whose views on women are well known in Denmark, to perform. During his 15-minute routine he ridiculed—to thunderous applause—various female politicians, praised the IT sector for excluding women, and gave men credit for inventing everything but the rolling pin. The tone of the routine is probably best captured by the following line, as translated by a member of the audience: 'You are the last bastion in IT, boys. Hiss it through your teeth. Shut your fucking face, bitch.'[18]

One of the women present at this event was a well-known Danish female blogger and radio programme host who is a frequent commentator on computer technology. She criticized the comedian's routine on her blog, which at first attracted a number of comments from both men and women who criticized Dell for having hired the comedian in the first place. Eventually a number of men who had enjoyed the performance weighed in with insults directed at the female blogger. They wrote comments like 'empty-headed blogger', 'poor little school girl feminist', 'angry little lady', and 'shut up bitch'.

Women are not oblivious to these occasional outbursts, which reveal a strong cultural undercurrent of resistance to female ambition in Western societies that are supposedly committed to equal opportunities for men and women. Young heterosexual women have good reason to be sceptical about how easy it is to find men willing to swim against the current with them, and they weigh their options accordingly.

[16] 'Careers and Marriage', Forbes, 23 August 2006.
[17] Konick (2006).
[18] Toft (2012).

Beneath the surface: unconscious influences on ambition

There is still more that goes into understanding the forces pushing us to conform to traditional gender norms. As explained in Chapter 4, unconscious gender bias causes both men and women to undervalue the talents, abilities, and contributions of girls and women. Sociologists explain that merely being female—and in racist societies, a person of the minority skin colour—creates the expectation that you have less to contribute to task performances than white males, unless you have some other externally validated source of prestige—like winning a Nobel Prize in physics. Sociologists call these expectations 'status expectations'. Status expectations contribute to the creation of prejudice, which can be understood as a cognitive bias that privileges those of already high status. In other words, when you have higher expectations of men than women, you tend to perceive whatever they do more favourably than whatever women do.

In a study of women's ambitions, psychiatrist and author Anna Fels described a number of ways in which cognitive gender bias is expressed throughout a lifetime, from pre-school through adulthood.[19] Her description brings the stiff headwind of cultural gender expectations plainly into view.

Her analysis of women's ambitions starts with an understanding of what ambition is. She presents substantial evidence from research in developmental psychology indicating that ambitions are formed on the basis of a combination of two things: mastery of a skill and social recognition of one's accomplishments. Fels refers to a longitudinal study by the renowned psychologist Jerome Kagan and his co-author Howard Moss. They examined the relationship between the tendency to strive to master selected skills on the one hand, and social recognition on the other—concluding that there was a high positive correlation between mastery and recognition. In other words, people who set out to master skills need recognition of their accomplishments in order to persevere. Recognition

---

[19] Fels (2004).

is what fuels the next stage of learning. Without earned affirmation, the motivational engine needed to drive long-term learning and performance runs out of fuel.

Fels then comes to the discouraging part. She argues that while women are no longer denied access to training and education, white, middle-class women (Fels did not study women of colour) lose steam as they deal with the conundrum of retaining the appearance of being feminine, which requires subordinating needs for recognition to those of others—particularly men—while at the same time striving for the recognition necessary to get the next promotion or the next bonus.

For proof, Fels points to the psychological instruments used for studies of gender. The most famous and widely applied psychological measure of femininity, masculinity, and androgyny is the revised Bem Sex Role Inventory (BSRI). The test includes 60 descriptive adjectives—20 masculine traits, 20 feminine traits, and 20 neutral traits—that subjects use to rate themselves. The traits were originally chosen from 200 personality characteristics by 100 male and female undergraduates, mostly white and middle-class, at Stanford University in the 1970s. The students were asked to rank the desirability of 200 traits for men and women in American society. The traits chosen for femininity are:

> Yielding, loyal, cheerful, compassionate, shy, sympathetic, affectionate, sensitive to the needs of others, flatterable, understanding, eager to soothe hurt feelings, soft-spoken, warm, tender, gullible, childlike, does not use harsh language, loves children, gentle, and—rather redundantly—femininity.

Fels suggests that two basic tenets of femininity emerge from these adjectives: 1. Femininity exists only in the context of a relationship. 2. Giving is the chief activity that defines femininity. These two tenets mean that women are expected to provide recognition for others rather than seek it for themselves. At work they must relinquish recognition to the men with whom they work. If they compete with men for high-visibility positions or speak as much as men at meetings, they may put their femininity at risk. Assertive, competitive women are regularly caricatured as either asexual and unattractive, or promiscuous and seductive.

In contrast, the BSRI adjectives selected to define masculinity do not presuppose participation in a relationship or giving to others:

> self-reliant, strong personality, forceful, independent, analytical, defends one's beliefs, athletic, assertive, has leadership abilities, willing to take risks, makes decisions easily, self-sufficient, dominant, willing to take a stand, aggressive, acts as a leader, individualist, competitive, ambitious, and—again, rather redundantly—masculinity.

Fels suggests that if masculinity is defined by these traits, a man can be solitary and masculine, but he cannot be in a relationship that involves overt dependence or being influenced by others without putting his sexual identity at risk.

Of course, cultural attitudes have changed (largely due to the women's movement) since these adjectives were selected to define femininity and masculinity. According to Fels, women no longer identify themselves solely in terms of the traditional feminine traits. College women have been shown to identify with more of the masculine traits in recent years, though they haven't dropped any of the feminine ones. More people have also realized that certain situations call for both masculine and feminine traits.

But there are still many situations where the traditional division of traits seems to push and/or pull men and women back into their traditional roles—such as when couples begin to have children or when bonuses and promotions at work are allocated. While certainly a number of the barriers that have kept women from mastering a subject—such as exclusion from professional schools or the habit of doing business and advancing careers inside men-only clubs—have been eliminated or reduced, the pressure remains on young women to relinquish opportunities for recognition in the workplace in order to maintain their feminine identity—both in their own and in others' eyes. For example, many women feel foolish soliciting appropriate acknowledgement of their contributions and accomplishments whereas most men seem to feel entitled to recognition and make sure they get it. Many women also feel as if they're demanding too much—putting their needs ahead of others—when they ask for appropriate support—in the form of money, time, promotion, flexibility at work or at home—to pursue their own career goals.

This pressure is not just in women's heads. Men—and other women—participate in daily interactions that constantly remind women to stay in their place. Sociologists suggest that one process in which men remind women to refrain from seeking recognition or expressing ambition is to engage in behaviour that constructs women as 'others' who do not belong in male-dominated environments.[20]

Gendered 'politeness' norms, such as opening doors, pulling out chairs, helping women on with coats may seem innocuous—even positively polite—but in some contexts, especially in male-dominated working environments where men behave this way towards their female peers, they may contribute to the 'othering' of women by constructing them as requiring more care than men. The same norms serve as reminders of men's independence and autonomy—real or imagined. Finally, when women do not display a sufficient number of feminine traits, or refuse male 'help', they may be penalized by being labelled too masculine, abrasive, or difficult, and denied the promotion or resources they seek.

The end result of the cultural pressure on women to relinquish the limelight and minimize their achievements is diminished social recognition for those achievements—as compared to, for example, their physical appearance or nurturing behaviour. Fels points out that in a world where it is not considered feminine to seek recognition and celebrate their own achievements, 'The personal and societal recognition [women] receive for their accomplishments is quantitatively poorer, qualitatively more ambivalent, and, perhaps most discouraging, less predictable.'[21] Women who conform to the feminine traits of the BSRI cannot get the recognition they need because they've learned not to seek it. Women who do not conform to the feminine traits of the BSRI may not get the recognition they deserve because they are regarded as unpleasant and mannish. They get criticism instead.

[20] Schwalbe et al. (2000).
[21] Fels (2004: 59).

A natural consequence of this dynamic is that girls and women tend to underestimate their abilities. Fels observes:

> Despite the fact that girls' and women's achievements, particularly in the academic sphere, frequently outstrip those of their male peers, they routinely underestimate their abilities. Boys and men, by contrast, have repeatedly been shown to have an inflated estimation of their capabilities. Paradoxically, these inaccurate self-ratings by both women and men seem to be accurate reflections of the praise and recognition they receive for their efforts.[22]

With less recognition and less confidence in their abilities, women give up their ambitions.

Running into a stiff headwind

If we put all of this together, it comes down to this: in the case of men's and women's choices, gendered expectations exert a strong force on our choices like a stiff wind. You can choose to run down the road with a stiff headwind—and risk getting blown off course—or you can choose the one with the wind at your back.

Sociologist Peter Blau has argued that the constraints imposed by society on the individual must be conceptualized as a force opposing individual motivation.[23] Picking up on this theme, structural sociologists like Ronald Burt have tried to show that while we may feel that we have freedom to make individual decisions and have some control over our destinies, the collective force of social norms makes it difficult to choose a path that contradicts those norms.[24] When we make choices about such things as careers and family, these sociologists suggest that we choose one alternative instead of another by comparing ourselves and our options to those in structurally similar positions. People *choose* the best alternatives with the information they have. The fact that people choose does

---

[22] Fels (2004: 59).

[23] Blau (1977).

[24] Burt (1982).

not mean they have either enough information to decide well or that the options available include choices that effectively serve their interests. The process of comparing your own options with the alternatives of similarly situated others contributes to the development and perpetuation of social norms.[25]

Making these comparisons is not an entirely rational calculation of material interests. Feelings of relative deprivation or advantage evolve from these comparisons, which leads us to make choices based on whichever decision ends up *feeling* right. It is impossible to predict which decision is rationally correct, so the one that feels right makes the decision easier to accept, even when it entails letting go of what had seemed like an important part of one's identity and life plan.

When people say that women have all the same opportunities as men to rise to the top, and the only thing holding them back is their own choices, they forget the different traits we assign to masculinity and femininity, and how organizations have traditionally catered to masculine traits. Women aiming for positions of authority—even when they have plenty of ambition—are like athletes running into a headwind while also jumping over fallen trees. As the stories and research about women's choices presented in this chapter have demonstrated, ambition is not enough to change social structures and processes that conspire to exclude or marginalize you.

Of course there are some women—even those with children—who make it all the way to the top. We have spoken with a number of them. But they do not make it to the top simply because they have the ambition. They also had good luck, plenty of support among friends and family, as well as recognition at the crucial moments.

Rather than focusing on which partners women choose to marry and have families with, or on how they can walk the tightrope between masculinity and femininity, we need to acknowledge that we all participate

[25] Risman (2004).

in a system that defines work, masculinity, and femininity in such a way that women are excluded from positions of authority, and men are not expected to participate in the care of their own children to the same degree as women. Gender is part of the social fabric which men and women weave together. It is a collective force opposing individual motivation. Changing it requires collective efforts and collective solutions.

Key points and guiding principle

- Most male executives do not have to choose between careers and children: they have both, while substantially fewer female executives do not have children.
- Many executives and employers assume that women with young children do not aspire to careers in top management.
- Girls and women routinely underestimate their abilities, even when they outperform their male peers, while boys and men tend to have inflated estimations of their capabilities.

Guiding principle: *Ambition is genderless.*

6

Truce

Sheryl Sandberg revealed that before she published *Lean In*, some people, especially other women in business, cautioned her against speaking out publicly about the importance of increasing the number of women in positions of power. And when she did speak out about it, she did indeed upset both men and women who took offence at her thesis.[1]

We have had similar experiences. In our capacities as university scholars and leaders, both of us have spoken with students, colleagues, and employees about the importance of addressing gender imbalances in university leadership and employment. We can confirm that talking about this subject upsets people. Sometimes voices were raised, faces reddened, arms crossed, eyes rolled, or all of the above happened—and we've seen both men and women react this way.

Why do people get so upset about this issue?

Sandberg says some criticize her for focusing on what women can do for themselves because that seems to be blaming the victim (women). Others criticize her because they say it is easy for her to talk about 'leaning in' given that she had the financial and personal resources to get all the help she needed, while most women don't.[2]

As for us, the two most common explanations from people who don't like to hear what we're saying is that it seems as if we are promoting

[1] Sandberg (2013: 10).
[2] Sandberg (2013: 11).

discrimination against men and lowering standards of quality 'just' to bring in more women. To them, gender balance sounds as if it involves taking away opportunities, power, prestige, and even money from men and giving them to women in order to even the score between men and women—without regard to individual merit or individual responsibility. Some seem to feel that they are being blamed for intentional discrimination against women.

All of these criticisms share two basic assumptions: first, that achieving gender balance requires identifying victims and perpetrators of unfair treatment and, second, that men and women are basically on opposite sides of that equation. No one likes being treated unfairly and no one likes being suspected of treating others unfairly. So, naturally, people get upset.

But here's the point that most people miss. Changing the way we think about gender is not a zero-sum game, where one side wins. Gender is not defined by men or women in isolation from each other. As the previous chapters have shown, gender is defined in relationships between men and women. Both men and women participate in producing the social norms that define 'masculinity' and 'femininity'. Given that public debates about gender inequality have tended to focus on women's under-representation in leadership positions and in well-paid male-dominated occupations, most people have the impression that all this talk about gender equality or gender balance (or whatever people end up calling it) is just about helping women compete with men—fairly or unfairly. They rarely consider how men might benefit from closing gender gaps.

In this chapter we want to show how gender balance can benefit men as well as women and take a closer look at the reasons people give when they caution us against speaking out about the need for gender balance.

Making the economic pie bigger for everyone
The evidence does not support the belief that gender balance or gender equality is a zero-sum game, in which men lose and women win. We cited in Chapter 1 various studies showing that increasing women's participation in the economy benefited the entire economy. Without the women who entered the workforce in the USA between 1970 and 2009,

the US economy would be 25% smaller today. We explained how increasing American women's workforce participation to 84% in all the states would be equivalent of increasing GDP by 3–4% and that the potential for economic growth is even more in Europe and Asia. We also pointed to research indicating that, in the corporate world, 'the key levers and drivers for innovative processes are positively influenced by having 50/50 proportions of men and women in teams'.[3] Most workplaces do NOT have that 50/50 balance right now. Clearly there's at least some room for more women in leadership and male-dominated occupations—and this means there is a potential for more economic growth that can, if distributed equitably, benefit everybody. Everyone, men and women, stand to gain.

If that's true, what happens if we *don't* achieve gender balance? No one can predict the amount of growth in any economy. We see examples of that all the time. Economists forecast the rate of growth for the year, often disagreeing with each other, and then, by the end of the third quarter, we find out who was right—if anyone.[4] One thing seems pretty certain given what we know about the growth that occurs when men and women participate equally in economic life: the economic pie may get bigger than it is now, stay the same, or get smaller, but it won't get as big as it would if we achieve gender balance. In other words, no one—including men as a group—would be better off without gender balance.

The masculine mystique: a prescription for loneliness, depression, and ill health

There's another reason why it's a mistake to think that women gain only at the expense of men. For all the power and wealth concentrated in men's hands, there is substantial evidence suggesting that men, as a group, aren't very happy the way things are. According to statistics from the World

---

[3] Lehmann Brothers Centre for Women in Business (2007).

[4] Here's a typical example. Szu Ping Chan, 'Economic Rebound May Speed Rate Rise', *The Telegraph*, 9 November 2013.

Health Organization (WHO), men commit suicide at a higher rate than women in just about every developed country.[5] In Europe and the USA, men are four to five times more likely to commit suicide than women. Globally, men have higher rates of alcoholism, and harmful use of alcohol is the leading risk factor for male deaths in the age group 15–59 years.[6] Men also make up the vast majority of both victims and perpetrators of all types of crime, including homicide, and are more likely to be killed in the street.[7]

These are gender gaps of a different kind from those we normally take into account when evaluating gender balance arguments. A number of studies have shown increasing evidence that common beliefs about appropriate masculine and feminine behaviour are significant contributing factors to men's health problems. The WHO wrote in one report:

> [M]en and boys who adhere to more rigid views about masculinity (such as believing that men need sex more than women do, that men should dominate women and that women are 'responsible' for domestic tasks) are more likely to report having used violence against a partner, to have had a sexually transmitted infection, to have been arrested and to use [alcohol and/or drugs].[8]

These statistics and studies support the idea that gender balance is not simply about giving women the same access to wealth and power as (many) men have. The kind of gender balance we are talking about is really something quite different. It requires developing different notions of masculinity and femininity in order to enable more men and women to live happy and healthy lives.

---

[5] World Health Organization (2013).

[6] World Health Organization (2011).

[7] United Nations Office on Drugs and Crime (2011). Jackson Katz, an American educator, author, filmmaker, and social theorist, who is recognized as one of America's leading anti-sexist male activists, has written a number of books on the subject of male violence and emphasizes the importance of framing it as a men's issue, rather than a women's issue.

[8] Barker et al. (2007).

Actually, this idea really isn't completely new, but it has yet to become mainstream thinking. Back in 1995, a book entitled *The Masculine Mystique*, by lawyer and environmentalist Andrew Kimbrell, made essentially the same argument.[9] Kimbrell pointed out that men die around seven years earlier than women and are more likely to die of heart disease, cancer, alcoholism, ulcers, and suicide. He noted that men are also less likely to graduate from college or to gain custody of their children after divorce. He suggested that these imbalances are the result of a 'masculine mystique' that requires 'real' men to be competitive, aggressive, violent, insensitive, and hyper-rational.

Since the mid-1990s, a number of UN-sponsored programmes and NGOs working on sexual and reproductive health, maternal mortality, children's health, and violence against women have affirmed the need to engage men and boys to address these issues. Evidence has confirmed that working with men and boys to challenge the 'masculine mystique' has positive effects not just on women and girls but also on men and boys. Well-designed programmes can change men's and boys' attitudes and behaviour in ways that benefit both men and women.[10]

Recent research on happiness and empathy support Kimbrell's thesis that by expecting 'real' men to be competitive, aggressive, violent, insensitive, and hyper-rational, we deprive men of the possibility of developing the personality characteristics and social skills necessary for living healthy, happy lives.

In their book *Born for Love*, author Maia Szalavitz and psychiatrist Bruce Perry summarize research suggesting that empathy—the ability 'to stand in another's shoes and care about what it feels like to be there'—is essential to health, creativity, intelligence, and productivity.[11] By allocating emotional expressiveness, caring, and empathy almost exclusively to girls, and not expecting boys to have or training them in the same skills, we set boys up for a lifetime of loneliness and ill health and girls for a lifetime of frustration.

---

[9] Kimbrell (1995).

[10] Promundo et al. (2010).

[11] Szalavitz and Perry (2010).

There is an overwhelming amount of evidence that relational health is the key to human joy, and that the most dependable route to relational health is through developing the ability to empathize. Luckily for us, the research also suggests that we are born with the genetic potential to become empathetic and humane. Humans evolved to be especially sensitive to social cues. In order for the relatively weak human species to survive, we had to form cooperative groups to hunt, gather, and protect one another from starvation, predators, and, unfortunately, other humans. To reproduce and to ensure that our exceptionally vulnerable babies survived, we needed to organize ourselves into caring collectives.[12]

Szalavitz and Perry assert:

> The resulting ability to read other people's intentions and to care about their plight—to empathize—helped us to become one of the most successful species on earth, the only one with the capacity to control its environment. Humankind would not have endured and cannot continue without the capacity to form rewarding, nurturing, and enduring relationships. We survive because we can love. And we love because we can empathize...[13]

However, the authors also point out that while we are born for love, we need to receive it and practise it ourselves as we grow from infants into adults. Consequently, boys raised to be insensitive, aggressive, or even violent do not learn some of the most basic lessons necessary to thrive in human society. They may be able to amass wealth and power, but happiness and good health are likely to elude them.

---

[12] Szalavitz and Perry (2010: 176–8). Szalavitz and Perry refer to research by anthropologist Sarah Hardy, who thinks that researchers' preoccupation with comparing human beings with great apes—like chimpanzees and orang-utangs—is a mistake, even though they are humans' closest surviving non-human ancestors, for a number of reasons. In particular, in contrast to humans, great ape mothers zealously guard their infants, rarely permitting even close relatives to pick them up because they know that both male and female chimps often kill unrelated babies. Great ape infants are nurtured exclusively by their mothers from four to seven full years. In contrast, in all human cultures, human mothers are happy to let relatives and friends hold their babies, and the human response to picking up virtually any new baby is tenderness and awe.

[13] Szalavitz and Perry (2010: 4).

By continuing to expect men to be less empathetic and caring than women, we teach boys to ignore their own emotional needs and the needs of others, and set them up to dominate others and die young and lonely. It's time to stop doing that, and we think a gender balance approach will help.

Gender balance: not just feminism in unisex clothes
Some people get upset by talk about promoting more women into leadership and better-paying male-dominated occupations because it reminds them of feminism, and they associate feminism with being anti-man. In fact, much of what we've been talking about in this chapter may sound like feminism or arguments everyone's heard since the 1970s women's movement. And quite frankly, it's amazing anyone admits to supporting a movement that seems to upset some people to the point that TV evangelist Pat Robertson once described feminism as a movement to 'encourage women to leave their husbands, kill their children, practice witchcraft, destroy capitalism and become lesbians'[14] and radio show host Rush Limbaugh described it as a movement 'to allow unattractive women easier access to the mainstream of society'.[15]

We do not share any concerns about alienating people by simply saying the words 'I'm a feminist' yet we do not want to label our ideas about gender balance as 'feminism'. We have two main reasons for distinguishing between our gender balance approach and what is usually referred to as feminism: (1) the word 'feminism' itself and (2) we think our approach is slightly different from the popular feminist movements of the past.

To the first reason, the online *Urban Dictionary* defines 'feminism' this way: 'Feminism is the belief that all people are entitled to the same civil rights and liberties and can be intellectual equals regardless of gender.' If having that belief makes you a feminist, then we're feminists. In fact, if that's all being a feminist is, then we're ardent feminists, who owe an immeasurable intellectual debt to feminism, and our gender balance approach is based on feminism.

[14] Traister (2012).
[15] Traister (2012).

Nevertheless, we have some difficulty with applying that word to the ideas we present in this book.

First, just the sound of the word 'feminism' makes it hard to shake the feeling that feminism doesn't have much to do with men. The 'fem' in 'feminism' is derived from the Latin word for 'woman', 'femininus'. That's where we got the word 'feminine' and the French get their word for 'woman'—'femme'.

Second, the *Oxford English Dictionary* (*OED*) says the word 'feminism' was derived from the French word 'féminisme' and that it has been used as a label for 'advocacy of the rights of women' since 1895. The *OED*'s current definition of 'feminism' is 'Advocacy of equality of the sexes and the establishment of the political, social, and economic rights of the *female* sex' (our italics).

For us, both the sound and past usage of the word make feminism seem like something for and about only women. Because 'feminism' seems to exclude men, it leads people to think 'women vs. men', forcing people to choose sides. And when you choose sides, you are setting things up for a zero-sum game that generates winners and losers. If feminists win, men lose. If feminists lose, men win.

One of the most significant differences between the strategies and achievements of the feminist movements of the past and our approach is that their focus has been on changing the way we think about women in order to improve women's lives, while we are looking at how changing the way all of us think about gender can improve both men's and women's lives. Feminist movements have rarely addressed both sides of the gender coin in any systematic way.[16]

---

[16] Of course some feminists have argued that feminism benefits both men and women and have written extensively about men in an empathic, rather than accusing, manner. See, for example, hooks (2000). A number of men, such as Jackson Katz and John Brougher, the founder of MaleFeminists.com, readily identify themselves as feminists, recognizing that feminist ideas have been and continue to be helpful in understanding the limitations and harms of masculine stereotypes.

We think it's time to do that. The gender gaps in leadership and other areas won't close without men's participation in the process, and they are not likely to participate unless men and women see themselves as partners, rather than adversaries, in the process. Men and women need to get away from this us-against-them-thinking and start thinking 'we'. Neither the word 'feminism' nor the history of feminist movements points clearly enough towards such a partnership.

We need to take a short tour of feminist history so you will understand what we mean.

First wave feminism: reformers and suffragettes

What has been dubbed the 'first wave' of organized feminist activism is the movement that emerged during the mid-nineteenth century and continued into the early twentieth century, peaking with the campaigns for women's right to vote in Europe and North America just after the First World War. The impetus for this movement began with women who sought to gain the same rights as men to vote, work, own property, and attend universities. As explained earlier, women at the start of the nineteenth century were not recognized as legal persons with the capacity to enter into contracts and own property. But the transition from agricultural to industrial economies required a mobile workforce, and single women became an important source of labour—particularly in the textile industry. The demand for labour generated a wave of legal reforms, one of which was to grant single women the right to enter into contracts, though most laws denying women equal civil and political status with men remained in place.

One legal doctrine in particular ensured women's inferior status in society: the doctrine of coverture, which incorporated a woman's legal identity into her husband's upon marriage. In the eyes of the law, a husband and wife were one person—and that person was the husband. The absorption of the wife's identity into the husband's was the underlying assumption of all aspects of matrimonial and family law until the last decades of the nineteenth century. As a result, a married woman could not own property, sign legal documents, enter into a contract, or do anything contrary to her husband's wishes. If a man permitted his wife to work, the laws of coverture required her to give her wages to him.

One of the decisive moments that helped generate the first wave of feminism in both the USA and Britain occurred in London in 1840 at the first international anti-slavery convention. The male delegates voted to exclude the female delegates from participating in the convention's proceedings even though these women had been nominated to serve as official delegates of their respective abolitionist societies. The men voted to require the women to sit in a curtained section where they could not be seen by the men, and the women were not even allowed to speak.[17] The experience inspired two American women who were present at the convention—Lucretia Mott and Elizabeth Cady Stanton—to join forces afterwards to organize an American women's rights convention in Seneca Falls, New York in 1848.[18]

The Seneca Falls Convention was the first time women gathered explicitly to explore the idea of organizing one broad campaign for their rights. Elizabeth Cady Stanton drafted the ideological blueprint for the movement in the form of a Declaration of Sentiments, which was adopted unanimously by the convention participants.

The Declaration of Sentiments followed the framework of the United States Declaration of Independence and quotes a substantial part of its text, but with a twist—it included women.[19] The Declaration of Independence proclaims that all *men* are created equal. The Declaration of

[17] Stanton (2010: 77).

[18] Stanton (2010: 78).

[19] It is probably not entirely coincidental that it also resembles the Déclaration des droits de la femme et de la citoyenne (Declaration of Women's and Female Citizens' Rights) published by the French author Olympe de Gourges in September 1791. The French Revolution's Constitution had just been adopted and de Gourges reacted promptly to the fact that women were excluded from the new French concept of citizenship. Her Declaration is copied from the French Declaration of the Rights of Men (Déclaration des droits de l'homme et du citoyen) except that in all the places where 'men' had been written, de Gourges added 'and women'. Olympe de Gourges was sentenced to death and executed in 1793.

Sentiments proclaimed that all men *and* women are created equal and have equal rights to 'life, liberty and the pursuit of happiness'. Like the Declaration of Independence, the Declaration of Sentiments also asserted that without the consent of the governed, or by failing to secure men's *and women's* rights, the government loses its legitimacy, and it is the duty of the governed to 'throw off such government'.

The Declaration of Sentiments also included a list of violations of women's rights as evidence of the fact that 'The history of mankind is a history of repeated injuries and usurpations on the part of man towards woman, having in direct object the establishment of an absolute tyranny over her.' The list consisted of 16 charges against 'man'. These included the denial of the right to vote, the denial of the right to enter into contracts, and the denial to married women of the right to own property, including the wages they earned. The list also charged men with denying women access to college and professional educations as well as 'nearly all the profitable employments', paying 'scanty' wages for the few jobs women were permitted to have, and applying a more lenient moral code to themselves than to women. It pointed out that the 'moral delinquencies which exclude women from society are not only tolerated but deemed of little account in man'. The list concluded by asserting that '[man] has endeavoured, in every way that he could to destroy [woman's] confidence in her own powers, to lessen her self-respect, and to make her willing to lead a dependent and abject life'.[20]

This Declaration of (Women's) Independence served as a blueprint for feminist activism in both the USA and the UK, and it inspired feminist activism in Scandinavia and continental Europe. Women in the USA, the UK, Scandinavia, and continental Europe began to campaign for married women's property rights, the right to university education, and the right to vote. It took five decades, but by 1900 nearly all the states of the USA, the UK, and the countries of Scandinavia and continental Europe had granted married women the right to own property. By 1930 nearly

---

[20] 'Declaration of Sentiments' (1848).

all of these countries had granted women the right to vote.[21] A few European countries began admitting women to their universities in the early 1900s—and some even earlier.[22]

The second wave: paving the way for professional women

First wave feminists achieved their primary goals—eliminating sex discriminatory laws that prohibited women from voting and owning property—but women continued to be systematically excluded from public life well into the twentieth century. The rights to vote and own property seemed to have little impact on the nineteenth-century cult of domesticity we talked about in Chapter 2. Instead, it took on a distinctly twentieth-century flavour after the Second World War.

When soldiers came back home from the war, they went back to their jobs, which women had taken in their absence. Most of the women went home. Most white men could earn enough to support their families without the need for additional income from wives. By this time, medical and technological developments had freed women from the hard physical labour, dangers of childbirth, and illnesses that had burdened women in the nineteenth and early twentieth centuries.[23] Ladies' magazines and journals began portraying dedication to the 'housewife-mother' role as the epitome of feminine fulfilment. The American housewife was:

---

[21] In 1918 the British Parliament passed an Act granting the vote to women over the age of 30 who were householders, university graduates, or wives of householders. Two years later, all adult American women won the right to vote, but it took another ten years before all British women gained the right to vote on the same terms as men. Norway, Denmark, and Sweden granted women the same voting rights as men in 1913, 1915, and 1921 respectively. A few countries did not grant full voting rights to women until after the Second World War, and a few held out well into the twentieth century: Switzerland in 1971 and Liechtenstein in 1984.

[22] Rowold (2010). By 1914 Oxford and Cambridge were the only British universities refusing to grant degrees to women, and most women undergraduates were studying at co-educational universities. Bush (2005).

[23] Friedan (1977: 13).

... healthy, beautiful, educated, concerned only about her husband, her children, her home ... As a housewife and mother, she was respected as a full and equal partner to man in his world. She was free to choose automobiles, clothes, appliances, supermarkets; she had everything that women ever dreamed of.[24]

This picture of fulfilled feminine identity was not limited to ladies' magazines and journals, though. It was widely accepted throughout American society, and even the most progressive politicians openly promoted it throughout the 1950s. One of them was Adlai Stevensen, a famous American politician, diplomat, and two-time presidential candidate, noted for his intellect, eloquent speeches, and promotion of progressive causes in the Democratic Party. In a speech he gave at the 1955 graduation ceremony at Smith College, an elite women's college in Massachusetts, Stevensen advised the all-female audience to embrace the role of mother and housewife. His speech is striking for its unapologetic portrayal of 1950s America's limited view of women's role in society:

> The point is that whether we talk of Africa, Islam or Asia, women 'never had it so good' as you. In short, far from the vocation of marriage and motherhood leading you away from the great issues of our day, it brings you back to their very center and places upon you an infinitely deeper and more intimate responsibility than that borne by the majority of those who hit the headlines and make the news ... [The woman's job is to] inspire in her home a vision of the meaning of life and freedom ... to help her husband find values that will give purpose to his specialized daily chores ... to teach her children the uniqueness of each individual human being. ... This ... you can do in the living room with a baby in your lap or in the kitchen with a can opener in your hand. ... I could wish you no better vocation than that.[25]

But this unrealistic image of happy and pedagogical housewives began to crumble by 1960 when the national media started reporting that

---

[24] Friedan (1977: 13).
[25] As quoted in Friedan (1977: 53–4).

unhappiness among American housewives had reached epidemic proportions.[26]

The national media traced the root of housewives' unhappiness to everything from incompetent appliance repairmen to inappropriate education.[27] One popular theory was that more and more housewives were college educated, which made them unhappy in their role as housewives. A number of educators proposed as a solution that women should no longer be admitted to four-year colleges and universities. Others suggested women should just be given more realistic preparation for making the transition from college student to housewife. Psychiatrists and sexologists suggested that maybe women just needed to have better sex and offered technical how-to advice.

In 1963, Betty Friedan offered a radically different diagnosis in her landmark book, *The Feminine Mystique*. Friedan believed the problem lay in cultural norms defining marriage and motherhood as the pinnacle of achievement for successful women. Friedan called this view of womanhood 'the Feminine Mystique' and traced its emergence to the end of the Second World War.[28] She believed that American housewives' unhappiness was due to the widespread cultural belief that women have only one true nature—passive, nurturing, and maternal. As a result, many women believed that happiness lay in conforming to these characteristics, and, as a consequence, delivered their lives and identities into the hands of men. To be feminine was to be defined by and dependent upon men.

Friedan argued in her book that the remedy was not less education or sexual counselling, but 'a drastic reshaping of the cultural image of femininity'. Women's identity needed to be redefined—without redefining masculinity—in a way that would enable them 'to reach maturity, identity, completeness of self, without conflict with sexual fulfilment'.[29]

---

[26] Friedan (1977: 17–18).
[27] Friedan (1977: 17–19).
[28] Friedan (1977: 12–14).
[29] Friedan (1977: 351).

The Feminine Mystique had a huge and immediate impact. It was published in both the USA and the UK in 1963, spending six weeks on the *New York Times* best-seller list. The first paperback edition sold 1.4 million copies, and in 1964 the first foreign language translation—in Danish— was published. Suddenly women who were dissatisfied with their roles as housewives and mothers had a name for the cause of their dissatisfaction and a new vocabulary to start talking about what they could do to feel better. A second wave of feminism activism soon began gathering momentum.

Organizing to fight for women's right to equal treatment

In the same year as the publication of *The Feminine Mystique*, the US Congress passed the Equal Pay Act, prohibiting sex discrimination in pay. In 1964 it passed the Civil Rights Act, prohibiting discrimination in employment on the basis of sex, marital status, and other grounds. But, as Friedan's book so painfully documented, the new legislation landed in a culture where most people still believed that women should quit working when they got married—or at least when they had children. Most employers were slow to take these laws seriously. They had been happily taking advantage of the assumption that women—even college graduates—didn't need or want careers. Many refused to employ women with pre-school children because they believed mothers with young children should not work full time.[30]

Not only did employers refuse to hire mothers—or even fired women when they became pregnant—but they also routinely refused to hire or promote women to better-paying jobs normally held by men. In 1960 more than half a million women worked for the federal government, but made up only 1.4% of the employees in the top four pay grades.[31] In the private sector, the few women who broke into male-dominated

---

[30] The US Supreme Court held this particular practice to constitute illegal sex discrimination in *Phillips v. Martin Marietta*, 400 U.S. 542 (1971).

[31] Collins (2010: 20).

professions were assigned to low-profile, low-paid jobs in 'women's' specialties. Female journalists were given the women's page, women doctors were channelled into paediatric medicine, and women lawyers were kept away from the courtroom.[32]

Perhaps worst of all, the Equal Employment Opportunity Commission (EEOC), the government body charged with enforcing these laws, was slow to enforce them to their fullest intent. One of the first signs that the EEOC was not taking sex discrimination seriously was its ruling that the new law permitted job announcements that distinguished between men's and women's jobs, even if there was no rational basis for a distinction.[33] An advertising agency, insurance company, or bank could advertise that they needed a man to fill a professional position, despite the fact that a woman could do the very same work.

A number of women in government became frustrated with the slow progress, so in 1966, they organized with Betty Friedan during a conference in Washington, DC to talk about what to do.[34] They decided to form a national advocacy group for women modelled on the National Association for the Advancement of Colored People. They called it the National Organization for Women (NOW) and elected Friedan as its first president.

Like the suffragettes almost 60 years before, one of the first things the new organization did was to organize picketing of EEOC offices in cities around the country. Friedan announced that NOW would take on the legal cases of women claiming sex discrimination in employment—even though it didn't have any legal staff yet.[35] They found lawyers among the many underemployed female lawyers—and NOW won its first case in 1969.[36]

---

[32] Collins (2010: 20–1, 26).
[33] Collins (2010: 82).
[34] Collins (2010: 84–5).
[35] Collins (2010: 85–93).
[36] Weeks v. Southern Bell Telephone Co., 408 F.2d 228 (5th Circuit Court of Appeals).

While NOW was pursuing its litigation strategy, a small group of women who called themselves the New York Radical Women was organizing a protest against the 1968 Miss America Pageant in Atlantic City, New Jersey. The Miss America Pageant had been the most watched programme on television in the early 1960s, and, in 1968, many still regarded Miss America as the icon of American womanhood. As the pageant's theme song said—Miss America was 'the queen of femininity'. The contestants were judged on three things: beauty, talent, and poise. They had to look good in both bathing suits and ball gowns, they had to display some kind of talent, and they had to be able to answer questions about themselves and their views on the meaning of life on live television without losing their composure. It was, in many ways, a testament to the fact that the Feminine Mystique was alive and well in 1968 America.

The contest infuriated many women, who were sick and tired of American culture's preoccupation with female beauty to the exclusion of female achievement. So when the New York Radical Women announced their protest, hundreds of women from around the country drove in cars and rented buses to Atlantic City to picket on the famous boardwalk. They marched carrying signs with slogans like 'No more beauty standards—everyone is beautiful!'[37] They threw bras, mops, girdles, pots and pans, and *Playboy* magazines into a big garbage can, and would have burned it all, but the police stopped them.[38]

It was no accident of history that a number of feminists began to pursue more militant strategies in 1968. The same year was marked by strikes and radical student demonstrations that erupted in the spring all across Europe and North America, anti-war protests in America, the assassination of Martin Luther King, and the raised fists of two African American athletes during the ceremony awarding their medals at the 1968 Olympics in Mexico City.

Almost all the women behind the protest at the Miss America Pageant had participated in and helped organize strikes, marches, and sit-ins

---

[37] Collins (2010: 193).
[38] Freeman, 'No More Miss America! (1968–1969)'.

in support of civil rights, student power, and opposition to the war, but had often found themselves sitting silent in such political meetings.[39] The male organizers and participants of these meetings treated the women among them in much the same way as the male delegates to the London anti-slavery convention had treated the female delegates. At one political convention in the 1960s, a number of the women proposed a resolution on women's rights, but the male committee in charge of deciding which resolutions would go on the agenda rejected it. When the women tried to challenge the decision on the convention floor, the men simply ignored them. One of the women—Shulamith Firestone, who later published a landmark book in the feminist movement, *The Dialectic of Sex* (1970)— rushed to the podium only to be greeted by the chairman who patted her on the head and said, 'Cool down, little girl. We have more important things to do here than talk about women's problems.'[40] Women may have got the vote 50 years before, but they still had no power or influence. And there seemed to be no twentieth-century male counterpart to the nineteenth-century male abolitionist William Garrison.[41]

These new feminist activists demanded access, on an equal basis with men, to every aspect of social life—business, the arts, sports, politics, science, and academia.[42] Second wave feminism—or the women's liberation movement, as it was called at that time—was united on that point. All the women engaged in that movement recognized each other as feminists by virtue of that agreement.

---

[39] Collins (2010: 183).

[40] Collins (2010: 183).

[41] Garrison was also a passionate advocate for equal treatment of men and women. Unlike many other abolitionist societies, his American Anti-Slavery Society admitted women as full participating members. He was also present at the London Convention when the male delegates voted to exclude the women from the proceedings. In protest, he declared, 'After battling so many long years for the liberties of African slaves, I can take no part in a convention that strikes down the most sacred rights of all women', and he refused to sit with the men. Stanton (2010: 77).

[42] Collins (2010: 181).

Women vs. men: drawing the battle lines

Feminists' focus on gaining equal access to every aspect of social life caused many—both feminists and non-feminists—to perceive feminism as being primarily concerned with women. Men did not figure much at all in feminist rhetoric. When they did, they were often cast as women's oppressors.

Feminist reformers, like Betty Friedan and the women who joined NOW, believed the main problem for women was that men discriminated against women in employment.

The more radical contingent that grew out of the Miss America protests was represented by organizations like the 'Redstockings'.[43] These feminists believed that women's problems weren't just the result of the 'feminine mystique' or discrimination in employment. Rather, they believed women's problems were the inevitable result of patriarchal culture—a social system in which human beings are artificially divided into two fixed and distinct gender categories, which are placed in a hierarchical relationship based on the principle of male domination. The Redstockings' Manifesto proclaimed—in rhetoric reminiscent of Elizabeth Cady Stanton's Declaration of Sentiments:

> All power structures throughout history have been male-dominated and male-oriented. Men have controlled all political, economic and cultural institutions and backed up this control with physical force. They have used their power to keep women in an inferior position. All men receive economic, sexual, and psychological benefits from male supremacy. All men have oppressed women.[44]

---

[43] The name 'Redstockings' represented the joining of two historical movements: the feminist movement of the nineteenth century, whose participants had been pejoratively labelled 'bluestockings', and the revolutionary movement inspired by Communism, signified by the colour red.

[44] 'Redstockings Manifesto', 7 July 1969.

These radical feminists believed that patriarchy makes male domination and female passivity synonymous with femininity and masculinity. As a result, they argued, male domination seems romantic and sexy, and women become willing participants in their own oppression.[45]

For these feminists, achieving women's 'final liberation from male supremacy' required the development of 'female class consciousness through sharing experience and publicly exposing the sexist foundation of all our institutions'.[46] In contrast to feminist reformers like Betty Friedan and the women in NOW, who were not interested in reforming the personal relationships between men and women, radical feminists focused on all the daily interactions between men and women, in both the private and public spheres. They coined new phrases—like 'the personal is political' and the 'politics of housework'—to articulate how women's second-class status in society was the result of male domination in personal relationships as well as in society at large. In books, articles, and public protests, the radicals denounced any practice they believed to be part of the system of male supremacy.

By the end of the 1970s, yet another group of radical feminists began promoting the view that male supremacy arose from devaluation of women and all things feminine. According to these feminists, liberation from patriarchy required revaluing 'femininity'. They explicitly promoted rejection of the values and virtues culturally associated with men—aggression, autonomy, hierarchy, domination, and violence—and instead promoted the values and virtues culturally associated with women—community, caring, sharing, emotion, trust, and peace.[47]

Slowly, public opinion began to generalize radical feminism's pro-female/anti-male programme to all feminists and by the 1980s feminism had become—in many people's imaginations—nearly synonymous with man-hating women who disrespected stay-at-home mums.

---

[45] Grant (2006).

[46] Redstockings Manifesto, 7 July 1969.

[47] Tong (2007).

A third wave?

From the suffragettes who campaigned for women's right to vote in the nineteenth century to women fighting for the right to do 'men's' jobs at 'men's' pay and recognition of the value of 'feminine' qualities, feminist movements have been instrumental in improving the lives of women— as well as, perhaps more indirectly, the lives of men. Feminist activism— collective action by women who are convinced that they are just as capable and worthy of respect as men and should have the same rights and opportunities as men—has won important legal rights, including the right to vote, the right to equal pay for the same work, the right to attend the same universities and enrol in the same programmes, the right to participate in sports, and the right to be considered for employment in any job. The foundational ideas that women can, some women must, and many women want full-time paid and meaningful work outside the home hardly seem novel any more. These are the results of the work of both reformist and radical feminists. This is indeed a history to be proud of.

Looking back over this history, we can see that first and second wave feminists achieved these results by following adversarial strategies targeting first the state and then the culture of male supremacy. First wave feminists accused the state of institutionalizing and enforcing male power over women by denying them the vote and property rights. Second wave feminists targeted the culture of male supremacy when they pointed out that just getting the right to vote and own property had not changed the basic cultural belief that women were not men's equals and should not be treated as such, let alone as breadwinners.

The reformist feminists targeted the establishment (employers, courts, educators, government officials, cultural institutions) because it continued to operate according to blatantly sexist norms that blocked women's access to full participation in the public sphere outside the home. Their strategy was to use the law—specifically anti-discrimination legislation— as a lever for forcing open the doors to better jobs and educational opportunities. They believed that legislation and its enforcement could be used to change people's mind-sets and pave the way for cultural change.

Radical feminists set out more directly against the agents and beneficiaries of male supremacy—men. It was a risky strategy. It achieved many important things, but at a price. The political became quite personal. Men, both as a group and as individuals, were treated as opponents—if not outright enemies. There was a time in the USA and Europe when that strategy may have made sense; there were a lot of men—perhaps even a large majority of them—who believed that women should not participate on an equal footing with them in business, academia, or politics and did everything in their power to keep women out.

Things have changed dramatically since then. Many men have embraced some, if not most, of the ideas advocated by reformist and even radical feminists—such as the importance of education and meaningful work for women, sharing childcare responsibilities, and women's sexual freedom and agency.[48] And as a result, many women—though still far from enough—have found the strength and resources to make full use of the changed cultural landscape and have achieved high positions in business, politics, and academia.

Of course there are men who still cling to the past, but opposition to the feminist project is not just a male phenomenon. As we show in Chapter 7, organized and vocal female opposition to many feminist ideas began to emerge in the 1980s. It hardly makes sense any more to claim that men are always the oppressors of women or that feminism, as it has been practised, necessarily always represents all women's interests. It just isn't that simple.

As we see it, the main obstacle to achieving gender balance isn't the government or men. It is the very human tendency to categorize people and to subscribe to the social norms that define those categories in our everyday interactions, and underlying that, a visceral fear of social exclusion. We enforce these norms by exacting a price or bestowing a reward

---

[48] The website Men and Feminism, http://www.mfeminism.com/, whose managing editor and editor are men, and whose regular contributors consist of a man and a woman, presents a wealth of material focusing on the ways in which men engage positively with feminism and feminist ideas. Its Facebook group, Men and Feminism, has attracted more than 30,000 'likes'.

in the common currency of social interaction: criticism, insults, giving or withdrawing recognition, friendship, respect, admiration, or intimacy. Just talking about behaving in ways that do not conform to social gender norms can result in social penalties. Both men and women participate in all these interactions and share the tendency to stereotype. Just think for a minute about how you, your family, friends, colleagues, or acquaintances react to women you perceive as being 'mannish', or to men you perceive as being 'girlish'.

On the other hand, think for a minute about how much our ideas about feminine and masculine behaviour have changed. As late as 1977, two-thirds of Americans believed that it was 'much better for everyone involved if the man is the achiever outside the home and the woman takes care of the home and family'. By 1994, two-thirds of Americans rejected this notion.[49] A 2011 survey showed that over two-thirds of Europeans (69%) *disagreed* with the statement that 'women are less interested than men in positions of responsibility'.[50] In four European countries, the number of interviewees disagreeing with the statement that women are less interested than men in positions of responsibility grew dramatically just since 2009: Sweden (from 68% to 84%), Ireland (from 69% to 81%), Portugal (from 64% to 74%), and Cyprus (from 64% to 73%).[51]

We do not deny that men as a group have more power and more wealth than women as a group,[52] and that some issues still call for the confrontational strategies of feminist activism—such as when the US Senate holds a hearing into the epidemic of sexual assault on women in the military and most of the witnesses are men (11 of the 12 in the first panel).[53] Nor

---

[49] Coontz (2013).

[50] European Commission (2012).

[51] European Commission (2012).

[52] We are also well aware that comparisons across different categories—race and class in particular—clearly show that many white women have more power and wealth than many black men, and most wealthy men *and* women, of whatever race, have more power and far more opportunities to live healthy and productive lives than the poor.

[53] Bump (2013).

do we reject the idea that women sometimes need to engage in collective, female-only action in order to attract attention to a particular problem that obviously affects the health and well-being of women far more than men—such as access to safe and reliable contraception, safe and legal abortion services, or female circumcision. Feminism is not obsolete when there are still women in the world without the right to vote, the right to an education, or the right to control what happens to their own bodies without answering to male or state authority. However, we are convinced that the main obstacles to closing gender gaps in leadership and occupations won't be eliminated by following a confrontational strategy that pits women against men.

Both men and women express frustration at the way gendered expectations about the way men and women should work interfere with their ability to find the right mix of work and private life. Here's an example. A Ph.D. student at Copenhagen Business School recently interviewed groups of practising lawyers in firms in Denmark as part of a project on how lawyers define their professional identities.[54] When one group of young lawyers discussed the subject of work/life conflicts, the female lawyers in the group saw it as a gender issue, and said they hesitated to talk about it at work because they did not want to be considered weak women who are not sufficiently committed to their careers.

To the surprise of the women in the group, however, the men felt they had the same problem. They felt equally torn between their work, their families, and their roles as caring dads/husbands/partners. The women were simply not aware that their male colleagues struggled with the same issue—an absence of role models who had figured out how to strike the balance differently from the older generation of mostly male lawyers who had relied on their wives to run their households and look after the children.

---

[54] Conversation with Ph.D. student, Inger Høedt Rasmussen. Her Ph.D. thesis, 'Developing Identity for Lawyers: Towards Sustainable Lawyering', is on file with the authors and is expected to be published in Denmark in 2014.

This example teaches us an important lesson. If we construct the under-representation of women in leadership or in certain occupations strictly as a feminist issue or a question of women's rights, we are unlikely to find the common interests between men and women that can convert the two genders into allies, rather than enemies in the process of changing the way we work and live together.

We want to encourage rethinking the way we talk about men and women—to move from the rhetoric of a conflict between the sexes to the more inclusive rhetoric of gender balance. Some feminists are wondering if they need to find a different name for their ideas in order to include men and other gender issues—for example, the problems of homosexuals and transgender people.[55] A lot of men have been raised with feminist ideas about women's sexual agency, access to contraception, abortion, divorce, sharing childcare and housework, and, as we'll show in the next chapter, a number of women have rejected them, so it clearly doesn't make sense to talk about gender imbalance or gender inequality as springing from a conflict between men and women. In short, we believe closing the gender gap requires that we stop fighting and find new allies across the lines of the battle of the sexes. It's time to call a truce and collaborate in the process of achieving gender balance.

Key points and guiding principle

- Gender balance is not a zero-sum game; men will benefit as well as women.
- Gender gaps in leadership and gender-segregated occupations won't disappear without men's participation in finding solutions.
- Eliminating gender gaps and gender-segregated occupations requires focusing on gender, giving equal attention to men and women.

Guiding principle: *Make peace, not war.*

---

[55] Chaudhry (2013); Jessica G. (2008)

7

Wrestling with God and Mammon

In our conversations with managers in different organizations about gender balance, a number of them express reluctance to invest much time or effort into doing anything to promote it by pointing out that a number of women—including female colleagues—say they don't want to pursue top positions because they believe that their primary role in society is to be wives and mothers. Or they point out that a number of their female colleagues have expressed dislike for any kind of 'positive action' for the purpose of increasing the numbers of women in top positions or male-dominated occupations because they don't want any special treatment. They want to make it 'on their own'.

We do not deny that a substantial number of women may disagree with the whole point of this book. A recent survey of American adults showed that one-third of all women aged 18–34 said that being successful in a high-paying career or profession is not 'one of the most important things' or 'very important' in their lives.[1] There are also a number of women who actively oppose the idea that we need to do anything to get more women into leadership positions. A high-profile conservative American think tank, Independent Women's Forum, regularly criticizes suggestions that business or government needs to do anything to promote more women into leadership. Its basic position on the subject is that women's calls for

---

[1] Two-thirds of women in that age group, as compared with 59% of young men, answered the question positively. Patten and Parker (2012).

more women in leadership positions amount to whining and begging for special treatment.[2]

Female opposition to initiatives intended to increase women's participation in business and public life is nothing new, though. When women all over the world joined together to campaign for the right to vote in the nineteenth century, some women organized themselves to campaign against it. In the USA, small groups of women protesting against state legislation giving women the right to vote joined forces in 1911 to form a nationwide *anti*-suffrage organization, the National Association Opposed to Woman Suffrage (NAOWS).[3] At its peak, NAOWS attracted an estimated 350,000 members. After the Second World War, both right- and left-wing Greek women demanded the right to vote and the right to hold political office, but right-wing women insisted that a woman's place was still in the home.[4] The first female minister in Greek government declared in a pre-election speech that 'A woman's first duty is to her family' and 'You must not consider that women who participate in political life are going to abandon their homes and their families, as some women have enjoined us to do in the past'.[5]

The women's liberation movement of the 1970s likewise encountered female opposition. Politically and socially conservative women in many countries opposed feminist campaigns to eliminate the remaining legal barriers to women's access to educational and employment opportunities as well as to contraception and legal abortion. In the USA, female opposition to the women's liberation movement found national expression in two women's organizations, the Eagle Forum and Concerned Women for America, both of which actively lobbied against passage of an amendment to the US Constitution which would have elevated protection from sex discrimination to a constitutional right.

---

[2] See, for example, Hays (2012).
[3] Maddux (2004).
[4] Vervenioti (2002: 115–26).
[5] Vervenioti (2002: 115–16).

In South America a substantial number of women supported General Pinochet's 1973 coup against Salvador Allende's Marxist government in Chile, largely because Pinochet opposed Allende's feminist-supported policies on birth control, abortion, and pornography.[6] Similarly, in France in the 1980s, Front National (FN), a right-wing political party, began actively opposing the idea that women should pursue full-time careers. It campaigned on a platform that included a promise to encourage French women to stay home by paying them a 'maternal salary'. A female member of the party formed an organization, Cercle National Femmes d'Europe (National Circle of European women; CNFE), in order to support FN's campaign to promote what they considered traditional marriage and families.[7]

History shows that women are not a single interest group. Women have very different experiences and opinions about what women's interests are. Women do not agree, and probably never will agree, that we need to do anything proactively about gender gaps in education, business, or politics. Should that disagreement among women stand in the way of measures to promote gender balance? In this chapter we take a closer look at some of the reasons for female opposition to gender balance initiatives and suggest a strategy for dealing with it in a respectful and constructive way.

Introducing the women of the opposition
To understand why some women oppose campaigns to bring more women into leadership positions or achieve a more balanced distribution of men and women across occupations, we want to take a close look at the women who have opposed modern campaigns for women's rights in both Europe and the USA. Political scientists and sociologists claim that

---

[6] Power (2002).
[7] Lesselier (2002).

these women can be grouped into two categories: 'social conservatives' and 'laissez-faire conservatives'.[8]

Social conservative women believe that men and women are essentially different and that these differences are at least biologically determined, if not directly ordained by God. As such, no argument can be regarded as a legitimate basis for genderless roles in society. Furthermore they believe that immorality is the main cause of social problems.[9]

Laissez-faire conservative women are committed to strong principles of individual freedom and responsibility. They reject collective interests based on gender, or other subgroup identities like race or sexual orientation, particularly when people invoke them to claim rights to government protection or support. They believe that social problems arise primarily as a result of too much government intervention in private life and in the market.[10]

The two most prominent conservative women's organizations in the USA—Concerned Women for America (CWA) and Independent Women's Forum (IWF)—represent these two categories of female opponents. We focus on CWA and IWF because they are very well organized, exercise substantial influence in American politics, and provide the clearest examples of what social and laissez-faire conservative women think about gender-related issues. There are no other comparable women's organizations in Europe, although there are certainly a number of politically active conservative European women who express the perspectives and interests that characterize social or laissez-faire conservative groups.

CWA was founded in 1979 by Beverly LaHaye, the wife of a prominent American evangelical Christian pastor. LaHaye got the idea of forming a women's organization to oppose feminist activism after she watched

[8] American sociologist Rebecca Klatch came up with these names for these two perspectives in her book, *Women of the New Right* (1987). That female opponents of feminist or gender balance initiatives tend to fall into one of these two categories is also indicated by Bacchetta and Power (2002: 7–8).

[9] Bacchetta and Power (2002: 7–8); Klatch (1987: 26–31).

[10] Schreiber (2002).

a television interview with Betty Friedan, author of *The Feminist Mystique* and founder of the feminist organization, National Organization for Women. Friedan's claim to represent American women's interests provoked LaHaye into action. She resented the idea that Friedan or any other feminist thought they could claim to represent her interests. The feminist agenda, to LaHaye, was 'anti-God' and 'anti-family', and she did not want any part of it. She knew many other women who shared her evangelical Christian beliefs and founded the organization to oppose Friedan and NOW.

Today, CWA is just as large and just as engaged in the political process as NOW. It has a professionally staffed office in Washington, DC, members in all 50 states, and claims to be the largest grassroots women's organization in the USA with approximately 500,000 members. From all visible evidence, the women of the CWA are mostly white fundamentalist evangelical Protestants who are passionately opposed to abortion, most forms of contraception, and civil rights for homosexuals.[11] CWA's mission 'is to protect and promote biblical values among all citizens—first through prayer, then education, and finally by influencing our society—thereby reversing the decline in moral values in our nation'.[12]

IWF is a much smaller organization, though hardly less influential than CWA. IWF grew out of the activism of a group of women who defended the nomination of Clarence Thomas to the US Supreme Court against allegations he had sexually harassed a staff attorney when he was chairman of the Equal Employment Opportunities Commission. As of 2008, IWF numbered approximately 20,000 members, most of whom are professional women with strong ties to the administration of former president George W. Bush.[13] The organization advocates for limits on federal social programmes and business regulations and increased private sector

[11] Schreiber (2008: 26). The number '500,000' represents the number of people reported by CWA to have ever been members.
[12] Concerned Women for America, mission statement.
[13] Schreiber (2008: 26).

involvement in the provision of public goods and services. IWF's website proclaims its mission to be:

> to expand the conservative coalition, both by increasing the number of women who understand and value the benefits of limited government, personal liberty, and free markets, and by countering those who seek to ever-expand government in the name of protecting women. IWF is a non-partisan, [...] research and educational institution. By aggressively seeking earned media, providing easy-to-read, timely publications and commentary, and reaching out to the public, we seek to cultivate support for these important principles and encourage women to join us in working to return the country to limited, Constitutional government.

Like CWA, IWF is expressly anti-feminist and claims to speak for those women whom feminists do not represent. An IWF board member explained that she and her colleagues founded the organization 'because it seemed . . . that feminist groups by and large spoke to a very radicalized minority'.[14] A CWA staff member similarly asserts that American women hear feminists 'saying we represent women in America, what American women think. And these women are saying this is not what I believe and not what I think . . . so they have looked for a place where they can get information that states their point of view, and they have found that in CWA.'[15]

Don't mess with God or Mother Nature

Social conservatives firmly believe that a strict division of gender roles is part of the natural order and that dire consequences will follow if we try to ignore those differences. Whether they believe these differences are ordained by God or Nature, the resulting world-view is the same: Tampering with traditional gender roles is asking for trouble.

In their view, men and women are different in essential and immutable ways, and it's a mistake to try to get men and women to do anything that

---

[14] Schreiber (2008: 44).

[15] Schreiber (2008: 43).

doesn't match their natural abilities, whatever they happen to be.[16] The consequences for society are dire—even catastrophic. For the women's organization (CNFE) within the French right-wing party, Front National, the whole of Western civilization depends on protecting men's and women's ability to fulfil their natural roles.[17] For the Christian women of the CWA, any departure from Christian fundamentalist teachings about gender roles or anything else 'is at the root of the glaring injustices of modern American public policy'.[18]

If asked about what exactly are the natural and essential differences between men and women, social conservatives answer primarily by referring to tradition or religion. Christian social conservatives reject scientific findings that do not support fundamentalist Christian views because they are nothing more than 'irrational secularism based on an unthinking and cruel relativism'.[19] Secular social conservatives are similarly unimpressed by scientific explanations that contradict their views on natural gender differences. They are primarily concerned with preserving traditional gender roles and social values. These do not require a scientific explanation. They are simply right and necessary for everyone's safety and security.

Social conservative women, regardless of nationality or religion, exalt motherhood and idealize heterosexual marriage and family, viewing it as the locus of women's power and self-realization.[20] The family—and women's role within it—is often depicted as 'the pillar of society, the bastion of society's security, order, and naturalized hierarchy, or a microcosm of society or of all humanity'.[21] The CNFE in France works for the revalorization of traditional feminine functions, advocating traditional femininity and opposing what they view as feminism's 'masculine model'

---

[16] Bacchetta and Power (2002: 7–8).
[17] Lesselier (2002: 131).
[18] Concerned Women for America, Core Issues.
[19] Concerned Women for America, Core Issues.
[20] Bacchetta and Power (2002: 8).
[21] Bacchetta and Power (2002: 8).

for women. Connie Marshner, one of the architects of social conservative women's opposition to feminist initiatives in the USA, claims that the traditional caregiver role ennobles women. In a speech delivered at a Family Forum conference in the early 1980s, Marshner said:

> A woman's nature is, simply, other-oriented. . . . To the traditional woman self-centeredness remains as ugly and sinful as ever. The less time women spend thinking about themselves, the happier they are . . . women are ordained by their nature to spend themselves in meeting the needs of others. And women, far more than men, will transmit culture and values to the next generation. There is nothing demeaning about this nature: it is ennobling.[22]

For these women, arguments that men and women are equally capable of caring for and meeting the needs of children and others contradict the essence of their understanding of themselves as women and their purpose in life.

For social conservatives who base their views on religion, arguments that gender roles need not be so distinct are also plainly wrong. Religious social conservatives believe distinct gender roles are decreed by God in the Holy Scriptures. Arguments that contradict these religious beliefs are doomed to fail. Rational argument simply fails in the face of religious beliefs like those preached by Jerry Falwell, one of the most well-known pastors and leaders of the American Christian fundamentalist evangelical movement. Falwell wrote:

> Scripture declares that God has called the father to be the spiritual leader in his family. . . . Good husbands who are godly men are good leaders. Their wives and children want to follow them and be under their protection. The husband is to be the decision maker and the one who motivates his family with love.[23]

CWA's website provides a lesson in how adamant religious social conservatives are in their beliefs about gender. In line with the basic tenets

---

[22] As quoted in Klatch (1987: 45).
[23] Falwell (1981: 110–11).

of fundamentalist evangelical Christianity, CWA points to biblical support for all its positions on political and social issues. Fundamentalist evangelical Christians believe that the Bible is to be read and understood as the literal word of God. CWA explains that God is the source of our knowledge of what is right and wrong, and that we can discover what is right and wrong by accepting Jesus Christ as our personal saviour and studying the Bible. They find biblical support for the idea that Christians should not follow any kind of philosophy or moral code that depends on non-biblical sources in this passage from the Book of Colossians in the New Testament: 'See to it that no one takes you captive through hollow and deceptive philosophy, which depends on human tradition and the basic principles of this world rather than on Christ.'[24]

A number of other passages in the Bible contain detailed instructions about family life, gender norms, and relationships between men and women from which evangelical fundamentalist Christians draw lessons for today. The CWA spells it all out on its website in a section on marriage and family. CWA declares, 'God made marriage between a man and a woman',[25] implying that homosexual marriage is un-Christian and immoral. It continues, 'Populating the earth is a mandate from God, not a threat to humanity.'[26] This statement implies that in order for women to obey God, they must embrace their reproductive role instead of seeing it as a problem—regardless of their life situation. Furthermore, according to CWA, 'God holds parents accountable for raising their children', which

---

[24] Colossians 2:8.

[25] CWA quotes Matthew 19:4–6 for support:

And He answered and said to them, 'Have you not read that He who made them at the beginning made them "male and female", and said, "For this reason a man shall leave his father and mother and be joined to his wife, and the two shall become one flesh"? So then, they are no longer two but one flesh. Therefore what God has joined together, let not man separate.'

[26] CWA quotes Genesis 1:27–8:

So God created man in His own image; in the image of God He created him; male and female He created them. Then God blessed them, and God said to them, 'Be fruitful and multiply; fill the earth and subdue it; have dominion over the fish of the sea, over the birds of the air, and over every living thing that moves on the earth.'

supports the view that daycare is not a Christian solution to the problem of combining parenting and full-time work.

The implications of such biblical assertions are clear. Women should not pursue careers to the extent it keeps them from having children or if it means letting someone else care for their children, even if the caregiver is the father. In short, women must assume the role of caregiver and men are to assume the role of breadwinner. Efforts to ensure the availability of affordable daycare, contraception, and safe, legal abortions are seen as attempts to keep women from fulfilling the role God intends for them. To encourage anything that distracts women from marriage and children is to encourage immorality.

Men and women who believe in the truth of evangelical Christian interpretations of the Bible are not interested in supporting or promoting anything that challenges these principles. For them, living according to different moral principles is morally wrong and will lead to nothing but misery, immorality, and even social collapse.

Some social conservatives do not identify specifically with these evangelical Christian principles, but they arrive at the same conclusion by a different route. They believe that trying to bring about gender equality in all areas of life is contrary to Nature. Any deviation leads to the same dire consequences as those feared by their Christian cohorts. The meaning of life for social conservatives is defined by these fundamental guiding principles, and there is no room for compromise. To stray from them renders their lives empty, meaningless, and dangerous.

Don't mess with the market: female disciples of Hayek and Friedman

Conservative women in the laissez-faire category of female opposition have a more complicated relationship with feminist activism. These women are not as interested in prescribing specific gender roles as they are in minimizing any government involvement in business and family life.[27]

---

[27] Klatch (1987: 147–8).

Laissez-faire conservative women thus oppose feminist campaigns for state-subsidized childcare, mandatory maternity and paternity leave, and prohibitions against pregnancy discrimination. Their opposition is not motivated by concerns that such initiatives would dismantle traditional gender roles. Rather, they are concerned simply about government encroachments on personal freedom. While feminists see these initiatives as strategies for overcoming the difficulties women have had in combining both motherhood and full-time paid careers, laissez-faire conservative women see them as interfering in men's and women's self-determination.

Laissez-faire conservative women believe that men and women are equal. They applaud the idea that every individual should do everything within his or her power to rise to the level of his or her talents. They just have to do it without government help or 'special' treatment. IWF asserts on its website:

> IWF believes passionately in women's equality and that women deserve every opportunity to pursue their vision of happiness. IWF rejects the view of women as a victim-class in need of special government protection or support, and objects to those who try to expand government power in the name of women.[28]

To the extent there are gender gaps, they are best left to the efforts of individual men and women to close them.

Instead of religious Scripture as the basis for their views, laissez-faire conservatives rely on a political ideology inspired primarily by the writings of two academic economists—Friedrich Hayek and Milton Friedman. Hayek's most famous book, *The Road to Serfdom*, published in 1944, argued that democracy is only possible in a system based on free disposal over private property.[29] According to Hayek, free disposal over private property is a guarantee against collectivist political ideologies, like

---

[28] Independent Women's Forum (2013).
[29] Hayek (1944: 69–70).

Communism, which he regarded as leading inevitably to repression and ultimately totalitarianism. '[T]he close interdependence of all economic phenomena makes it difficult to stop planning just where we wish . . . once the free working of the market is impeded beyond a certain degree, the planner will be forced to extend his controls until they become all comprehensive.'[30]

Milton Friedman wrote something quite similar 18 years later in his book, *Capitalism and Freedom*:

> Historical evidence speaks with a single voice on the relation between political freedom and a free market. I know of no example in time or place of a society that has been marked by a large measure of political freedom, and that has not also used something comparable to a free market to organize the bulk of economic activity.[31]

Belief in the unity of political and economic freedom rests on a strong version of individualism and the absence of state coercion. In order to believe that you can maximize freedom through the absence of state coercion, you must believe that each individual exists as a self-contained entity, consisting of a core self that exists prior to any interaction with family, friends, and the rest of society. This core self is thought to be impervious to history, culture, or society. That way, the individual is motivated solely by his or her own preferences, which arise from within the self—not as a result of social forces. Individual differences with regard to the objects we desire and the amount of effort we are willing to put into satisfying our wants are believed to account for the dynamism of free markets.

According to this version of individualism, attempts to substitute my preferences for yours or vice versa are not just futile; they're pernicious because they interfere with the operation of the market. We must allow individuals to seek fulfilment of their desires by using their natural talents to achieve them. We must not assume that we know what other people want, or get in the way of people's efforts to pursue their own

---

[30] Hayek (1944: 117).
[31] Friedman (1962: 9).

goals. Differences in preferences and natural talents plus differences in individual effort explain the differences in outcomes—not social forces. Because the amount of effort expended is a matter of individual choice, and because most people believe that effort should be rewarded, unequal outcomes are to be expected and are morally justifiable.

For Hayek and Friedman, human freedom exists even in the face of fierce competition or private power. Impersonal forces—the 'invisible hand' of the 'market'—define the conditions of competition among individuals. Because these forces cannot be controlled by individuals and because they affect all individuals, they are not seen as constraints on any single individual's freedom. Everyone is free to pursue his or her vision of the good to the same extent as anyone else. Impersonal forces establish the rules of the game, and individual talent and effort determine the outcome. That is not to say life is always fair, or that individuals never misuse their economic power, but it is, according to this view, far better to assume that in general, everyone gets what they deserve. The only alternative to this arrangement, according to Hayek and Friedman, is state-sponsored coercion. To believe that government can intervene in this process to achieve greater equality of outcomes is the first step down 'the road to serfdom'.

IWF represents women who have adopted a strong version of Hayek's and Friedman's perspective. One of the best examples of how this perspective shapes the way women understand the issue of women's relative absence from leadership positions is a blog post by Charlotte Hays on IWF's website.[32] The blog salutes Danielle Pletka of the American Enterprise Institute for rejecting criticism directed at right-wing think tanks for the absence of women from policy positions. The blog post is written in reply to an article in *The Washington Monthly* by Anne Kim, managing director for policy and strategy at the Progressive Policy Institute. Kim pointed out that at the American Enterprise Institute, only eight out of 60 resident scholars are women, as is only one of the institution's top five officials, while the Heritage Foundation's 'senior management' page shows 15

[32] Hays (2012).

white men and only two women, neither of whom hold policy positions. The blog quotes Pletka's reply to Kim's article:

> Why are some people so obsessed with counting up their seats? What do they think they're missing? . . . Are we going to be better served by more women economists? More chicks in foreign policy? More high heels pondering the education mess? Tell me, what are you looking for here except more entitlements, more special treatment, more set asides, more demeaning quotas? Who wants to be hired because they're a woman? I'll tell you: A woman who knows she isn't the best for the job and is looking for preferential treatment. You want to work here at AEI? Great. Send me your awesome resume, show me your platinum degrees, hand over your testimony, your writing, and your collection of super op-eds. Oh, don't have that? Then sit down, and shut up.[33]

In essence, Pletka is arguing that the current gender composition of senior management in these organizations reflects actual differences in individual effort, talent, and interest. If the same number of women as men put in the necessary effort, gender balance will be achieved.

The facts do not support the thesis

One of the most distinguished academic economists of the twentieth century was Paul A. Samuelson, the first American to win the Nobel Prize in economics in 1970. He was educated at the University of Chicago by Friedrich Hayek, who also won the Nobel Prize in 1974. From Hayek, Samuelson learned that 'business freedoms and personal freedoms have to be strongly linked, as a matter of both brute empirical fact and cogent deductive syllogism', and, for a long time Samuelson believed what he was taught.[34] But as he later wrote in a 1983 paper published in *The American Economist*, he gradually 'had to acknowledge that the paradigm could not fit the facts'.[35] As an example of the lack of fit between theory and

---

[33] As quoted in Hays (2012).
[34] Samuelson (1983).
[35] Samuelson (1983: 7).

facts, Samuelson pointed out that the highly regulated social democratic Scandinavian countries were certainly at least as free, if not freer, than the USA. He acknowledged that '[c]ontrolled socialist societies are rarely efficient and virtually never freely democratic', but, on the other hand, some of the freest markets were established and maintained by fascist dictatorships:

> Indeed, after mid-century the finest archetypes of efficient free markets have often been quasi-fascist or outright fascist societies in which a dictatorial leader or single party imposes a political order—without which imposition the market could not politically survive. Chile with its military dictatorship cum-the-Chicago boys is only one dramatic case.[36]

Samuelson concluded, 'I am primarily a theorist. But my first and last allegiance is to the facts'.[37]

We two authors agree with Samuelson. We are also committed to paying attention to the facts. For us, 'facts' are claims supported by substantial scientific evidence. We're not talking about absolute certainties here. We're talking about what the preponderance of historical and scientific evidence indicates. We don't think either of the conservative perspectives outlined above is tenable in light of the facts as we understand them.

As we hope previous chapters have shown, there are a number of facts that prevent us from accepting either the social conservative or laissez-faire conservative understanding of gender roles. In Chapter 3, we explained that scientific research on biological explanations for psychological and behavioural gender differences has not generated sufficient evidence to support the view that men and women are all that different from each other—naturally, substantially, and essentially speaking. Men and women are at the minimum not so different from each other that we should give up on closing the existing pronounced gender gaps in leadership, career patterns, or occupation.

---

[36] Samuelson (1983: 7).

[37] Samuelson (1983: 7).

In Chapter 4 we presented the scientific findings indicating that much of what we think of as inborn gender differences may actually stem from learned preferences and behaviours. And we learn them without realizing that we do so—or that there are alternatives to what we're learning. We do not claim that all gender differences are learned or socially constructed and that biology plays no role. We merely claim that the available scientific evidence so far indicates that gender roles are far more flexible and subject to change than many people tend to believe.

Nor do we believe that the facts support the strong version of individualism underlying laissez-faire conservative opposition to feminist activism. The research described in Chapters 4 and 5 contradict the laissez-faire conservatives' belief that individuals are perfectly free to 'choose' their career paths and achieve their goals regardless of gender norms. Men's and women's capacity to act freely and independently from dominant gender norms is not unlimited. Indeed, it seems quite constrained. We all internalize the images, insults, stigmas, and stereotypes associated with gender and other identity categories—cultural, ethnic, racial, and sexual—to some degree. Granted, we do not all internalize the *same* gender norms. Much depends on the people we meet, our education, our life experiences, and our own personalities. However, the research on the effects of negative stereotypes indicates that the possibility of self-realization can be substantially constricted by the individual's incorporation of negative stereotypes into his or her own self-understanding—unless they are consistently counteracted by some other positive norms.[38] In short, the perfect world of strong individualism does not exist.

Respecting our differences

We have no illusions that we can persuade religious social conservatives that they need to adjust their beliefs to scientific facts. That is simply not in the nature of religion. Religion is, literally, a matter of faith, not scientific evidence.

---

[38] Hawkesworth (1984).

Likewise, we probably cannot persuade secular social conservatives—those who simply believe that it is best to follow traditional gender norms—to adjust their views to the facts. Their commitment to traditional gender norms is based on the closed-door belief that those norms are right and natural. Even with overwhelming and incontrovertible evidence to the contrary, they feel no compulsion to change their minds. Therein lies the problem. For them, no such evidence exists, nor will it ever.

Laissez-faire conservatives have a rather intellectual commitment to the belief that individuals are in control of their own destinies—so we should treat them that way. Even if some of them might come around to agreeing that culture and socialization constrain individual freedom, it is likely that few would step over to the other side and abandon their philosophy that people must be treated *as if* they were free from all constraints. It's clear they fear the potential for state coercion more than any consequences of failing to achieve gender balance. Their cost–benefit analysis—if we can call it that—always ends up in favour of radical individualism.

These are all fundamental assumptions that support anti-feminist views. No one is likely to give up such fundamental assumptions without considerable struggle. It is akin to trying to remove one of the cards at the bottom of a house of cards—the whole deck collapses.

For most people, that kind of change in perspective does not happen overnight or without rather far-reaching consequences. A fundamentalist evangelical Christian would have to find a new church or perhaps a new God. A laissez-faire politician would have to find a new political party to represent or give up politics all together. A policy analyst in a think tank would have to give up his job. Stepping anywhere outside the circle of their beliefs, most social and laissez-faire conservatives would find themselves looking for new friends—maybe even new jobs.

The struggle to hang on to our fundamental assumptions about the world is probably a key reason that conflicts about gender balance generate so much heat. Any attempt to persuade the opposition runs into the wall of resistance that protects those fundamental assumptions from attack. The futility of rational argument between people starting from different fundamental values provokes so much frustration that both sides often find themselves resorting to name-calling and personal insults.

As a strategic matter, it's counter-productive for anyone, no matter which side of the issue you're on, to engage in those kinds of debates. It makes everyone look and feel bad. Everyone starts digging foxholes instead of trying to figure out how to bridge the gaps. Far better to recognize what the disagreement is really about—a clash in fundamental assumptions— and agree to disagree than to resort to name-calling and personal insults.

Nevertheless, our position is . . .

We do not, and cannot, claim to speak for all women, nor do we expect all women to agree with us. Women do not constitute a homogeneous group. They have different world-views, different experiences, different problems, and different priorities. However, women's heterogeneity is not a good reason to withhold support or take action to promote gender balance in leadership and occupations, for a number of reasons.

First, gender balance is not a women's issue alone. It is a social issue that affects everyone. Ensuring the conditions for economic prosperity is for the good of humanity, and we believe that gender balance is one of those conditions. The fact that some women may oppose gender balance initiatives is really no less and no more worrisome than the fact that some men may also oppose them.

Second, social movements that have brought about profound change have never achieved their goals because at some point everyone agreed. A critical mass is all that's needed. Just look at what feminists and other activists have achieved despite strong, sometimes even violent, opposition. The right to vote for ex-slaves and women and the elimination of racial segregation are just two examples of enormous change brought about despite strong opposition.

Third, logical, fact-based arguments alone are just as unlikely to change the minds of our opponents in the social and laissez-faire conservative categories as they are to motivate anyone to actually get up and do something to promote gender balance. No matter how much we want to believe that we can think completely rationally, without any disturbing interference from our emotions, human beings are just not built that way. The different regions of the brain that control different aspects of our lives—the amygdala, which controls things like heart rate without our thinking about it, the midbrain that regulates sleep, appetite, pleasure, motivation, and attention, the limbic system that is critically involved with relationships and emotion, and the cortex, which allows us to master language, engage in abstract thought and planning—work together so that it is impossible to actually separate 'rational thought' from emotion.[39] If our brains didn't work that way, we wouldn't be able to choose among available alternatives. We would not be able to decide if one alternative were 'better' than the other because arriving at any decision that requires valuing anything—even an idea—as 'good' or 'bad' requires feeling.[40]

Finally, as any good actor, dancer, or musician can tell you, effective human communication does not necessarily take place through language, let alone well-formulated arguments. We communicate a great deal through subtle cues in posture, expressions, and tone of voice—or simply through example, by acting things out. That's one of the reasons why, as we show in the next chapter, we cannot simply rely on legislation or court decisions to establish the conditions for gender balance.

Key points and guiding principle

- Social movements that have brought about profound changes for the better—like the movements to abolish slavery and give women the right to vote—did not achieve their goals because everyone agreed.
- Rational arguments alone are not enough to change the minds of people whose religious beliefs and political ideologies are inconsistent with gender balance.
- Gender balance is a social issue that affects everyone, not just women.

Guiding principle: *Expect female opposition.*

---

[39] Szalavitz and Perry (2010: 18).
[40] Szalavitz and Perry (2010: 18).

8

Illusions of Justice

When we interviewed executives and human resource managers for this book, we asked all of them what they thought accounted for the fact that women were clustered in administrative jobs and middle management in their organizations, and men dominated the upper levels of management. None of them said they thought it was due to sex discrimination. None of them reported ever having a case of sex discrimination in their organizations, either. That second fact alone is remarkable, considering what the labour market looked like just a half century ago.

Back then, medical and law schools banned female students or limited their numbers to a handful per class. It was entirely legal to refuse to hire women or pay women less than men for the same jobs. Many employers did both. They justified paying women less with the argument that women didn't need the same pay as men because if they were single, they lived with their parents, and if they were married, they were just bringing in extra money. Newspapers offered cafeteria jobs to women with journalism degrees from the best schools in the USA. Law firms offered female law school graduates secretarial jobs. Newspapers facilitated this kind of discrimination by dividing their job announcements into those for men and those for women. Many states had laws that did not allow married women to go into business without their husbands' permission or get credit without male co-signers.[1] European countries were no better.[2] All this was going on just 50 years ago.

[1] Collins (2010).
[2] Nielsen and Halvorsen (1992).

The US Congress passed the Equal Employment Opportunities Act in 1964, which prohibited sex and race discrimination in employment. Many European countries signed international agreements banning sex and race discrimination in the 1960s and 1970s, which required them to pass national legislation banning discrimination.[3] After 1964, if an American woman didn't get a job because the employer decided to give the job to a man, she could take the employer to court and get financial compensation or, in some cases, even the job itself. Before 1964, only one woman, Katharine Graham of the *Washington Post*, had ever been the CEO of a Fortune 500 company; only the Russians had sent a woman into space— in 1963; all the judges on the US Supreme Court and the European Court of Justice were men; and all the heads of state in North America and Europe were men.[4] Now we've seen a number of women in all these roles.

Now everyone knows it's illegal for employers and businesses to treat men and women differently solely on the basis of their sex. Women can— as a matter of law, at least—get credit, insurance, and any education or job they want. None of that is reserved for men any more. If women think they're being discriminated against, they can sue someone. You might think that that would be enough of a deterrent for businesses to do everything necessary to close remaining gender gaps. After all, businesses usually pay attention to lawsuits that can impact the bottom line.

As we showed in Chapter 1, though, there are still pronounced gender gaps. The existence of laws prohibiting sex discrimination is apparently not enough to close them. A number of the executives and managers we have spoken with say that it must be because these gender gaps are not caused by sex discrimination, and suggest that it's because of women's choices. It is true, after all, that even though there are male- and female-dominated categories of positions in their own organizations, they have not been and are not defending themselves against sex discrimination

[3] Roseberry (2002).

[4] '50 Famous Firsts in Women's History', Encyclopedia Britannica blog, accessed 20 November 2013. Katharine Graham first took over the management of the *Washington Post* in 1963 to replace her husband, Philip Graham, after he committed suicide.

lawsuits. The assumption seems to be that these problems are due to something which employers have no legal or moral obligation to do anything about.

Like all the other popular excuses for gender gaps and imbalances, relying on sex discrimination law as the measure of an organization's ability and obligation to eliminate them assumes far too much about law's efficacy and far too little about managers' ability. Two cases—one from a Danish study of male nurses, the other based on our own interviews with a group of women at a European university—indicate why such assumptions have little basis in fact.

Men in a woman's world

In 2012, a Danish newspaper reported that figures from 2008 showed that only 6% of all social workers in Denmark were men.[5] The figures are slightly better in childcare. In 2010 16.7% of the employees in this sector were men, but they are unevenly distributed, with the smallest minorities of men in daycare institutions for small children. Only 1.5% of the care-givers in Danish public daycare for infants under the age of three were men. In daycare institutions for children between the ages of three and six, they made up 6.1% of the employees.

This kind of pronounced occupational segregation by gender is not limited to the caring professions. Even though Denmark ranks number eight on the 2013 World Economic Forum's Gender Gap Index, making it one of the top ten countries in the world as far as sex equality goes,[6] it still has one of the most gender-segregated labour markets in the world. More than 60% of the economically active are employed in occupations where there is less than 25% of the opposite sex.[7]

An interesting qualitative study of Danish men's experiences with working in the caring occupations suggests that perceptions of gender

[5] Schmidt (2011).
[6] World Economic Forum (2013).
[7] Holt et al. (2006).

norms—not occupational preferences—play a decisive role in sorting men and women into different occupations. In the study, 35 Danish men working in the caring occupations were interviewed about their reasons for choosing, staying in, or leaving these occupations.[8] One of the biggest hurdles for these men to overcome when they decided to enter these occupations appears to be the fact that their sexual orientation and motivations receive a lot of attention. More to the point—a surprising number of people seem to think that men who go into nursing are gay, and paedophilia is just a thought removed from the idea of men working with children.[9] The fear of stigmatization that these perceptions raise may be enough to keep many men away from these occupations. Add that to the fact that these occupations pay lower than male-dominated occupations, and they become even less attractive.

The same study notes that many of these men consciously try to avoid stigmatization by playing up stereotypical masculine traits. They are accorded more authority than their female colleagues and find it easier to pursue management positions if they do. They also tend to specialize within their occupation in areas that are especially physically demanding, require knowledge of technology or especially assertive, take-charge behaviour. So, for example, more men work as nurses and medical technicians in emergency rooms and trauma centres than in oncology units.

Men who do not display stereotypical masculine behaviour have a harder row to hoe. The women they work with still expect them to display all the traditional masculine characteristics.[10] So, for example, female nurses expect their male colleagues to do small repairs and help lift patients, even though these are not typically part of a nurse's job

[8] Warming (2012).

[9] A Danish movie released in 2012, *The Hunt* (*Jagten*), directed by Thomas Vinterberg and starring Mads Mikkelsen, is a dramatization of the damaging effects of this fear. The story is about a man who works in a local kindergarten in a small Danish village and becomes the target of mass hysteria after being wrongly accused of sexually assaulting a child.

[10] Schmidt (2011).

description. It is hard for a male nurse to say he would rather call a porter than help a patient over into her bed—particularly if there are other male nurses who do it.

Is any of this sex discrimination? If a man gets so tired of this kind of treatment that he decides to leave the profession, can he sue someone? Who? If you have a hard time answering those questions, you already know a lot about why sex discrimination law is not particularly effective in addressing occupational segregation or other kinds of sex discrimination.

Women in a man's world

In 2009 a group of 25 female faculty members at a large European university gathered to talk about why they thought women were not advancing to the top of the academic hierarchy as quickly as men.[11] Nearly 50% of the Ph.D. students at the university were women, but the percentages decreased on the way up the hierarchy ending at about 17% of the full professors. These figures are not unique to universities in much of Northern Europe. Since the 1990s, the majority of university graduates in Europe and the USA have been women, but the average percentage of women in senior academic positions in European universities was still only about 15% in 2009.[12] Only one European country—Finland—has exceeded 20%. The average percentage of full professors at American universities as of 2006 was around 24%.[13]

Some of the women at that November meeting in 2009 said it seemed to them that the male professors choose to help the male Ph.D.s and junior professors more often than the female Ph.D.s and junior professors. Since there are more male professors than female professors, this means, of course, that women don't get the same encouragement and support as the men. Lack of encouragement and support by experienced

---

[11] This case is based on our interviews with facilitators at this meeting and their notes of this meeting.

[12] European Commission (2009).

[13] West and Curtis (2006).

faculty can have very real negative consequences. One of the assistant professors in the group said that she was one of the few women in the group of Ph.D. students with whom she had studied who had continued with her research career. She said that while she and her classmates were working on their Ph.D.s, the men expressed unequivocal ambitions to pursue careers as university scholars after completing their Ph.D.s, and the women expressed a lot of uncertainty. The women were uncertain about whether they would be able to get university positions. They started looking for other jobs as they approached completion of the Ph.D. programme—and accepted other jobs when offered.

Another participant in the meeting indicated that senior faculty may actually directly discourage women from pursuing academic careers. Some women at the meeting said that they were advised by senior female faculty—many of whom are single and childless—not to have children until they got tenure. No one had ever heard of any male colleagues who had received that kind of advice.

Some of the younger women present complained that their male colleagues commented on their clothing and appearance in ways that made them feel uncomfortable. All of the women agreed that it was difficult to tell their male colleagues they didn't like this behaviour because they knew how the men would react. The women expected to be laughed at or told that they were being too sensitive. Their perception was based on experience, not imagination. One of the young women said that she had been directly propositioned by a senior professor in front of her younger male colleagues. When she protested, they simply laughed.

The stories told by these university women echo findings published in 2012 by the League of European Research Universities (LERU).[14] LERU reports that over the course of their careers, women face a number of different biases that are relatively small, and often not obvious in individual cases. However, when combined, they create a leaky pipeline to the top. Both the lack of mentoring by senior faculty and the unwanted sexual

---

[14] League of European Research Universities (2012).

attention might be enough to discourage many women from making their careers in academia, and as the LERU report says, 'many mole hills together become a large mountain.'

Even if we can point to a few of the 'mole hills' that may combine into insurmountable obstacles for some of the women seeking higher positions in the academic hierarchy, the question of whether the female university faculty members at that meeting in 2009 could obtain effective redress under anti-discrimination law is not easy to answer. The women at the meeting had all concluded that they couldn't.

Proving it in court

The first question anyone thinking about bringing a sex discrimination case needs to consider is, 'Is it worth the time, money, and frustration?' In both Europe and in the USA, the answer seems to be, in most cases, 'No'. The Network of European Legal Experts in the Field of Gender Equality, which advises the European Commission on gender equality issues, has asserted that 'there are remarkably few claims compared to the scale of gender inequality' revealed by statistics.[15] In many of the countries of the EU, the number of gender discrimination cases before the courts has remained in single figures:

> Several reasons for this emerge from the reports from the Member States. First, the complaints-led model requires the perpetrator to be identified and proof that the law has been breached. . . . Problems of proof are exacerbated . . . by . . . difficult questions as to appropriate comparisons. A second and particularly significant deterrent is the fear that by initiating legal proceedings, the victim will be exposed or stigmatized as a nuisance. Thirdly, judicial procedures are slow and, in most Member States, costly. Fourthly, in most Member States, remedies are retrospective and the amount of compensation available is not sufficient to deter the perpetrator nor make it worth the victim's while to pursue a case.[16]

[15] Fredman (2009: 1).
[16] Fredman (2009: 1–2).

In the USA, the abysmal success rate of discrimination cases is likely to deter many people from seeking legal redress. Employment discrimination plaintiffs obtain fewer pre-trial settlements and therefore have to proceed to trial more often and lose far more often than other plaintiffs.[17] The same holds for appeals.[18] More successful employment discrimination cases undergo appeal than other types of cases. When judgements are appealed, employment discrimination plaintiffs tend to lose—regardless of whether they won or lost at trial. So even when they win, they lose, and when they lose, they're unlikely to obtain a reversal on appeal. These are shockingly low odds when compared with just about every other category of litigation. The only other category of cases with worse odds for plaintiffs is prisoner lawsuits alleging violations of prisoners' rights.[19]

In case you think the low success rate of discrimination cases in the USA indicates that there really isn't much discrimination after all, and that discrimination lawsuits are being brought by greedy lawyers on behalf of hypersensitive women and minorities crying wolf, consider a recent study of some of the common explanations for the low success rate. The author of the study, law professor Katie R. Eyer, says that the hypersensitive-plaintiffs-and-ambulance-chasing-lawyers argument simply cannot explain the full range of negative outcomes for the following reasons:[20]

- A number of empirical studies comparing objective standards for evaluating the merits of cases with the actual case outcomes show no correlation between merit and outcome. Even cases that meet the US Equal Employment Opportunities Commission's own criteria for pursuing discrimination claims are dismissed before they go to trial at higher rates than other kinds of cases.

---

[17] Clermont and Schwab (2009).
[18] Clermont and Schwab (2009: 103).
[19] Eyer, (2012).
[20] Eyer (2012: 1286–9).

- Qualitative studies examining the characteristics of dismissed cases have shown that even cases based on direct evidence of racist or sexist attitudes—such as racist or gender-based slurs uttered by supervisors—are routinely dismissed as a matter of law.
- Since discrimination cases are dismissed on pre-trial motions at a higher rate than other kinds of cases, you would expect that the cases that do go to trial are stronger than the average case in other categories. Not so. The cases that do go to trial are more rarely won (28%) than other categories of cases (45%) that go to trial.
- Given the high failure rate of cases all the way through trial, you might expect that the few discrimination plaintiffs who actually win trial victories would be more likely to win post-trial appeals. Again, not so. They also suffer a higher rate of reversals on appeal than for other kinds of cases—41% versus 28%.
- The best cases actually go to trial, it seems. Data on the average size of discrimination settlements show an average settlement recovery of only $14,000 before trial and $30,000 during litigation while individual awards in tried cases are at least three to five times the size of those figures. And that's before adding attorneys' fees and costs.

Legal scholars have created a cottage industry of identifying and listing virtually every possible feature of anti-discrimination law that may be responsible for the abysmal success rates.[21] While they undoubtedly offer many constructive criticisms and suggestions for improvements in the law, their research does not provide an empirical basis for concluding that legal reform will improve the success rate of anti-discrimination cases.

Professor Eyer says that empirical research on when and how people perceive discrimination suggests that a substantial part of the problem lies outside legal theory and doctrine—in people's resistance to attributing negative outcomes to discrimination.

---

[21] Eyer (2012: 1285–6).

We don't believe it when we see it

In the interviews we completed to gather material for this book, we noticed that many of the people with whom we spoke could identify gender-related attitudes and behaviours they believed posed obstacles or extra burdens for men or women, but only the most blatant discriminatory behaviours were labelled as such. It seemed that no one wanted to apply the label 'discrimination' to anything but the most clear-cut cases, even though we promised them and their organizations anonymity.

Social psychological research in the USA provides some empirical support for our hunch that sex discrimination law is not a good tool for eliminating sex discrimination or any of its effects precisely because people resist attributing negative outcomes to discrimination. A number of studies suggest that women and members of minority groups under-perceive discrimination more than they perceive it.[22] In fact, psychologists have found that people are quite clearly *un*willing to make attributions to discrimination[23] even in the presence of quite compelling facts. Among both minorities and non-minorities, the likelihood of explaining adverse outcomes as being the result of discrimination is minimal when the circumstances do not clearly indicate that someone *intended* to harm women or minority group members because of their sex or other characteristics. Even where minority group members are significantly harmed as a result of thoughtless or stereotyped, but not deliberately malicious, behaviour, most people simply do not perceive it as discrimination.[24]

A study involving pairs of Canadian university students consisting of one white student and one aboriginal student provides an example of this phenomenon.[25] The students were grouped together for the

[22] Kaiser and Major (2006).

[23] 'Attributions to discrimination' is a term of art used by psychology scholars to describe the likelihood of whether people will characterize the cause of a particular negative outcome as being based on discrimination or as based on some other cause. Eyer (2012: 1293).

[24] Eyer (2012: 1293, 1299–1300).

[25] Vorauer and Kumhyr (2001).

purpose of interacting in 'get-acquainted' conversations. Before being paired, the white students were given a test that measured racial prejudice. The students were then classified as either high in prejudice or low in prejudice towards aboriginals. The researchers found that aboriginal students paired with high-prejudice whites felt worse after their conversations than the aboriginal students who interacted with low-prejudice white students. Interestingly, the aboriginal participants who interacted with a highly prejudiced partner did *not* perceive that they had been targets of prejudice. Instead they were critical of themselves. The authors of the study interpreted their findings as supporting the hypothesis that in everyday life members of low-status groups are unlikely to detect prejudice, and instead take responsibility for the negative emotions they feel as a result of their exposure to prejudice.

The results of this study of aboriginals echo the findings concerning women's formation and retention of their ambitions discussed in Chapter 5: when women do not display a sufficient number of feminine traits, or refuse male 'help', they may be penalized by being labelled too masculine, abrasive, or difficult, and denied the promotion or resources they seek.[26] Rather than labelling such penalties as sex discrimination, many women are likely to accept the penalties as reasonable responses to their behaviour.

Why are people so reluctant to pull the 'discrimination' card? There are a number of factors that may be at work.

Some scholars assert that recognizing that you have experienced discrimination exacts a high psychological price because it forces you to suspend or even abandon fundamental, adaptive beliefs about the social world, such as the belief that people generally get what they deserve—that there's a rough correspondence between effort and talent on the one hand and rewards on the other.[27] This kind of meritocratic ideal is especially strong in knowledge industries like academia, making it very difficult for both male and female academics to identify instances of gender bias.

[26] Schwalbe et al. (2000).
[27] Kaiser and Major (2006: 804–5).

Most people would rather interpret negative career outcomes as personal failures than accept the idea that their failures are linked to their membership in a stigmatized and devalued social group.[28] To do so is to acknowledge that the social world is not as meritocratic as we like to believe. Simple, isolated instances of unfairness are not enough to usurp a meritocratic belief system, but recognizing the occurrence of discrimination suggests systematic unfairness that targets entire categories of people. For those who believe they have achieved all their successes by the strength of their own merit, recognizing the existence of discrimination seriously challenges their belief in their own ability to live out their career dreams—or, if they are members of the dominant group, it undermines their self-perceptions as competent and hardworking people who deserve their success.

We blame the victim, not the discriminator

Not only do we not believe in it when we see it ourselves, but we also think badly of people who claim they have experienced discrimination. Social psychology research has produced substantial evidence that minorities and white women who complain about discrimination as the cause of negative outcomes are often disliked, viewed as troublemakers, or as having problematic personalities.[29] The negative perception of someone claiming discrimination does not depend on the merits of the case, either. In one notable study, the male participants liked a woman less when she challenged as sexist a male colleague's remarks that really were sexist, but did not dislike her if she challenged as sexist other remarks that had no apparent connection to gender. Oddly enough, confronting behaviour as sexist when it really isn't does not provoke the same degree of hostility as when the behaviour is obviously sexist.

The results of another study indicate that women and minorities are at least instinctively, if not explicitly, aware of the risks involved in challenging discriminatory behaviour. In this study, researchers studied the

---

[28] Eyer (2012: 1304).

[29] Brake (2005).

reactions of two groups of female subjects to sexual harassment.[30] One group of women was asked to read an account of a job interview in which a male interviewer asked a female interviewee several sexist and inappropriately sexual questions. The women were then asked how they would have responded if they had been posed such questions. Most of them asserted that they would have refused to answer the questions, confronted the interviewer, or reported him to a higher authority.

The second group of female subjects participated in actual interview situations with a male interviewer, who was presented as someone participating in the evaluation of their qualifications for a research assistant position. These women were then subjected to the same discriminatory questions featured in the earlier part of the study. Not one of the subjects in this part of the study confronted the interviewer or refused to answer the questions. Instead, most of them simply answered the questions. Some tried to avoid answering the question directly or politely asked why the interviewer was asking a particular question. Even these interviewees ultimately answered the questions without further objection. In follow-up debriefing, the most common emotional response reported by these women was fear, not anger, contrary to what the other group of women had predicted about how they themselves would react.

The gap between how women expect themselves to react and how they actually react in real life may act as a kind of suppressant on their ability to both recognize and complain about discriminatory treatment.[31] People who experience discrimination, but who are afraid to confront it, even though they always believed they would, experience cognitive dissonance. In order to make sense of the situation, they have to suppress some part of the incident. In this process, the pressure not to confront bias can inhibit the perception of bias. If you *believe* that you would react with anger and confront the perpetrator of discrimination, you are likely to doubt that the experience was actually discriminatory or to minimize the effects of

---

[30] Woodzicka and LaFrance (2001).
[31] Brake (2007).

the discriminatory behaviour if you *react* to actual discrimination with fear and passivity instead of the anger you thought you would feel.

Our case of the female faculty members seems to match this account of how sex discrimination often goes unreported. None of the female faculty members at that meeting in 2009 had reported their experiences of sexual harassment to management. In fact none of them characterized it as sexual harassment or sex discrimination. They didn't like the behaviour, and they would have liked it to stop, but the only action they took was to talk to a colleague about it.

We're not as smart as we think

Another factor militating against successful outcomes in discrimination cases relates to the limits of human cognitive capacity. Psychological research has established that when we judge new situations, we engage in cognitive processes that employ a number of short-cuts that make us less rational than we would like to think.[32] Human beings simply do not have the cognitive capacity to evaluate fully all the information about every situation they meet. Instead of evaluating every situation individually, we rely heavily on the categories and mental prototypes that we have developed through our own experience. The stories in this book's Chapter 4, about how young children identify biological sex, illustrate this point. Their understanding and experience of gender generally includes little awareness of the importance of anatomical differences, so they tend to identify girls and boys according to clothing, toys, and hairstyles, instead of anatomy—until they gain enough experience to learn otherwise. We never outgrow the need to compare incoming data with pre-existing cognitive templates, however. We modify our cognitive templates as we gain experience, but we always have them, and we continue to depend on them to help us to interpret what is going on around us.

---

[32] Nobel Prize-winner and Princeton professor Daniel Kahneman, and his colleague, the late Stanford professor Amos Tversky, are the most well-known proponents of this research. For an approachable overview of their research, see Kahneman (2011). For an overview of older research as it relates to perception of discrimination, see Krieger (1995).

Researchers have also found that for all of us, certain explanations are more or less likely to come to mind when faced with a particular outcome. This phenomenon is called 'cognitive accessibility'.[33] Which explanations are more or less 'cognitively accessible' depends on a number of factors. These include things like the extent to which you believe discrimination is relatively common or whether you recently experienced something that you perceived as being discriminatory.

How easily accessible—how quickly an explanation comes to mind—is also interpreted by most people as indicating that that explanation is correct. Think about a recent situation that you tried to explain to yourself and then changed your mind. Your reasoning goes something like this, 'The first thing that popped into my mind was X, but after thinking about it, I realized it was Y.' Many times we don't even get to the alternative explanation because it's sufficiently cognitively inaccessible to produce the feeling that it simply can't be true.

Both the fact that we operate with cognitive templates and tend to settle on the first explanation to come to mind impacts the extent to which people are more or less likely to recognize discrimination. Researchers who have studied how people perceive discrimination have found that people do in fact construct cognitive templates of what constitutes discrimination and that these templates influence the interpretation of a particular set of events as discriminatory or non-discriminatory. This means that if a factual situation does not contain significant elements of your cognitive template for discrimination, you will not recognize the situation as being discriminatory. On the other hand, the same situation may fit someone else's cognitive template perfectly, allowing them to perceive the discriminatory aspects of the situation.

Since we build our cognitive templates on the basis of our own experiences and knowledge, people are obviously not going to perceive all situations the same way. However, researchers have found that most people

---

[33] Baron (2008: 153–5).

seem to apply cognitive templates of discrimination that contain the following elements:[34]

- Discrimination always harms the victim in some tangible and measurable way.
- The harm must be intended by the person(s) doing the discriminating.
- Discrimination occurs only when the victims are unable to do anything about that part of their identities that is targeted for discriminatory treatment.
- Perpetrators of discrimination are always members of a majority group and victims are always members of a minority group.

The problem with this template is that it describes a much narrower category of cases than what anti-discrimination law defines as illegal discrimination. That means that people who experience treatment that actually violates anti-discrimination law are unlikely to recognize it as such, that those who engage in behaviour or practices that have disadvantaged men or women because of their sex are unlikely to recognize that they have unlawfully discriminated against someone, and that judges and juries may have difficulty applying the law.

In the next section, we apply this template to our two cases so you can see why that's true.

Where's the harm?
It is difficult to identify the harm in either of our cases.

The female faculty who were at the meeting in 2009 were still working. They had not been so adversely affected by the sexist comments and lack of mentoring that they felt compelled to leave. The women complained about it, but they did not feel harmed—just irritated or offended.

The male nurses and male childcare workers did not complain about sexual harassment—just the fact their female colleagues expected them

---

[34] O'Brien et al. (2009). Similar conclusions, although they do not purport to describe a template, are found in Major and Sawyer (2009: 94–9).

to perform stereotypically male tasks at work and that family members, acquaintances, and the people they cared for sometimes questioned their masculinity or suspected their motives for working with children. While that kind of pressure is not overtly sexual, it falls squarely within the definition of gender-based harassment, which is explicitly prohibited in European countries and defined simply as 'unwanted conduct related to the sex of a person' which 'occurs with the purpose or effect of violating the dignity of a person, and of creating an intimidating, hostile, degrading, humiliating or offensive environment'.[35]

The law does not require people to produce evidence of psychological harm in order to win a sexual or gender-based harassment case.[36] Nevertheless the female faculty members, like many others, seem to think that if it isn't so bad that they feel forced to quit, then it isn't worth making a fuss, and it certainly isn't illegal sexual harassment. Similarly, the men don't claim to be harmed. They just don't like the masculine stereotypes that get applied to them. They don't use the word harassment to describe that kind of behaviour, either.

The reactions of both the men and women in our two cases are strikingly similar to the results of studies on women's responses to sexual harassment.

[35] Article 2(2) of Directive 2002/73/EC of the European Parliament and of the Council of 23 September 2002 amending Council Directive 76/207/EEC on the implementation of the principle of equal treatment for men and women as regards access to employment, vocational training and promotion and working conditions.

[36] The US Supreme Court held in *Harris* v. *Forklift Systems, Inc.*, 510 U.S. 17 (1993), that the plaintiff could bring a sexual harassment claim without showing serious psychological harm. In the European Union, the plaintiff only has to show that the conduct *either* had 'the purpose *or* effect of violating the dignity of a person, and of creating an intimidating, hostile, degrading, humiliating or offensive environment'. In the European Union, this rule applies to all Member States according to Article 2(2) of Directive 2002/73/EC of the European Parliament and of the Council of 23 September 2002 amending Council Directive 76/207/EEC on the implementation of the principle of equal treatment for men and women as regards access to employment, vocational training and promotion and working conditions.

In a study of two independent samples of female employees, 447 from a private company and 300 from a university, most of the women who answered yes to questions about whether they had experienced behaviours that fitted the description of sexual harassment in the past 24 months, answered 'no' to the question of whether they had been sexually harassed in the same period of time.[37] These women simply did not see themselves as victims of harassment.

Research has shown that the most common responses to sexual harassment are coping strategies that manage the thoughts and emotions associated with the harassment rather than confronting the harasser or reporting the behaviour to management.[38] Besides denying that the behaviour has any effect, victims of harassment may also reinterpret the behaviour as benign, try to forget about it, and/or, less commonly, blame themselves. The female faculty members who met in 2009 engaged all these coping strategies. They focused on managing their own responses to the behaviour rather than confronting it directly.

What many people don't realize, though, is that even mild forms of sexual or gender harassment have been associated with a variety of negative short- and long-term outcomes.[39] The study described above showed that sexual harassment, even at low frequencies, exerts a significant negative impact on women's psychological well-being, including job attitudes and work behaviours. Women who had reported a moderate level of harassment also reported significantly worse outcomes than those women who had not been harassed. The study's findings regarding the employee sample from the university is especially interesting. Those women described primarily low-level, relatively mild, hostile environment harassment, consisting of sexist put-downs and offensive sexual remarks—much like the stories told by the women in our case from the European university. The women in the study could be distinguished from those who had not

---

[37] Schneider et al. (1997).

[38] Schneider et al. (1997: 403–4).

[39] Schneider et al. (1997: 412–13).

experienced sexual harassment based on differences in their job-related attitudes and behaviours and psychological well-being.

Furthermore, most research on sexual harassment reports that approximately 50% of women in any particular sample have experienced unwanted and offensive sex-related behaviours at work or school, but fewer than 20% of these women label themselves as having been sexually harassed.[40] No similar studies have been done of male victims of gender harassment. The research indicates that whether women label their experiences as sexual harassment or not, the outcomes are the same.[41] Both groups experience negative outcomes—including physical, psychological, and work-related problems—attributable to the experiences of harassment.

Finally, studies of sexual and gender-based harassment show that sexual harassment occurs most frequently in areas dominated by one sex.[42]

If these research findings are reliable, they suggest that one significant factor contributing to the occupational and vertical gender segregation exemplified by our two cases may well be behaviour that fits the legal definition of gender-based or sexual harassment, but it just isn't perceived that way because there is no obvious harm.

Who intends harm?

If it's difficult to see the harm in the behaviours complained about in these two cases, it's equally difficult to find any indication of an intention to harm men or women because of their sex. The female professor advising the female Ph.D. student to postpone childbearing until she gets tenure undoubtedly believes she's helping the student to plan her career. It may be the strategy she herself pursued, given that most people give advice based on their own experience.

---

[40] A number of studies are cited in Magley et al. (1999).

[41] Magley et al. (1999: 399–401).

[42] Schultz (1998).

The male professors who seem to prefer to mentor junior male faculty probably don't necessarily form their preferences out of a conscious intent to harm women.[43] Their preferences may just as likely spring from a genuine wish to help the junior colleagues they think they can help most easily.

The female colleagues of men in caring occupations, who expect them to be able to lift heavy objects, take charge, and fix things, may form those expectations based on their own personal experience of gender roles. If female nurses do not perform those tasks themselves either at work or at home, but have always relied on men to do them, they are almost bound to see these tasks as inherently masculine, making it reasonable and appropriate—in their eyes—to expect their male colleagues to perform them. Besides, as the Danish study showed, many men in caring occupations seem to welcome the opportunity to fulfil these expectations as a way of confirming their masculinity in contrast to the more stigmatizing perceptions they may meet in the surrounding society.[44]

Similarly, the male members of the university faculty who make sexist jokes and comment on their female colleagues' appearance and bodies, or even proposition them, may well be treating their female colleagues according to the way they treat all women—indeed the way many men are portrayed as treating women in movies, music videos, and

---

[43] It may be true, as Yale law professor Vicki Schultz has argued, that many male workers in male-dominated occupations, consciously or unconsciously, may view not only their jobs, but also the male-dominated composition and masculine identification of their work, as forms of property to which they are entitled, and regard women as interlopers in their territory. Harassment, sexual or not, is a way of defending their territory. Schultz (1998: 1755–61). She writes, at p. 1760: 'Motivated by both material considerations and equally powerful psychological ones, harassment provides a means for men to mark their jobs as male territory and to discourage any women who seek to enter. By keeping women in their place in the workplace, men secure superior status in the home, in the polity, and in the larger culture as well'.

[44] Warming (2012).

advertisements.[45] Most women have encountered this kind of behaviour before they even start their careers. Listening to jokes about blondes, wolf whistles, comments on female anatomy—whether it's their own or someone else's—is part of being female in a society where most people are heterosexual, men are expected to be the initiators of sexual relationships, and women generally try to make themselves attractive to men. It can be difficult to discern an intention to harm women behind this kind of behaviour in the workplace when it matches normal, and for the most part, accepted behaviour outside the workplace.

Most people are unaware of the research indicating that even mild forms of this kind of behaviour in the workplace can actually have negative effects on women's careers. It seems unlikely that any of the men would answer yes to the question, 'Did you intend to cause these women to feel alienated and lose interest in their work and maybe eventually leave your workplace?' Intentional or not, though, the effects remain the same.

Where are the powerless victims?

The women like those in our case, who have achieved Ph.D.s and embarked on academic careers, are not prone to seeing themselves as powerless victims. They regard themselves as professionals and have proven that they have the determination and talent to complete lengthy and demanding advanced degree programmes. When presented with the women's complaints about lack of mentoring, male colleagues suggest

---

[45] An example of how some men seem not to understand the effect of such behaviour, was seen in the French National Assembly in 2012, when Cécile Duflot, the country's housing minister, faced hooting and catcalls when she stood up to deliver a speech on 17 July, ostensibly because she was wearing a blue-and-white flowered dress. The male legislators, who participated in the heckling later said they were merely showing their appreciation for her attire and that they did not regard their conduct as harassment. 'France Passes New Law on Sexual Harassment', *Al Jazeera*, 31 July 2012. The reactions of the male legislators to complaints about their behaviour are much like the reactions complained about by the women in our university case.

that women passively wait for mentoring, while men seek it out, and many female academics wonder if they're right. Perhaps they just need to be a bit more active in seeking out mentoring. After all, there is nothing inherent in being female that prevents women from finding mentors, and these highly educated women, of all women, are most likely to be aware of their right to equal treatment.

Similar things could be said about men in female-dominated caring occupations. Powerlessness and masculinity generally do not go together in the popular imagination, and the career paths of many of the men in these occupations indicate that in fact they do quite well if they cultivate traits traditionally associated with masculinity.

Neither female academics nor men in caring occupations seem particularly powerless. Those who remain in their occupations are persistent and stubborn, while those who don't choose those occupations, or leave them, have arguably made rational decisions to seek their fortunes elsewhere—in workplaces or occupations where they don't have to spend so much energy on figuring out how to fit into a workplace where the gender norms of the opposite sex dominate.

Women don't do sex discrimination, and real men *can't* discriminate against men

The female professor's advice to avoid having children until achieving tenure certainly has the effect of discouraging all but the most determined female academics—and she would never give the same advice to a male academic. Clearly this is gender-biased treatment that produces a gender-biased result, but it falls outside popular culture's discrimination template because the senior professor is female, and women are generally perceived to be the targets, not the perpetrators, of sex discrimination.

As for the men working in female-dominated caring professions, it may be difficult for many people to perceive their female colleagues' expectations of stereotypical masculine traits and behaviour as constituting any kind of sex discrimination for two reasons. First, these men don't fit the template because they don't belong to the sex generally perceived as the target of discrimination. Second, *both* men and women share expectations of stereotypical masculine traits. There may be male doctors and porters, family members and friends who share the same expectations and make the same comments and exert the same kind of pressure to conform to stereotypical masculine behavioural norms. When both men and women display gender-biased behaviour, it doesn't look like the discrimination defined by the template. Men can't discriminate against men on the basis of their sex according to that definition. It's illogical.

And yet, it seems that those kinds of expectations, whether they are expressed by men or women, contribute to the barriers that segregate the sexes into male- and female-dominated occupations. Isn't that what anti-discrimination law is supposed to stop?

Going beyond compliance

Given the difficulties in perceiving and proving discrimination, it seems obvious that mere compliance with the law—meaning avoidance of discrimination lawsuits—is not an effective strategy for closing the remaining gender gaps. Some legal scholars have argued that because the successful discrimination cases tend to represent a very narrow category of cases, where there is clear evidence of conscious, intentional discrimination by an individual perpetrator, they support a cultural narrative that portrays the world of employment as meritocratic and discrimination as aberrational.[46] As one law professor puts it:

> In the dominant narrative, the [woman] failed to get the raise, promotion, or opportunity because she was not sufficiently competent or deserving. On the fewer occasions when the alternative narrative prevails, there are usually enough smoking gun comments to suggest that one or more bad actors intentionally and malevolently took sex into account.[47]

Thus, the way anti-discrimination law has developed reinforces the view that we don't need to worry about persistent gender gaps because they

---

[46] Crenshaw (1988); Freeman (1990); Becker (1989).
[47] Brake (2007).

are the result of a presumptively meritocratic labour market. People basically get what they deserve, except if they are unlucky enough to encounter the exceptional employer who intentionally and malevolently treats women worse than men. The discrimination narrative does not direct our attention to all the phenomena that contribute to the processes that create and entrench gender gaps in pay, occupations, and leadership. It has us looking for bad guys and victims, when what we need to be looking at is how even people acting without any malicious intent do and say things that erect gender barriers to entry or promotion or both in certain occupations and put caps on pay. Because we're so used to it, we don't see it, we learn to navigate in it, think it's normal, and get angry and offended when anyone suggests there might be something discriminatory going on.

Box 8.1 Facilitating gender balance with proactive measures

Examples of proactive measures include:

- Evaluating existing practices to determine whether they perpetuate or cause gender segregation in the workplace, such as low-level harassment and gender role expectations.
- Assessing all new policies for their impact on gender equality.
- Appointing an equality ombudsperson for the organization, who would be charged with the responsibility of receiving and resolving gender-equality-related complaints and disputes.

In order to ensure that such proactive measures are regarded as managerial imperatives, rather than merely optional, cosmetic, or bureaucratic exercises, they should be linked to appropriate incentives, sanctions, and mechanisms for accountability, such as linking them to managers' performance evaluations.[48]

---

[48] Fredman (2009: 75).

Achieving a better gender balance in organizations of all kinds requires understanding that gender imbalances are the result of a number of complex processes, not the bad behaviour of a few men or women with bad intentions. When that understanding falls into place, it becomes easier to go beyond the limitations of legal compliance and start thinking about how to actually facilitate gender balance. Proactive measures, like those described in Box 8.1, are one way to go beyond the limits of legal compliance.

Key points and guiding principle

- Many people believe that the law prohibits only intentionally discriminatory behaviour, but gender imbalances are not necessarily the result of intentional discrimination.
- Many people who are victims of discrimination do not recognize it as discrimination.
- Many people who could claim discrimination never do because it's too expensive, time consuming, and unpleasant.

Guiding principle: *The law is not enough.*

9

Trailblazing

After reading the first eight chapters of this book, we hope you can see why gender balance is a necessary condition for good governance in all our social institutions—business, education, and government. We hope you agree that in order to make correct and effective decisions, which are the hallmark of good governance, we need to counteract the myths, assumptions, and anachronisms that lull people into accepting gender imbalance as the way things have to be. The counter-arguments we have presented in this book have led us to develop seven guiding principles that can help do that. They are:

1. Leave the past behind.
2. Bring men and women back to Earth.
3. If it feels right, it might be wrong.
4. Ambition is genderless.
5. Make peace, not war.
6. Expect female opposition.
7. The law is not enough.

During our research for this book, we came across a number of leaders who behave and speak in ways that conform to some of these principles in some areas or some situations. One organization stands out from all the rest, though, because it has been working in conformity with *all* of these principles throughout the entire firm since the late 1990s.

Meet IBM: gender balance and diversity pioneer

IBM has a long history of being a leader when it comes to including women and minorities in its workforce. It hired its first professional women in the 1930s and appointed its first female executive in the 1940s. Nevertheless, when Lou Gerstner became IBM's new CEO in 1993, he still didn't like the way his senior executive team looked. In fact, he felt it didn't reflect the diversity of the market for talent or the universe of IBM's customers and employees. To fix that, he launched a diversity task force initiative in 1995.

The story of IBM's remarkably successful diversity initiative is by now well known among HR and diversity managers. Harvard Business School professor David Thomas published an article about it in *Harvard Business Review* in 2004.[1] He described how IBM invested a significant amount of time and money in the initiative. Eight task forces, each comprising 15–20 senior managers, were formed. The members of the task forces came from all the different business units of the company and represented eight demographic employee constituencies—Asians, blacks, Hispanics, white men, GBLTs (gays/bisexuals/lesbians/and transgender), Native Americans, people with disabilities, and women. Each task force was also assigned one or two HR employees and a senior HR executive for administrative support, plus a lawyer for legal guidance.

The initial assignment for the task forces was to research and report back to the CEO and the Worldwide Management Council (WMC) on four questions:

- What is necessary for your constituency to feel welcome and valued at IBM?
- What can the corporation do, in partnership with your group, to maximize your constituency's productivity?

---

[1] Thomas (2004).

- What can the corporation do to influence your constituency's buying decisions, so that IBM is seen as a preferred solution provider?
- Which external organizations should IBM form relationships with to better understand the needs of your constituency?

They were given six months to complete this assignment. At the end, the task forces met on 1 December 1995 to share their findings.

Whether you measure it in terms of increased diversity or in terms of bottom-line results, the diversity strategy that emerged from the task forces has been enormously successful.

In terms of increased diversity, the number of female executives increased by 370% between 1995 and 2004. Fifty-two per cent of IBM's WMC—the top 52 executives who determine corporate strategy—is composed of women, ethnic minorities born in the USA, and non-US citizens. The number of self-identified LGBT executives increased by 733%, and the number of executives with disabilities more than tripled.

In terms of bottom-line results, these can be traced in large part to the task forces' numerous suggestions for capitalizing on demographic diversity as a way to develop new markets or expand existing ones. For example, the women's and ethnic minorities' task forces recommended establishing a group focused on developing the market of multicultural and women-owned businesses in the USA. IBM followed their advice and by 2001, those two markets accounted for more than $300 million in revenue for IBM as compared with $10 million in 1998.

Today, IBM is widely regarded as representing the gold standard for diversity management, including gender balance.

The bigger picture: Ashby's Law of Requisite Variety
When Harvard professor David Thomas asked Gerstner what he thought accounted for the success of IBM's diversity strategy. Gerstner replied, 'We made diversity a market-based issue. . . . It's about understanding our markets, which are diverse and multicultural.' We think what Gerstner meant is that he, top management, and the task forces were committed to making it work because they could see a connection between

diversity and business success. But we also hear something else in Gerstner's answer. He was making a connection between diversity in the market and diversity in IBM, which to us sounds a lot like *Ashby's Law of Requisite Variety*, one of the cornerstones of systems theory.[2]

Put simply, Ashby's Law of Requisite Variety holds that a system's ability to deal with change in the environment depends on the variety of actions which are available to it internally. In order to survive, if not thrive, in complex markets, a company's strategy and management must be as diverse as the market they are serving. In other words, IBM's ability to adapt to change depends on the range of the alternatives it can think up and execute. This is what good governance looks like. Applied to a business, the Law of Requisite Variety means that diversity in the market requires diversity in the organization. Good governance requires gender balance because the market is composed of roughly equal numbers of men and women.

In 1996, around the time Lou Gerstner was effectively putting into practice Ashby's Law of Requisite Variety, management guru Gary Hamel made a related argument in a cover article for the *Harvard Business Review*.[3] He pointed out that organizational pyramids are generally based on experience. This means that the people at the top of a given organizational pyramid are likely to represent the least diversity of experience, the largest investment in the past, and display the greatest reverence for the reigning business dogma in their industry. Hamel saw this as a problem because, as he put it, 'experience is valuable only to the extent that the future is like the past. In industry after industry, the terrain is changing so fast that experience is becoming irrelevant and even dangerous.'

This boils down to the same logic as the Law of Requisite Variety. When an organization's environment is stable and homogeneous, it has no need for diversity. But when an organization's environment is complex, which often includes being characterized by a high degree of diversity, good

---

[2] Ashby (1956).
[3] Hamel (1996).

management can be achieved only by making sure managers reflect the same degree of diversity as the organization's environment instead of simply representing a lot of experience.

Lou Gerstner certainly believed there was a connection between diversity within IBM and being able to connect with new markets. He asked the task forces to find it, but he didn't have the proof ahead of time. He had a hunch. He may have known about Ashby's Law of Requisite Variety, or he may have talked with Gary Hamel. We don't know, but at any rate, the IBM task forces produced what he was looking for. IBM itself became proof that diversity and gender balance 'pay off'.

We have encountered a handful of leaders who have made similar commitments to gender balance based on their hunch—an intuitive understanding of Ashby's Law of Requisite Variety—rather than on well-documented individualized business cases for their companies. In all these instances, they have brought about changes that resulted in substantial progress towards gender balance although they all chose different ways of doing it.

Meet Novartis CEO, Joe Jimenez: laser focus on female leadership talent

Novartis Pharmaceuticals is a multinational based in Basel, Switzerland and on its website you can find a wealth of information about its commitment to diversity and inclusion. For example, its Diversity and Inclusion Report for 2012 states that 69% of Novartis employees agree that diversity increases the quality of their decisions and 63% see a strong business case for a diverse and inclusive organization.[4] The report itself does not include a detailed business case. Instead you find interviews and quotes from various high-level executives that reveal a great deal about what drives Novartis to invest so much effort into promoting diversity and inclusion. For example, the report includes an interview with Novartis Division Head David Epstein, who says:

---

[4] Novartis (2012).

If Novartis Pharmaceuticals has employees who all look and sound like each other, our organization will work fine, but we will never be great, and we will never do anything really revolutionary and game changing. Another reason that diversity and inclusion is so important is that the world has shifted. Much of the growth opportunity in healthcare comes from emerging markets. Patients in those markets need to be included in trials to make sure we are developing the right medicines for them.

Like Gerstner, Novartis executives and employees have an intuitive understanding of Ashby's Law of Requisite Variety. The idea that their organization, including top management, should reflect the diversity of the markets in which it operates, seems like common sense to them. They don't need to see beforehand a direct impact on the bottom line to believe it's important enough to warrant significant effort on everyone's part.

The way Novartis has tackled the issue of promoting women into leadership is an example of this approach. In 2010 Novartis launched the Executive Female Leadership Program (EFLP) in partnership with Duke Corporate Education. CEO Joe Jimenez had approached Cynthia Emrich, a consultant at Duke, about developing a programme for female leadership talent, saying that the company really needed to do something to get more women into leadership because women constituted a substantial part of the market for Novartis products. In his view, getting more women into top management was a strategic imperative.[5] He didn't ask a consultant to demonstrate how investing in the advancement of women in the company would have a positive impact on shareholder value. It was just common sense to him.

That Novartis' top management takes the advancement of women very seriously—as a strategic imperative—is evident in the way the programme is put together. The EFLP is not a one-off seminar or training course. It is a 12-month, hands-on learning experience that demands considerable time and commitment on top of the participants' normal jobs. Each year, 30 women from different functions and Novartis sites around

---

[5] Emrich (2013).

the world are nominated for the EFLP. Fifty per cent of the programme is led or co-led by the CEO and executive committee. A mentor from the top 200 senior leaders is handpicked to give each participant advice and candid feedback throughout the year. The women meet for three face-to-face sessions over the course of the programme. The rest of the time is spent working in small project teams and individually with mentors and coaches.

The small teams are one of the centrepieces of the EFLP. They work on real-time business issues that are important to the company. The teams are expected to present their recommendations to top managers, who give their immediate feedback. During the three face-to-face sessions and the team projects, EFLP members work directly with David Epstein, Division Head of Novartis Pharmaceuticals, and other members of the Pharmaceuticals Executive Committee. EFLP members can also choose an external coach to discuss such topics as their management style, work–life balance, or issues with their teams or supervisors.

The time and resources invested in the EFLP reflect top management's commitment to gender balance as a strategic imperative for the company, not just a desire to look good or to 'help' women.

Meet Arne Norheim, IBM Executive in Scandinavia
When we met Arne Norheim, he was Country Manager for IBM Infrastructure Services in Denmark. Since then he transferred to Norway, where he is currently (as we write this in 2013) Director of General Business and Operations for IBM in Norway. Arne's career with IBM began in St Louis, Missouri in the late 1990s. He arrived not long after Gerstner's task forces had delivered their results and the diversity strategy was in full swing. He told us that IBM made it clear from the beginning of his employment that diversity was very important to the business. He and all the managers, including top management, had to take classes about anti-discrimination law and received training in diversity issues.

Although Arne came from Norway, where a commitment to sex equality is practically part of the national identity, he found himself feeling deeply challenged by IBM's diversity strategy. His commitment to sex equality was based on the belief that human beings, male and female, are essentially the same and should be treated the same. So IBM's commitment to recognizing *differences* between men and women, and between ethnic and other demographic categories, fundamentally challenged his beliefs. He was also troubled by the fact that every woman and member of the different minority categories had to have a career plan, but not white men. White men were basically left to their own devices, he felt. At first he saw it as a threat. He felt that he, as a white man, was being put at a disadvantage in comparison to his female and minority colleagues, and so he worried about his own career. But as time went by, he began to see things differently.

One reason for the change in his perspective was his own wife's experience in a male-dominated environment in a small executive recruitment agency where she was earning almost twice his salary. What she went through in her career helped him see the value of IBM's approach. The men in Nina's office continually made sexist jokes. When she came back from maternity leave, she wanted to continue breastfeeding, and had to pump her breasts while at work. She could not pump her breasts in the bathroom because her pumping device needed a power plug. The only room offered to her for that purpose was a meeting room with a window facing out into the hallway. Nina and her secretary considered covering the glass wall with paper, but found it impractical. Instead she got access to the server room and pumped while sitting among the servers, and keeping the door locked from the inside. Everyone knew what she was doing when she went to the server room, and her male colleagues would make jokes about her enlarged breasts and snicker as she went to and from the server room.

At IBM, that kind of behaviour could get you fired. Arne told us about one of his male colleagues who wanted to date a woman in their department. Arne's colleague stopped by her desk a couple of times to ask her out. Both times she said no. After the second time, their manager called Arne's colleague to his office. When he got there, his manager told him he had to stop asking this woman out. If he did it again, he'd be fired. Arne also heard a story about how Gerstner fired one of his own C-suite executives after he told an off-colour ethnic or sexist joke in a private meeting where only the two of them were present. According to the story Arne heard, Gerstner escorted the executive out of the building.

By the time Arne was transferred to IBM in Sweden in 2004, he had become utterly convinced that recognizing, respecting, and valuing diversity and gender balance was the right way to do things. He had come to realize that being a white, able-bodied heterosexual man gave him certain advantages in his career—especially in white, male-dominated organizations. He recognized that in those environments, men like him often have the same interests and have an easier time finding things to talk about, which makes it easier for them to network and navigate in the organization.

So when Arne arrived at IBM Sweden and went to his first management meetings attended solely by men, he was quite surprised. There was not a single woman in management outside the human resource department. When he asked why there were no women, he was told, 'We can't find any qualified women. Women don't want to become managers.'

He decided he would just have to show them they were wrong. The first manager he hired was female, even though she was not the best qualified candidate on the list if he had judged her solely on the basis of her experience and academic credentials. But he believed that she had other important qualities that would contribute to the team and that she could learn what she needed to learn on the job.

Arne's decision to hire this woman provoked different reactions. Four women stopped him in the hallway after the decision was announced to thank him, telling him that it was 'ground-breaking'. He heard a few women grumbling that the woman he hired 'didn't deserve it'. But Arne remained unfazed, and his newly appointed female manager performed well and was soon joined by more female managers.

Although Arne insists that his commitment to diversity and gender balance has nothing to do with morals, it also doesn't seem to have much to do with the specific business goals of IBM in Scandinavia either. He didn't hire the woman in Sweden after conducting an analysis of how increasing the number of female managers would help them develop new female markets. He had simply come to accept the idea that something different happens when you put men and women together as compared with highly gender-segregated teams. He had experienced himself how IBM was able to make good business decisions because its management teams look something like the people in the markets where it does business: roughly equal numbers of men and women representing various ethnicities, ages, religions, disabilities, and sexual orientations.

Lou, Joe, Arne, and the seven guiding principles

In our view, such stories about people like Lou, Joe, and Arne demonstrate that gender balance initiatives will not go anywhere in an organization unless led from the top by individuals who sincerely believe, or at least have a sincere hunch, that having roughly equal numbers of men and women in leadership positions is a high priority strategic issue for the organization.

By the time we wrote these cases, we had listened to the stories of many leaders in different industries in different countries going through the same journey. Many have become stuck along the way. In our experience, Arne, Lou, and Joe are, unfortunately, lonely heroes.

But we also think that many people, like these three, who believe that men and women are basically equal and should be treated as equals, are ready and able to make similar commitments to gender balance. They just need to have a compass to help them find the way. They need to be assured and reminded that gender imbalance is inimical to good governance and that it is not ordained by nature, the economy, or completely impervious to change.

If after reading this book, you are beginning to see yourself as someone who can sincerely commit to the view that gender balance in leadership and gender-integrated occupations are necessary characteristics of well-governed organizations and societies, the seven principles presented at the beginning of this chapter will give you the compass you need to help you formulate your own strategy. These principles will guide you on your journey towards the intuitive understanding that led Lou Gerstner, Joe

Jimenez, and Arne Norheim to become gender balance and diversity leaders and role models.

When we look at how these three men approached the issue of achieving gender balance and diversity, we see a mind-set that matches our seven principles of gender balance. They believed that they could increase diversity in their management teams and that it was worth doing. They didn't blame gender imbalance or lack of diversity on factors beyond their control—like market forces, or a short supply of qualified and ambitious women or minorities. Believing that it is possible to do something about gender imbalances was just the first step on the journey that leads to gender balance. In order to go further, they had to:

1. *Leave the past behind.* A story told by an IBM executive to Professor Thomas illustrates one of the ways Gerstner did this:

   During a board of directors' dinner, I had to go to [my daughter's] 'back-to-school night', the one night a year when you meet the teachers. I had been at the board meeting that day. I was going to be at the board meeting the next day. But it was the dinner that posed a problem, and I said, 'Lou, I'll do whatever you want, but this is the position I am in', and . . . he didn't even blink. He said, 'Go to back-to-school night. That is more important'. And then . . . he told the board at dinner why I wasn't there and why it was so important . . . to make it possible for working parents to have very big jobs but still be involved parents. He never told me that he told the board. But the board told me the next day. They . . . said, 'You should know that Lou not only said where you were but gave a couple minute talk about how important it was for IBM to act in this way'.[6]

2. *Bring men and women back to Earth.* One of Gerstner's task forces recommended that IBM should organize computer camps for girls in order to encourage more girls to get into computer programming.

---

[6] Thomas (2004).

By implementing that recommendation, IBM acted according to the conviction that talent and interest in computers can be nurtured in both sexes. Similarly, neither Jimenez nor Norheim ever seemed to think that women are genetically coded to be nurturers rather than leaders.

3. *If it feels right, it might be wrong.* Gerstner realized that by ignoring differences among different demographic groups, IBM had lulled itself into promoting a very homogeneous group of men into leadership positions. Norheim recognized that the common interests between men may make it easier for them to form the personal bonds that lead to promotions while leaving women out in the cold.

4. *Ambition is genderless.* Instead of accepting the under-representation of women in leadership positions as an expression of lack of female ambition, Gerstner understood it as a signal that something wasn't working well for women in the organization. Jimenez introduced a programme that pulled women up. Norheim looked and found female leaders, where his predecessors could not.

5. *Make peace, not war.* Gerstner and Jimenez pushed their diversity and gender balance initiatives in terms of markets, rather than right and wrong. It wasn't about 'helping' women, and by implication, making things harder for men. Norheim eventually realized that he wasn't losing out to women and minorities—they were just competing with him as his equals.

6. *Expect female opposition.* Norheim did not waver in his commitment to gender balance in the face of women's criticism of his decision to promote the first woman to management in the Swedish branch of IBM.

7. *The law is not enough.* Gerstner realized that by blindly following anti-discrimination law's admonition to treat everyone equally, IBM had filtered women and minorities out of the leadership pipeline. He believed IBM had to do more than the law required in order to advance gender balance and diversity. Neither Jimenez nor Norheim referred to legal obligations of non-discrimination when they talked about their commitments to gender balance. In fact Norheim

recognized that his previous commitment to 'equal treatment' had kept him from seeing how much easier it was for men like him to pursue their career goals than for women and minorities.

Meet A&C: an average company

A&C is a pseudonym for a Scandinavian branch of a leading US-based consulting firm. It is a good example of how gender balance initiatives run out of steam when top management does not believe that gender balance is fundamentally important to their organization or that it is achievable.

A&C had 235 partners as of April 2013. Only 20 of them—just 8%—are women. The low number of female partners is surprising given that female graduates from relevant degree programmes at Scandinavian universities hit 50% about ten years ago. Indeed, 50% of the firm's new hires for a number of years already have been women, and 22% of its middle managers are now women. A&C has been trying to address its gender imbalance problem with several different initiatives, including flexible work arrangements, maternity coaches, six months of paid maternity leave and about three months of paid paternity leave, but these don't seem to be doing the trick.

At an employee meeting with top management not long before we wrote this, one of the female senior consultants asked the firm's CEO whether he saw the low percentage of female partners as a problem for the firm. He replied, 'No. We can still meet our business goals.' 'Aha,' you may be thinking. 'A link between gender balance and business goals seems to be missing. That's why A&C is still male-dominated.' But is this really what should stop A&C from putting some muscle behind their gender balance initiatives?

We interviewed both the (male) CEO and the (female) HR manager of A&C, and both of them expressed a belief that men and women are equally capable. They indicated that they would like to see a larger percentage of women among the partners than the current meagre 8%. The CEO had even signed a public pledge to work on increasing the number of women in senior management as part of a voluntary initiative launched by the national government. On the other hand, the CEO had said at the company's town hall meeting that A&C could meet its business goals with or without more female partners. This contradictory message indicates top management had no clear picture of why gender balance was important to the organization. Instead, A&C seemed to think of gender balance as being primarily a moral issue.

When we dug a little deeper into A&C, we found lots of evidence that the moral case for gender balance just isn't compelling enough to get people to change the practices that keep most of the female consultants there from rising to the top of the company's hierarchy. One of A&C's female senior consultants, we'll call her Maria, told us that she experienced the firm as being rather oblivious to gender issues in a number of respects.

For instance, the overall culture of the company seldom supports or values women. Maria told us that the social activities of the firm—both those for employees and for clients—tend to focus on things like golf, running, hunting, and sailing. Not surprisingly, very few, if any, of the female employees or clients participate in those activities. There are no cultural activities like concerts or wine tastings or anything else that might appeal to both men and women equally. Even the merchandise the firm makes available for gifts and for employees' own use follows the pattern of the firm's social activities. While there are gender-neutral things like umbrellas and tote bags, most of the merchandise is hunting equipment and sports-related items for men such as clothing for golf, running, and sailing. There is no clothing for yoga or fitness or other activities that more women might be interested in.

Another problem is that A&C, like most companies in professional services, expects employees to engage with clients before and after working hours and to do team-building activities, which inevitably end up being sports. Participating in the activities outside work hours is especially challenging for the women in comparison to the men because most of the men with children have wives who take most of the responsibility for childcare and the household. Their wives don't work, or they work part time, or they have jobs that don't require them to participate in social activities before and after work. Meanwhile, the female employees with children typically have husbands who work full time. At most, their husbands will take responsibility for half of the childcare and household chores. This situation traps most women into not being able to take part in after-hour work activities to the same degree as their male colleagues.

Finally, Maria told us that while the women are given several months' paid maternity leave, they often must take an additional few months with public maternity benefits as provided by national law. They need to do this, at least in part, because it is difficult to find public daycare before their children are one year old. The men are only given a few weeks of paternity leave—probably because it is expected that their wives will take the rest of the year off—with full pay, and when the men go on leave, their colleagues and supervisors continue to call them at home and correspond with them by e-mail. The women on maternity leave don't get the same attention. By the time they come back to work, they feel as if they've fallen behind.

The basic message communicated to female employees is that they are not very important to the firm. However, when we asked the HR manager why female consultants were leaving the firm at higher rates than men, she did not identify any of these practices as problematic. She located the problem in women's perfectionism and in their difficulty with combining family life with the long hours that are the norm in this branch. She based her conclusions on the fact that most of the women leave the firm when they have children and that many of the women who come back to work express the feeling that they can't perform at the same level as before. They were accustomed to being able to match their male colleagues' performance (in terms of hours) before they left, but they don't feel they can keep up when they come back. She also speculated about whether women are genetically predisposed to perfectionism.

Because A&C's leadership seems to believe many or most of the popular justifications for gender imbalance we've identified in this book, A&C is unlikely to follow the examples of IBM and Novartis. Even when women have volunteered information about their negative experiences in the firm, A&C's management filtered it through the seven justifications for gender imbalance. For instance, A&C's head of HR thought the women in the firm lacked ambition. One senior consultant at A&C told us that she hesitated to say anything about gender issues in the firm for fear of being branded a feminist or 'one of those women who's out to get special treatment'. Her concern appears to be well-founded, given that the CEO told us that 'women are overachievers', and that some of the women in the company have become 'too edgy', which did not 'benefit themselves'. He found evidence of that in the fact that a number of female employees had expressed the feeling that they're 'not regarded well' by their male colleagues. Women seem unable to talk about their experiences in the firm without evoking the feeling that they blame the men in the firm for their difficulties.

The A&C case demonstrates that when both the corporate internal structures and the external social structures are stacked against women, moral arguments for gender balance are not enough. Tying gender balance to business results may help advance the rationale for gender balance, but when the business case is ambiguous or absent, it is not enough to bring about the necessary changes. Without the conviction that gender balance is fundamentally important to their companies, CEOs muster only half-hearted commitment to gender balance. They talk the talk, but do not walk it. The first thing A&C's top management needs to do is understand Ashby's Law of Requisite Diversity and its importance to good governance.

To get from there to effective action requires understanding where the obstacles to gender balance arise, and that understanding does not necessarily come just from understanding the governance case for gender balance. That's where our seven principles can help.

Let's see how they could guide a company like A&C towards a stronger and more effective commitment to gender balance. Here are some simple examples of how we would advise its leaders to apply the principles.

1. *Leave the past behind.* The CEO, the HR manager, and the women themselves need to realize that problems with balancing work and childcare commitments are not a women's issue. They are

organizational and social issues that require men's participation to solve. The firm ought to consider how the unequal social expectations regarding who provides childcare—mothers more than fathers—shapes the firm's expectations and practices. It needs to ensure that its expectations and corresponding practices regarding, for example, maternity and paternity leave and participation in after-work activities function just as well for mothers as for fathers, and for parents as for employees without children.

2. *Bring men and women back to Earth.* The HR manager seems to be a bit too willing to blame women's career difficulties on genetic differences. In this particular instance, it is pure and simple speculation on her part. Unfortunately it serves as a convenient excuse for her—and the firm—to avoid looking at the reality of how A&C treats its female employees.

3. *If it feels right, it might be wrong.* The extra-hours activities—especially the sports activities—are an example of something feeling right, but being wrong. For male partners and employees, these are perfectly natural ways of socializing with (male) clients and with each other. It feels comfortable and easy. But it has the effect of marginalizing their female colleagues—and perhaps potential female clients as well.

4. *Ambition is genderless.* Given that ambition is genderless, the firm's management should be more curious about why women, who are so ambitious before they go on maternity leave, suddenly seem to lose their ambition when they come back. Rather than believing they're not interested, or accepting the excuse that it's too hard to combine being a new mother with a career, they might ask what could be done to help them stay on track. They need to follow Arne Norheim's and Joe Jimenez's examples, and instead of waiting for women to step up, they need to pull them up.

5. *Make peace, not war.* The CEO's characterization of women who complain about feeling marginalized as 'too edgy' is a symptom of scars from the old battle of the sexes. Talking about gender imbalance in this firm invokes images of a conflict between men and

women. Instead, the firm's management needs to consider how their male employees may also benefit from the changes that need to be made to support their female employees' careers. The current practices around extra-hours socializing are equally difficult for many men who would like, or need, to take more responsibility for caring for their children. Men who are not particularly interested in any of the sports activities are also likely to feel burdened and possibly marginalized by the heavy emphasis on sports as a vehicle for team-building and client entertainment. By engaging in such a restricted range of social activities with employees and clients, the firm perpetuates a very homogeneous workforce and management culture. A&C should focus on matching the market environment in which it operates.

6. *Expect female opposition.* We did not find any evidence of the kind of female opposition described in Chapter 6. This fact demonstrates how our guiding principles are not to be forcibly acted on, but simply provide a new lens through which you can evaluate an organization's performance with regard to gender balance.

7. *The law is not enough.* This case is a perfect example of how anti-discrimination law is not enough to rectify the kinds of practices that lead to gender imbalance. This branch of A&C is located in a country that has passed anti-discrimination laws that in some respects are even stricter than American anti-discrimination law. Yet none of the female employees with whom we talked expressed any opinion about the legality or illegality of the practices they complained about, nor did they express any interest in bringing a lawsuit. They simply wanted the firm to listen to them and take some action. The firm's management itself seemed to feel quite sure that it was operating well within the limits of anti-discrimination law, and it might be, as a matter of fact. We've seen how the firm engages in a range of practices that have the effect of marginalizing its female consultants, but the risk of causing more conflict, costs of pursuing such claims, and slim chances of success deter them from bringing formal complaints of discrimination.

How to make our guiding principles work for you

We want to emphasize that these guiding principles do not work like rules or check lists. They merely guide your observations and thinking and suggest different routes of action. Keeping these guiding principles in mind, you can begin to look at your own situation to see if any of them might be relevant to your workplace or your private life. Think of them as 'rules of thumb' to help you counteract everyone's—including your own—tendency to simply accept gender imbalance as an immutable fact of life.

Our guiding principles are a bit like what are called judgemental heuristics, i.e. decision-making strategies that rely on intuitive, rather than scientific, assessments of situations to produce decisions or judgements. They are basically mental short-cuts. All of us use judgemental heuristics—whether we're aware of it or not—to enable rapid decision-making in complex situations where gaining a full understanding of all relevant factors is impossible.

You might be wondering if these kinds of mental short-cuts are more likely to lead to worse—not better—decisions. Nobel Prize-winning psychologist Daniel Kahneman and Stanford psychology professor Amos Tversky are among the leading proponents of this view.[7] Although they recognize that heuristics are often useful,[8] their studies have shown how certain kinds of heuristics often lead to certain kinds of errors or biases. For example, the resemblance of a child to the stereotype of a teacher or banker may be given too much weight in predicting what occupation the child will eventually choose, at the expense of other more relevant information—like intelligence, academic performance, and interests. Organizational scholars have also found evidence that heuristics impair decision-making in corporate acquisition and divestment decision processes,[9] strategic planning exercises,[10] and local city council decision-making.[11]

---

[7] Kahneman and Tversky (1973); Tversky and Kahneman (1974).
[8] Kahneman and Tversky (1996).
[9] Duhaime and Schwenk (1985).
[10] Barnes (1984).
[11] Drummond (1994).

We don't think our guiding principles are like these kinds of judgemental heuristics. The heuristics Kahneman and Tversky warn against are relatively static, deeply ingrained in our thinking habits, and largely unconscious. In fact, they are the kind of heuristics that probably generate gender bias; they are the beliefs and attitudes we have identified as standing in the way of gender balance. Our guiding principles, on the other hand, are grounded in the research-based narratives presented in each of the preceding chapters that counteract the judgemental heuristics that lead to gender-biased judgements. They are more like story headlines that you use to find different ways of understanding and talking about causes of gender imbalance and finding ways of addressing it.

Here are some examples of when you would want to employ our guiding principles. If you are about to decide how to fill a management position in your department and you are looking at internal candidates for the job, you should review these guiding principles if you discover that no women have made it onto your shortlist. If you are a professional woman thinking about your next career move, you should consider these guiding principles to help you see through the popular explanations for gender-segregated workplaces and the domination of leadership positions by men and identify opportunities you may not have considered otherwise. If you are getting ready to decide what to major in in college, you should make your decision with these principles in mind—whether you are male or female. Using these principles will give you the freedom to discover far more possibilities and opportunities than you might have dreamed of before.

We can't include examples of every situation where applying our guidelines is needed, nor how they might fit into your life. But we can give you some broad examples of signs indicating that you need to give these principles more attention. Here are some things to watch out for—principle by principle:

1. You need to figure out how to *leave the past behind* when high performers in your company or workplace don't take time off to take care of their children or elderly parents, or if you or the leaders of your organization agree with any of the following statements:

- In order to compete against the Chinese and Indians, everyone has to work long hours; no exceptions.
- We can't have flexible working conditions and be successful.
- In our society, it's more logical for women to take primary responsibility for childcare.

2. You need to think about how you can *bring men and women back to Earth*:
   - If you claim that there are more differences than similarities between the sexes.
   - When you invite a brain scientist to come and explain to your employees or colleagues why men and women are different.
   - When you use your own sons and daughters as evidence of gender differences, especially after having painted your son's room blue and your daughter's pink.

3. You need to reconsider whether something that *feels right is wrong*:
   - When your stereotypes about women and men are constantly confirmed in your mind, and you feel satisfied with that.
   - When someone tells a blonde joke, and you laugh without wondering why the butt of the joke is a blonde female.
   - When you hear yourself saying women are more caring, less competitive, and less egotistical than men.
   - When you use examples of your husband's or wife's behaviour to explain gender differences.

4. You need to remind yourself that *ambition is genderless*:
   - When you use sports or warfare metaphors during interviews of candidates for leadership positions.
   - When you realize that you haven't considered any, or hardly any, female candidates for a job.
   - When you're not surprised that no women apply.
   - When you hear yourself saying women just aren't interested in leadership positions.

5. You must remind yourself that *gender balance is about making peace, not war*:

- When you feel your body go into fight or flight mode every time you hear the word 'feminism', 'sex equality', 'sex discrimination', or 'gender balance'.
- When you think gender balance is only about helping women.
- When you worry that women are taking over, and men are falling behind.
- When you think work–life balance is a women's issue.

6. You need to consider whether you need to expect female opposition:
   - When you're afraid of provoking various religious or political groups if you suggest that occupational segregation is not just the result of individual choices or an expression of divine will.
   - When you're afraid of being called a feminist.
   - When a close friend or colleague tells a sexist joke, and you laugh even though you feel uncomfortable.
   - When you decide not to speak openly with your colleagues, friends, or employees about supporting gender balance because you've heard them grumble about special treatment for women or claim that it's contrary to their religious beliefs.

7. You need to remind yourself that *the law is not enough*:
   - When you think your organization supports gender balance because no one has ever complained about sex discrimination.
   - When you think that your organization will achieve gender balance if it treats men and women exactly the same.
   - When you think pregnancy and childbirth should be treated like an illness.
   - When you think your organization supports gender balance because you have never heard anyone say anything opposing equal treatment of men and women.

Gender balance requires knowledgeable leaders

We started this book by listing a number of gender imbalances in business, politics, and education. The problem is on the radar of business and political leaders in Europe. During the two years we've been writing this book, a number of initiatives intended to achieve gender balance in company boards of directors have been proposed. In October 2013, two key European Parliament committees voted in favour of Commissioner Viviane Reding's proposal for a European law that would require company boards to have a minimum 60/40 gender composition (that is, at least 40% but no more than 60% of either gender) by 2020.[12] The legislation has passed the European Parliament, but, as we write this, the 28-member Council of Ministers has not yet voted on the measure. Germany's two largest parties, Chancellor Angela Merkel's conservative bloc and the left-leaning Social Democrats, proposed legislation in November 2013 requiring German companies listed on the stock exchange to ensure that from 2016 at least 30% of supervisory board members are women.[13] Denmark passed legislation that went into effect on 1 April 2013 requiring the 1,100 largest Danish companies to set their own targets for increasing the number of women (or men, if they are under-represented) on their boards and to adopt a policy for increasing the numbers of the under-represented sex in the companies' management levels.[14] While the companies are free to set their own targets and develop their own policies, failure to include this information in their annual reports can be sanctioned with a fine.

Asian countries appear to be taking gender balance seriously as well. The number of women in senior management in China grew from 25% in 2011 to 51% in 2013.[15] Regionally, Asia Pacific leads with 29% (although Japan scored an abysmal 7%), compared to 25% in the European Union, 23% in Latin America, and 21% in North America.

An increasing number of women have also won national elections around the world. South Korea elected its first female president and the

---

[12] Quinn (2013).

[13] Torry (2013).

[14] Law number 1383 of 23 December 2012, amending the Company Act, the Annual Reports Act, etc. (*lov om ændring af selskabsloven, årsregnskabsloven og forskellige andre love*) and Law number 1288 of 19 December 2012, amending the Sex Equality Act (*lov om ændring af lov om ligestilling af kvinder og mænd*).

[15] Grant Thornton (2013).

number of female heads of government or heads of state has more than doubled—to a total of 17 women—since 2005.

As encouraging as the increased attention paid to women in leadership around the globe is, there are signs of equally strong resistance. First, the Nordic countries, which rank in the top ten for gender equality on other measures than leadership, do not have as many senior female managers as China, which is ranked 69th in the World Economic Forum's 2013 Global Gender Gap Report. Second, even when public attention is directed towards this issue and governments urge organizations to take action, little happens. Even though Norway passed a law in 2006 requiring 40% of the boardroom seats of companies traded on the stock exchange to go to women (or men in case of a female-dominated board of directors), and all public companies are now in compliance with the law, a large number of Norwegian publicly traded companies converted into private limited companies just before the mandatory quota went into effect, raising suspicions that they did so deliberately to avoid complying with the new law.[16] In 2009 women held only 17% of the board positions in the companies not covered by the law, growing only 2% from 15% in 2004, and, since the quota only applies to boardroom seats and not top management, only 11% of all company presidents in Norway are women.[17]

[16] In December 2003, the Norwegian Parliament passed a law requiring all public limited firms to have at least 40% representation of women on their boards of directors by July 2005, but non-compliance was not subject to any sanction; at the time women held only 9% of board seats. The quotas became compulsory on 1 January 2006, with a two-year transition period. Firms that did not comply by January 2008 would be forced to dissolve. Notices to comply were given to 77 delinquent firms in January 2008, and by April all public limited firms were in compliance with the law. The number of public limited firms in Norway in 2009 was less than 70% of the number in 2001. In contrast, the number of private limited firms, not affected by the quota, had increased by over 30%. Ahern and Dittmar (2012).

[17] European Commission's Network to Promote Women in Decision-making in Politics and the Economy (2011).

Similarly, the British government has adopted a completely voluntary approach to increasing the number of women in boardrooms, following the recommendations of a report drafted by Lord Davies in 2011. The report urges 25% female presence in boardrooms by 2015 for FTSE 100 companies.[18] However, the proportion of women on FTSE 100 boards has remained at about 17.4% since August 2012, and at current rates the 25% target will be missed.[19]

The previous eight chapters of this book have suggested eight reasons why progress is so slow:

1. Too many politicians, leaders, and managers regard gender balance as unimportant, a distraction from what they regard as the core concerns of business and politics.
2. Too many people believe that women's relative absence from leadership positions is due to the market's competitive forces requiring managers to prioritize work over family.
3. Too many people believe that the gender gap in leadership has something to do with differences between male and female brains.
4. Too many people expect boys and girls, men and women to behave in certain ways, and those expectations become self-fulfilling prophecies.
5. Too many people believe that men are simply more ambitious than women.
6. Too many people believe that drawing attention to gender gaps is the first salvo of a battle between the sexes.
7. Too many people worry about assertions that some women think gender balance is immoral, unjust, or politically unwise.
8. Too many people believe that legal prohibitions against sex discrimination are sufficient to address gender gaps in employment.

[18] Smedley (2013).
[19] Smedley (2013).

Telling women to 'lean in' is not a response to these disabling beliefs. It may help change the way *women* think and help *them* persist in the face of resistance, but that kind of advice 'targets only half the players and not the game'.[20] The guiding principles we present in this book target the *game*: gender.

The debates sparked by Sandberg and Slaughter in the USA and by politicians proposing quotas and passing legislation requiring organizations to set targets and make plans or pay a fine have breathed life into a debate that seemed to be running on recirculating stale air. The attention business and political leaders are giving this debate has opened a window for change.

If you believe that gender balance is important, you are one of the people who can lead the way through that window. Think about these seven guiding principles. Talk about them with your colleagues, board members, friends, and family. Use them as your compass to find your way around the jungle of explanations and excuses for the status quo. They will help you discover different ways of doing things, explain why it is necessary to make the changes you propose, and motivate others to help you. Use the foregoing chapters and seven principles as the grounds for what you claim to do and to provide a motivating force for your own and others' efforts to improve the governance of societies' institutions by closing the gender gaps in employment and leadership.

Do you want to adapt and implement the seven guiding principles in your organization? We can help.

www.ontheagenda.eu

---

[20] Benschop and Verloo (2011: 280).

Bibliography

ABC News (2012) 'Gillard Labels Abbott a Misogynist', 8 October. http://www.youtube.com/watch?v=ihd7ofrwQX0

Adams, Renee B. and Daniel Ferreira (2009) 'Women in the Boardroom and Their Impact on Governance and Performance', *Journal of Financial Economics* 94: 291–309.

Adams, Tim (2011) 'Testosterone and High Finance Do Not Mix: So Bring on the Women', *The Observer*, 19 June. http://www.guardian.co.uk/world/2011/jun/19/neuroeconomics-women-city-financial-crash

Ahern, Kenneth R. and Amy K. Dittmar (2012) 'The Changing of the Boards: The Impact on Firm Valuation of Mandated Female Board Representation', *Quarterly Journal of Economics* 127: 137–97.

Alfonsi, Sharyn and Claire Pedersen (2012) 'Is Dad the New Mom? The Rise of Stay-At-Home Fathers', ABC Nightline, 28 June. http://abcnews.go.com/US/stay-home-dads-dad-mom/story?id=16596365

Aquinas, Thomas (1947) *The Summa Theologica* (New York: Benziger Brothers).

Archer, John (2004) 'Sex Differences in Aggression in Real-World Settings: A Meta-Analytic Review', *Review of General Psychology* 8: 291–322.

—— (2006) 'Testosterone and Human Aggression: An Evaluation of the Challenge Hypothesis', *Neuroscience and Biobehavioral Reviews* 30: 319–45.

Ashby, W. H. (1956) *An Introduction to Cybernetics* (London: Methuen).

Augustine (1958) *City of God*, trans. Gerald G. Walsh, Demetrius B. Zema, Grace Monahan, and Daniel J. Honan, ed. Vernon J. Bourke (Garden City, NY: Image Books).

—— (2008) *Confessions*, trans. Henry Chadwick (Oxford: Oxford University Press).

Bacchetta, Paola and Margaret Power (2002) 'Introduction', in *Right Wing Women: From Conservatives to Extremists Around the World*, ed. Paola Bacchetta and Margaret Power (New York and London: Routledge), 1–16.

Barker, Gary, Christine Ricardo, and Marcos Nascimento (2007) *Engaging Men and Boys in Changing Gender-Based Inequity in Health: Evidence from Programme Interventions* (Geneva: World Health Organization). http://www.who.int/gender/documents/Engaging_men_boys.pdf

Barnes, James H. (1984) 'Cognitive Biases and their Impact on Strategic Planning', *Strategic Management Journal* 5: 129–37.

Barnett, Rosalind and Caryl Rivers (2004) *Same Difference: How Gender Myths Are Hurting Our Relationships, Our Children, and Our Jobs* (New York: Basic Books).

Baron, Jonathan (2008) *Thinking and Deciding* (Cambridge; Cambridge University Press, 4th edn).

Baron-Cohen, Simon (2004) *The Essential Difference: Male and Female Brains and the Truth About Autism* (New York: Basic Books).

Barsh, Joanna and Lareina Yee (2011a) 'Changing Companies' Minds about Women', *McKinsey Quarterly*, September. http://www.mckinsey.com/insights/organization/changing_companies_minds_about_women

—— (2011b) 'Unlocking the Full Potential of Women in the U.S. Economy', McKinsey and Company, April. http://www.mckinsey.com/client_service/organization/latest_thinking/unlocking_the_full_potential.

BBC News (2013) 'Men and Women's Brains Are "Wired Differently"', 3 December.

Becker, Mary E. (1989) 'Obscuring the Struggle: Sex Discrimination, Social Security, and Stone, Seidman, Sunstein & Tushnet's *Constitutional Law*', *Columbia Law Review* 89: 264–89.

Belkin, Lisa (2003) 'Q: Why don't more women get to the top? A: They choose not to', *The New York Times Magazine*, 26 October. http://www.nytimes.com/2003/10/26/magazine/26WOMEN.html

Bem, Sandra (1981) 'Gender Schema Theory: A Cognitive Account of Sex Typing', *Psychological Review* 88: 354–64.

—— (1983) 'Gender Schema Theory and Its Implications for Child Development: Raising Gender-Aschematic Children in a Gender-Schematic Society', *SIGNS: Journal of Women in Culture & Society* 8: 598–616.

Benjamin Jr., Ludy T. (1990) 'Leta Stetter Hollingworth: Psychologist, Educator, Feminist', *Roeper Review* 12: 145–50.

Benko, Cathleen and Anne Weisberg (2007) *Mass Career Customization* (Boston: Harvard Business School Publishing).

Benschop, Yvonne and Mieke Verloo (2011) 'Gender Change, Organizational Change, and Gender Equality Strategies', in *Handbook of Gender, Work and Organization*, ed. Emma Jeanes, David Knights, and Patricia Yancey Martin (Chichester: Wiley-Blackwell), 277–90.

Biletta, Isabella (2012a) 'Gender Gaps: Occupational Segregation Impacts and Challenges', presentation at the conference, 'Exchange of Best Practices on the Gender Pay Gap', 29–30 October, Limassol, Cyprus. http://www.eurofound.europa.eu/docs/events/2012/genderpaygap/segregation_ibi.pdf

—— (2012b) 'Tackling Gender Barriers in Employment', presentation at symposium organized by Centre for Parliamentary Studies, Brussels, 27 November, on file with the authors.

Blau, Peter (1977) *Inequality and Heterogeneity* (New York: Free Press).

Brake, Deborah L. (2005) 'Retaliation', *Minnesota Law Review* 90: 32–42.

—— (2007) 'Perceiving Subtle Sexism: Mapping the Social-Psychological Forces and Legal Narratives that Obscure Gender Bias', *Columbia Journal of Gender and Law* 16: 679–723.

Brizendine, Louann (2006) *The Female Brain* (New York: Broadway Books).

—— (2010) *The Male Brain* (New York: Broadway Books).

Brown, Peter R. L. (2005) 'Augustine and a Crisis of Wealth in Late Antiquity', *Augustinian Studies* 36: 5–30.

Brown, Richard D. (1972) 'Modernization and the Modern Personality in Early America, 1600–1865: A Sketch of a Synthesis', *Journal of Interdisciplinary History* 2: 201–28.

Brundage, James A. (1976) 'Prostitution in the Medieval Canon Law', *Signs* 1: 825–45.

Bump, Philip (2013) 'A Visual Guide to the Gender Diversity of the Senate's Hearing on Sexual Assault in the Military', *The Atlantic Wire*, 4 June. http://www.thewire.com/politics/2013/06/visual-guide-gender-diversity-senates-hearing-sexual-assault-military/65884/

Burt, Ronald S. (1982) *Toward a Structural Theory of Action* (New York: Academic Press).

Bush, Julia (2005) '"Special strengths for their own special duties": Women, Higher Education and Gender Conservatism in Late Victorian Britain', *History of Education* 34: 387–405.

Cahill, Spencer E. (1986) 'Language Practices and Self-Definition: The Case of Gender Identity Acquisition', *Sociological Quarterly* 27: 295–311.

Cameron, Deborah (2007) *The Myth of Mars and Venus: Do Men and Women Really Speak Different Languages?* (Oxford and New York: Oxford University Press).

'Careers and Marriage', *Forbes*, 23 August 2006. http://www.forbes.com/2006/08/23/Marriage-Careers-Divorce_cx_mn_land.html

Catalyst (2004) 'Women and Men in U.S. Corporate Leadership: Same Workplace, Different Realities?' http://www.catalyst.org/knowledge/women-and-men-us-corporate-leadership-same-workplace-different-realities

—— (2013a) 'Women CEOs of the Fortune 1000', 18 September. http://www.catalyst.org/knowledge/women-ceos-fortune-1000

—— (2013b) 'Women in Male-Dominated Industries and Occupations', 13 March. http://www.catalyst.org/knowledge/women-male-dominated-industries-and-occupations-us-and-canada

CBS News (2004) *60 Minutes*, 20 October.

Center for American Women and Politics (2013) Fact Sheet, 'Women in the U.S. Congress 2013'. http://www.cawp.rutgers.edu/fast_facts/levels_of_office/Congress-CurrentFacts.php, accessed 5 November 2013.

Chan, Szu Ping (2013) 'Economic Rebound May Speed Rate Rise', *The Telegraph*, 9 November. http://www.telegraph.co.uk/finance/bank-of-england/10437120/Economic-rebound-may-speed-rate-rise.html

Chatard, S. Guimond and L. Selimbegovic (2007) '"How good are you in math?" The Effect of Gender Stereotypes on Students' Recollection of their School Marks', *Journal of Experimental Social Psychology* 43: 1017–24.

Chaudhry, Lakshmi (2013) 'Call Me a Feminist: Or is it Time to Junk the F Word?', *Firstpost*, 9 July. http://www.firstpost.com/living/call-me-feminist-or-is-it-time-to-junk-the-f-word-941847.html

Clearfield, Melissa W. and Naree M. Nelson (2006) 'Sex Differences in Mothers' Speech and Play Behaviour with 6-, 9- and 14-Month-Old Infants', *Sex Roles* 54: 127–37.

Clermont, Kevin M. and Stewart J. Schwab (2009) 'Employment Discrimination Plaintiffs in Federal Court: From Bad to Worse', *Harvard Law and Policy Review* 3: 103–32.

Collins, Gail (2010) *When Everything Changed: The Amazing Journey of American Women from 1960 to the Present* (New York: Little, Brown and Company).

Concerned Women for America (2013) Mission Statement. http://www.cwfa.org/about.asp, accessed 13 November 2013.

Concerned Women for America (2013) 'Biblical Support for CWA Core Issues'. http://www.cwfa.org/coreissues.asp, accessed 7 December 2013.

Connor, Steve (2013) 'The Hardwired Difference between Male and Female Brains Could Explain Why Men are "Better at Map Reading"', *The Independent*, 3 December. http://www.independent.co.uk/life-style/the-hardwired-difference-between-male-and-female-brains-could-explain-why-men-are-better-at-map-reading-8978248.html

Coontz, Stephanie (2013) 'Why Gender Equality Stalled', *New York Times*, 17 February.

Correll, Shelley J. and Stephen Benard (2007) 'Getting a Job: Is There a Motherhood Penalty?', *American Journal of Sociology* 112: 1297–338.

Costa, Jr., Paul T., Antonio Terracciano, and Robert R. McCrae (2001) 'Gender Differences in Personality Traits Across Cultures: Robust and Surprising Findings', *Journal of Personality and Social Psychology* 81: 322–31.

Cott, Nancy (1977) *The Bonds of Womanhood: 'Woman's Sphere' in New England, 1780–1835* (New Haven: Yale University Press).

Cotter, David, Joan Hermsen, and Reeve Vanneman (2012) 'Is the Gender Revolution Over?', Council on Contemporary Families, online Gender Revolution Symposium. http://contemporaryfamilies.org/gender-sexuality/gender-revolution-symposium-keynote.html

Crenshaw, Kimberlé Williams (1988) 'Race, Reform and Retrenchment: Transformation and Legitimation in Antidiscrimination Law', *Harvard Law Review* 101: 1331–87.

Criscione, Valeria (2011) 'Paternity Rights . . . and Wrongs', *The Guardian*, 19 March.

Cuddy, Amy, Susan Fiske, and Peter Glick (2004) 'When Professionals Become Mothers, Warmth Doesn't Cut the Ice', *Journal of Social Issues* 60: 701–18.

Dabhoiwala, Faramerz (2012) *The Origins of Sex: A History of the First Sexual Revolution* (London: Allen Lane).

Davison, Heather K. and Michael J. Burke (2000) 'Sex Discrimination in Simulated Employment Contexts: A Meta-Analytic Investigation', *Journal of Vocational Behavior* 52: 225–48.

'Declaration of Sentiments' (1848). http://www.princeton.edu/~achaney/tmve/wiki100k/docs/Declaration_of_Sentiments.html, accessed 11 November 2013.

Desvaux, Georges and Sandrine Devillard (2008) 'Women Matter 2: Female Leadership, a Competitive Edge for the Future'. http://www.mckinsey.com/features/women_matter.

Desvaux, Georges, Sandrine Devillard-Hoellinger, and Pascal Baumgarten (2007) 'Women Matter: Gender Diversity, a Corporate Performance Driver', October. http://www.mckinsey.com/client_service/organization/latest_thinking/women_matter

Desvaux, Georges, Sandrine Devillard, and Sandra Sancier-Sultan (2010) 'Women at the Top of Corporations: Making it Happen', October. http://www.mckinsey.com/client_service/organization/latest_thinking/women_matter

Directive 2002/73/EC of the European Parliament and of the Council of 23 September 2002 amending Council Directive 76/207/EEC on the implementation of the principle of equal treatment for men and women as regards access to employment, vocational training and promotion and working conditions. http://eur-lex.europa.eu/LexUriServ/LexUriServ.do?uri=OJ:L:2002:269:0015:0020:EN:PDF

Donovan, Wilberta, Nicole Taylor, and Lewis Leavitt (2007) 'Maternal Sensory Sensitivity and Response Bias in Detecting Change in Infant Facial Expressions: Maternal Self-Efficacy and Infant Gender Labelling', *Infant Behavior and Development* 30: 436–52.

Drummond, Helga (1994) 'Too Little Too Late: A Case Study of Escalation in Decision Making', *Organization Studies* 15: 591–607.

Duhaime, Irene M. and Charles R. Schwenk (1985) 'Conjectures on Cognitive Simplification in Acquisition and Divestment Decision-Making', *Academy of Management Review* 14: 287–95.

Eagli, Alice and Linda Carli (2007) *Through the Labyrinth* (Boston: Harvard Business School Publishing).

The Economist (2006) 'The Mismeasure of Women', 3 August.

——(2013) 'Trouble at the Lab: Unreliable Research', 19 October.

Edwards, Catherine (2002) *The Politics of Immorality in Ancient Rome* (Cambridge: Cambridge University Press).

Eliot, Lise (2010) *Pink Brain, Blue Brain: How Small Differences Grow into Troublesome Gaps—And What We Can Do About It* (London: Oneworld Publications).

Emrich, Cynthia (2013) Presentation at Professional Development Workshop on Advancing Women in Leadership, Academy of Management Conference, 10 August, Orlando, Florida, on file with the authors.

Erhardtsen, Birgitte (2010) 'Direktør Ravnemor', *Berlingske Business*, 31 January, updated 30 May 2012. http://www.business.dk/karriere/direktoer-ravnemor

European Commission (2009) *She Figures 2009: Statistics and Indicators on Gender Equality in Science* (Luxembourg: Publications Office of the European Union). http://ec.europa.eu/research/science-society/document_library/pdf_06/she_figures_2009_en.pdf

—— (2012) 'Women in Decision-Making Positions', Special Eurobarometer 376/Wave EB76.1–TNS Opinion & Social, March.

European Commission's Network to Promote Women in Decision-Making in Politics and the Economy (2011) 'The Quota-Instrument: Different Approaches across Europe', working paper, June. http://ec.europa.eu/justice/gender-equality/files/quota-working_paper_en.pdf

Eyer, Katie R. (2012) 'That's Not Discrimination: American Beliefs and the Limits of Antidiscrimination Law', *Minnesota Law Review* 96: 1275–362.

Falwell, Jerry (1981) *Listen America!* (New York: Bantam Books).

Farberov, Snejana (2012) 'Number of stay-at-home dads has DOUBLED in past decade as "man-cession" bites', *Mail Online*, 17 June. http://www.dailymail.co.uk/news/article-2160638/Mr-Mom-generation-Number-stay-home-dad-DOUBLED-past-decade-amidg-changing-attitudes-ongoing-man-cession.html#ixzz22fyKykCu

Feingold, Alan (1994) 'Gender Differences in Variability in Intellectual Abilities: A Cross-Cultural Perspective', *Sex Roles* 30: 81–92.

Fels, Anna (2004) 'Do Women Lack Ambition?' *Harvard Business Review* 82: 50–60.

'50 Famous Firsts in Women's History'. Encyclopedia Britannica blog. http://www.britannica.com/blogs/50-famous-womens-history-answers/, accessed 20 November 2013.

Fine, Cordelia (2010) *Delusions of Gender: The Real Science Behind Sex Differences* (London: Icon Books and New York: W. W. Norton).

Florida, Richard, Charlotta Mellander, and Karen M. King (2011) 'The Rise of Women in the Creative Class', Martin Prosperity Institute, October. http://martinprosperity.org/media/Women%20in%20the%20Creative%20Class%20Oct%202011.pdf

Folbre, Nancy (2009) *Greed, Lust, and Gender: A History of Economic Ideas* (Oxford: Oxford University Press).

'France passes new law on sexual harassment', *Al Jazeera*, 31 July 2012. http://www.aljazeera.com/news/europe/2012/07/201273120465183720.html

Fredman, Sandra (2009) *Making Equality Effective: The Role of Proactive Measures* (Brussels: European Commission).

Freeman, Alan (1990) 'Antidiscrimination Law: The View from 1989', *Tulane Law Review* 64: 1407–41.

Freeman, Jo (n.d.) 'No More Miss America! (1968–1969)'. http://www.jofreeman.com/photos/MissAm1969.html.

Freeman, Nancy K. (2007) 'Pre-Schoolers' Perceptions of Gender Appropriate Toys and their Parents' Beliefs about Genderized Behaviors: Miscommunication, Mixed Messages, or Hidden Truths?' *Early Childhood Education Journal* 34: 357–66.

Friedan, Betty (1977) *The Feminine Mystique* (New York: Dell Publishing).

Friedman, Milton (1962) *Capitalism and Freedom* (Chicago: University of Chicago Press).

Galinsky, Ellen, Kerstin Aumann, and James T. Bond (2011) *Times are Changing: Gender and Generation at Work and at Home.* Families and Work Institute (August). http://familiesandwork.org/site/research/reports/Times_Are_Changing.pdf

Galinsky, Ellen, Kimberley Salmond, James T. Bond, Marcia B. Kropf, Meredith Moore, and Brad Harrington (2003) *Leaders in a Global Economy: A Study of Executive Women and Men.* Families and Work Institute. http://familiesandwork.org/site/research/reports/GlobalLeadersFullStudy.pdf

Ghoshal, Sumantra (2005) 'Bad Management Theories are Destroying Good Management Practices', *Academy of Management Learning and Education* 4: 75–91.

Goldin, Claudia and Cecilia Rouse (2000) 'Orchestrating Impartiality: The Impact of "Blind" Auditions on Female Musicians', *American Economic Review* 90: 715–41.

Good, Catherine, Joshua Aronson, and Jayne Ann Harder (2008) 'Problems in the Pipeline: Stereotype Threat and Women's Achievement in High-Level Math Courses', *Journal of Applied Developmental Psychology* 29: 17–28.

Grant, Judith (2006) 'Andrea Dworkin and the Social Construction of Gender: A Retrospective', *Signs* 31: 967–93.

Grant Thornton (2013) 'Women in Senior Management: Setting the Stage for Growth', Grant Thornton International Business Report. http://www.internationalbusinessreport.com/files/ibr2013_wib_report_final.pdf, accessed 7 December 2013.

Guerrera, Francesco (2010) 'The "Wall Street" Effect', *Financial Times*, 25 September.

Hamel, Gary (1996) 'Strategy as Revolution', *Harvard Business Review* 74: 69–82.

Harris v. *Forklift Systems, Inc.,* 510 U.S. 17 (1993).

Hawkesworth, Mary E. (1984) 'The Affirmative Action Debate and Conflicting Conceptions of Individuality', *Women's Studies International Forum* 7: 335–47.

Hayek, Friedrich (1944) *The Road to Serfdom* (Chicago: University of Chicago Press).

Hays, Charlotte (2012) 'AEI's Danielle Pletka Takes on Whiny Women', 12 July. Independent Women's Forum, http://www.iwf.org/blog/2788469/AEI's-Danielle-Pletka-Takes-on-Whiny-Women

Hemel, Daniel J. (2005), 'Summers' Comments on Women and Science Draw Ire', *The Harvard Crimson*, 14 January. http://www.thecrimson.com/article/2005/1/14/summers-comments-on-women-and-science/

Hines, Melissa (2004) *Brain Gender* (New York: Oxford University Press).

Holt, Helle, Lars Pico Geerdsen, Gunvor Christensen, Caroline Klitgaard, and Marie Louise Lind (2006) *Det Kønsopdelte Arbejdsmarked: En kvantitativ og kvalitativ belysning* (Copenhagen: SFI).

hooks, bell (2000) *Feminism is for Everybody: Passionate Politics* (London: Pluto Press).

Horowitz, Maryanne Cline (1976) 'Aristotle and Woman', *Journal of the History of Biology* 9: 183–213.

The Hunt (film, 2012) (Danish title: *Jagten*), directed by Thomas Vinterberg.

Hyde, Janet Shibley (2005) 'The Gender Similarities Hypothesis', *American Psychologist* 60: 581–92.

Ickes, William, Paul R. Gesn, and Tiffany Graham (2000) 'Gender Differences in Empathic Accuracy: Differential Ability or Differential Motivation?' *Personal Relationships* 7: 95–109.

Independent Women's Forum (2013) 'Feminism'. Issues. http://www.iwf.org/issues/feminism, accessed 7 December 2013.

Ingalhalikar, Madhura, Alex Smith, Drew Parker, Theodore D. Satterthwaite, Mark A. Elliott, Kosha Ruparel, Hakon Hakonarson, Raquel E. Gur, Ruben C. Gur, and Ragini Verma (2013) 'Sex Differences in the Structural Connectome of the Human Brain', *Proceedings of the National Academy of Sciences*. Published online before print 2 December 2013. http://www.pnas.org/content/early/2013/11/27/1316909110

International Monetary Fund (2005) 'The IMF's Approach to Promoting Good Governance and Combating Corruption—A Guide', 20 June. http://www.imf.org/external/np/gov/guide/eng/index.htm

Inter-Parliamentary Union (2013) 'Women in National Parliaments'. http://www.ipu.org/wmn-e/classif.htm, accessed 5 November 2013.

Jessica G. (2008) 'Gloria Steinem On Feminism, Sarah Palin: "It's Such An Insult"', *Jezebel*, 9 September. http://jezebel.com/5056307/gloria-steinem-on-feminism-sarah-palin-its-such-an-insult

Johnson, Jenna (2013) 'Paul Tudor Jones: In Macro Trading, Babies are a "Killer" to a Woman's Focus', *Washington Post*, 23 May. http://articles.washingtonpost.com/2013-2005-23/local/39465926_1_macro-two-women-successful-traders

Joy, Lois and Harvey M. Wagner (2011) 'The Bottom Line: Corporate Performance and Women's Representation on Boards (2004–2008)', *Catalyst*, 1 March. http://www.catalyst.org/knowledge/bottom-line-corporate-performance-and-womens-representation-boards-20042008

Kahneman, Daniel (2011) *Thinking, Fast and Slow* (New York: Farrar, Straus & Giroux).

Kahneman, Daniel and Amos Tversky (1973) 'On the Psychology of Prediction', *Psychological Review* 80: 237–51.

———— (1996) 'On the Reality of Cognitive Illusions', *Psychological Review* 103: 582–91.

Kaiser, Cheryl R. and Brenda Major (2006) 'A Social Psychological Perspective on Perceiving and Reporting Discrimination', *Law and Social Inquiry* 31: 801–30.

Kane, E.W. (2006) 'No Way My Boys are Going To Be Like That! Responses to Children's Gender Nonconformity', *Gender & Society* 20: 149–76.

Kanter, Rosabeth Moss (1977) *Men and Women of the Corporation* (New York: Basic Books).

Katz, Jackson (2013) http://www.jacksonkatz.com/index.html, accessed 11 November 2013.

Kay, John (2011) 'Why Economists Still Stubbornly Stick to Their Guns', *Financial Times*, 16 April.

Kimbrell, Andrew (1995) *The Masculine Mystique: The Politics of Masculinity* (New York: Ballantine Books).

Klatch, Rebecca (1987) *Women of the New Right* (Philadelphia: Temple University Press).

Klein, Kristi J. K. and Sara D. Hodges (2001) 'Gender Differences, Motivation, and Empathic Accuracy: When It Pays To Understand', *Personality and Social Psychology Bulletin* 27: 720–30.

Kling, Kristen C., Janet S. Hyde, Carolin J. Showers, and Brenda N. Buswell (1999) 'Gender Differences in Self-Esteem: A Meta-Analysis', *Psychological Bulletin* 125: 470–500.

Kolata, Gina (1995) 'Men and Women Use Brain Differently, Study Discovers', *New York Times*, 16 February.

Kolhatkar, Sheelah (2010) 'What If Women Ran Wall Street?', *New York Magazine*, 21 March. http://nymag.com/news/businessfinance/64950/

Konick, Kate (2006) 'Career Women Face Less Money, Less Marriage', ABC News, online edition, 7 September. http://abcnews.go.com/Business/CareerManagement/story?id=2395758&page=1#.UdMDGzsweSp

Krieger, Linda Hamilton (1995) 'The Content of Our Categories: A Cognitive Bias Approach to Discrimination and Equal Employment Opportunity', *Stanford Law Review* 47: 1161–248.

Law number 1383 of 23 December 2012, amending the Company Act, the Annual Reports Act, etc. (*lov om ændring af selskabsloven, årsregnskabsloven og forskellige andre love*) and Law number 1288 of 19 December 2012, amending the Sex Equality Act (*lov om ændring af lov om ligestilling af kvinder og mænd*). https://www.retsinformation.dk/Forms/r0710.aspx?id=144739

Lawson, Sandra (2008) 'Women Hold Up Half the Sky', Goldman Sachs Economic Research, Global Economics Paper No. 164. http://www.goldmansachs.com/our-thinking/focus-on/investing-in-women/bios-pdfs/women-half-sky-pdf.pdf

League of European Research Universities (2012) 'Women, Research and Universities: Excellence Without Gender Bias', July. http://www.leru.org/files/general/LERU%20Paper_Women%20universities%20and%20research.pdf

Lehmann Brothers Centre for Women in Business (2007) 'Innovative Potential: Men and Women in Teams—Executive Summary'. http://www.london.edu/assets/documents/facultyandresearch/Innovative_Potential_NOV_2007.pdf

Lesselier, Claudie (2002) 'Far-Right Women in France: The Case of the National Front', in *Right Wing Women: From Conservatives to Extremists Around the World*, ed. Paola Bacchetta and Margaret Power (New York and London: Routledge), 127–40.

Levy, Gary D. and Robert A. Haaf (1994) 'Detection of Gender-Related Categories by 10-Month-Old Infants', *Infant Behavior & Development* 17: 457–9.

Levy, Neil (2004) 'Book Review: Understanding Blindness', *Phenomenology and the Cognitive Sciences* 3: 315–24.

Livius, Titus (2006) *History of Rome*, books nine to twenty-six, trans. Daniel Spillan and Cyrus Edmunds (Fairford, UK: Echo Library).

Macrae, Neil and Galen V. Bodenhausen (2000) 'Social Cognition: Thinking Categorically about Others', *Annual Review of Psychology* 51: 93–120.

Maddux, Kristy (2004) 'When Patriots Protest: The Anti-Suffrage Discursive Transformation of 1917', *Rhetoric & Public Affairs* 7: 283–310.

Magley, Vicki J., Charles L. Hulin, Louise F. Fitzgerald, and Mary DeNardo (1999) 'Outcomes of Self-Labeling Sexual Harassment', *Journal of Applied Psychology* 84: 390–402.

Major, Brenda and Pamela J. Sawyer (2009) 'Attributions to Discrimination: Antecedents and Consequences', in *Handbook of Prejudice, Stereotyping, and Discrimination*, ed. Todd D. Nelson (New York and Hove, East Sussex: Psychology Press, 4th edn.), 89–110.

MaleFeminists.com. http://malefeminists.com/, accessed 7 December 2013.

Martin, Carol L. and Diane Ruble (2004) 'Children's Search for Gender Cues: Cognitive Perspectives on Gender Development', *Current Directions in Psychological Science* 13: 67–70.

Mason, Andrew D. and Elizabeth M. King (2001) 'Engendering Development through Gender Equality in Rights, Resources, and Voice', World Bank Policy Research Report (Washington, DC: World Bank). http://documents.worldbank.org/curated/en/2001/01/891686/engendering-development-through-gender-equality-rights-resources-voice

Men and Feminism. http://www.mfeminism.com/

Merrill-Sands, Deborah, Jill Kickul, and Cynthia Ingols (2005) 'Women Pursuing Leadership and Power: Challenging the Myth of the "Opt Out Revolution"', *CGO Insights*, Briefing Note Number 20, February, Center for Gender in Organizations, Simmons School of Management, Boston, MA. http://www.simmons.edu/som/docs/insights_20.pdf

Mondschein, Emily R., Karen E. Adolph, and Catherine S. Tamis-LeMonda (2000) 'Gender Bias in Mothers' Expectations about Infant Crawling', *Journal of Experimental Child Psychology* 77: 304–16.

Morin, Richard and Megan Rosenfeld (1998) 'With More Equity, More Sweat', *Washington Post*, 22 March.

Moss-Racusin, Corinne A., John F. Dovidio, Victoria L. Brescoll, Mark L. Brescoll, Mark J. Graham, and Jo Handelsman (2012) 'Science Faculty's Subtle Gender Biases Favor Male Students', *PNAS Early Edition*, open access edition, approved for publication 21 August. http://www.pnas.org/cgi/doi/10.1073/pnas.1211286109, accessed 29 June 2013.

Mother Goose (1916) *The Real Mother Goose* (Chicago: Rand McNally & Co.).

'Mother Goose Nursery Rhymes'. http://www.nursery-rhymes.org/nursery-rhymes/what-are-little-boys-made-of.html, accessed 26 November 2013.

Mundy, Liza (2012) *The Richer Sex* (New York: Simon & Schuster).

Nielsen, Ruth and Marit Halvorsen (1992) 'Sex Discrimination: Between the Nordic Model and European Community Law', in *The Nordic Labour Relations Model: Labour Law and Trade Unions in the Nordic Countries—Today and Tomorrow*, ed. Niklas Bruun, Boel Flodgren, Marit Halvorsen, Håkan Hydén, and Ruth Nielsen (Aldershot: Dartmouth Publishing), 180–220.

Novartis (2012) 'Perspective Changes Everything: Diversity & Inclusion Report 2012'. http://www.novartis.com/careers/diversity-inclusion/diversity-inclusion-report-2012.html, accessed 7 December 2013.

O'Brien, Laurie T., Alison Blodorn, AnGelica Alsbrooks, Reesa Dube, Glenn Adams, and Jessica C. Nelson (2009) 'Understanding White Americans' Perceptions of Racism in Hurricane Katrina-Related Events', *Group Processes & Intergroup Relations* 12: 431–44.

OECD (2012) *Closing the Gender Gap: Act Now* (Paris: OECD Publishing). http://dx.doi.org/10.1787/9789264179370-en

Patten, Eileen and Kim Parker (2012) 'A Gender Reversal on Career Aspirations: Young Women Now Top Young Men in Valuing a High-Paying Career', Pew Research Center, 19 April. http://www.pewsocialtrends.org/2012/04/19/a-gender-reversal-on-career-aspirations

Phillips v. *Martin Marietta*, 400 U.S. 542 (1971).

Pinker, Steven (2005) 'The Science of Difference: Sex Ed', *The New Republic Online*, 7 February. http://pinker.wjh.harvard.edu/articles/media/2005_02_14_newrepublic.html

Pinker, Susan (2008) *The Sexual Paradox: Troubled Boys, Gifted Girls and the Real Difference Between the Sexes* (New York: Scribner).

Poldrack, Russell A. (2011) 'Inferring Mental States form Neuroimaging Data: From Reverse Inference to Large-Scale Decoding', *Neuron* 72: 692–7.

Power, Margaret (2002) 'Right-Wing Women, Sexuality, and Politics in Chile during the Pinochet Dictatorship, 1973–1990', in *Right Wing Women: From Conservatives to Extremists Around the World*, ed. Paola Bacchetta and Margaret Power (New York and London: Routledge), 273–86.

Promundo, United Nations Population Fund, and MenEngaged (2010) *Engaging Men and Boys in Gender Equality and Health: A Global Toolkit for Action* (New York: UNFPA). http://www.unfpa.org/public/home/publications/pid/6815

Quinn, James (2013) 'EU Quota for 40 pc of Women on Boards Moves Step Closer', *The Telegraph*, 14 October. http://www.telegraph.co.uk/finance/newsbysector/banksand-finance/10378585/EU-quota-for-40pc-of-women-on-boards-moves-step-closer.html

Rasmussen, Inger Høedt (2014) 'Developing Identity for Lawyers: Towards Sustainable Lawyering', Ph.D. thesis, on file with the authors.

Ray, Rebecca, Janet C. Gornick, and John Schmitt (2009) 'Parental Leave Policies in 21 Countries: Assessing Generosity and Gender Equality', Center for Economic and Policy Research, revised version, June. http://www.cepr.net/documents/publications/parental_2008_09.pdf

Redstockings Manifesto (7 July 1969) http://www.redstockings.org/index.php?option=com_content&view=article&id=76&Itemid=59, last accessed 7 December 2013

Risman, Barbara J. (2004) 'Gender as Social Action: Theory Wrestling with Activism', *Gender & Society* 18: 429–50.

Roos, Johan (2006) 'The Benefits and Limitations of Leadership Speeches in Change Initiatives', *Journal of Management Development* 32: 548–59.

Roseberry, Lynn (2002) 'Equality Rights and Discrimination Law in Scandinavia', *Scandinavian Studies in Law* 43: 215–56.

Rosin, Hanna (2010) 'The End of Men', *The Atlantic*, July/August.

Rowold, Katharina (2010) *The Educated Woman: Minds, Bodies, and Women's Higher Education in Britain, Germany, and Spain, 1865–1914* (New York and London: Routledge).

Ruble, Diane N., Leah E. Lurye, and Kristina M. Zosuls (2013) 'Pink Frilly Dresses (PFD) and Early Gender Identity', *Princeton Report on Knowledge* 2, no. 2. http://www.princeton.edu/prok/issues/2-2/pink_frilly.xml, accessed 29 June 2013.

Sample, Ian (2013) 'Maps of Neural Circuitry Show Women's Brains are Suited to Social Skills and Memory, Men's Perception and Co-ordination', *The Guardian*, 2 December. http://www.theguardian.com/science/2013/dec/02/men-women-brains-wired-differently

Samuelson, Paul A. (1983) 'My Life Philosophy', *The American Economist* 27: 5–12.

Sandberg, Sheryl (2011) Barnard College Commencement, Tuesday, 17 May, New York City, Transcript and Video of Speech, 18 May 2011. http://barnard.edu/headlines/transcript-and-video-speech-sheryl-sandberg-chief-operating-officer-facebook
—— (2013) *Lean In* (New York: Alfred Knopf).

Saunders, Jennifer (2010) 'The Long-Delayed Post about Swiss School Schedules or: Are You People "Trying" to Make It Hard for Stay-At-Home Moms?', Magpie Days blog, 13 December. http://www.magpiedays.com/2010/12/the-long-delayed-post-about-swiss-school-schedules-or-are-you-people-trying-to-make-it-hard-for-stay-at-home-moms/

Sax, Leonard (2006) *Why Gender Matters* (New York: Broadway Books).

Schaffer, Amanda (2008) 'Mars, Venus, Babies, and Hormones', *Slate Magazine*, 3 July. http://www.slate.com/articles/health_and_science/medical_examiner/features/2008/the_sex_difference_evangelists/empathy_queens.html

Schiebinger, L., I. Klinge, I. Sánchez de Madariaga, and M. Schraudner (2011–13) 'Analyzing Sex', *Gendered Innovations in Science, Health & Medicine, and Engineering.* http://genderedinnovations.stanford.edu/methods/sex.html, accessed 7 December 2013.

Schmidt, Malin (2011) 'Mænd kan jo ikke have et kvindejob', *Information*, 26 February. http://www.information.dk/260673

Schneider, Kimberly T., Louise F. Fitzgerald, and Suzanne Swan (1997) 'Job-Related and Psychological Effects of Sexual Harassment in the Workplace: Empirical Evidence from Two Organizations', *Journal of Applied Psychology* 82: 401–15.

Schreiber, Ronnee (2002) 'Playing "Femball"', in *Right Wing Women: From Conservatives to Extremists Around the World*, ed. Paola Bacchetta and Margaret Power (New York and London: Routledge), 211–24.

—— (2008) *Righting Feminism: Conservative Women & American Politics* (New York: Oxford University Press).

Schultz, Vicki (1998) 'Reconceptualizing Sexual Harassment', *Yale Law Journal* 107: 1683–732.

Schwalbe, Michael, Sandra Godwin, Daphne Holden, Douglas Schrock, Shealy Thompson, and Michele Wolkomir (2000) 'Generic Processes in the Reproduction of Inequality: An Interactionist Analysis', *Social Forces* 79: 419–52.

'The Science of Gender and Science—Pinker vs. Spelke: A Debate', *Edge*, 16 May 2005. http://www.edge.org/3rd_culture/debate05/debate05_index.html

Sellers, Patricia (2003) 'Power: Do Women Really Want It?' *Fortune*, 13 October. http://money.cnn.com/magazines/fortune/fortune_archive/2003/10/13/350932/

Sen, Amartya (1990) 'More than 100 Million Women are Missing', *The New York Review of Books*, 20 December.

Serbin, Lisa A., Diane Poulin-Dubois and Julie A. Eichstedt (2002) 'Infants' Responses to Gender-Inconsistent Events', *Infancy* 3: 531–42.

Shteir, Rachel (2012) 'Breadwomen', *The New York Times*, 15 April.

Slaughter, Ann Marie (2012) 'Why Women Still Can't Have It All', *The Atlantic* (July/August). http://www.theatlantic.com/magazine/archive/2012/07/why-women-still-cant-have-it-all/309020/

Smedley, Tim (2013) '"Glacial" Rate of Progress Brings Calls for Quotas', *Financial Times*, 19 September. http://www.ft.com/intl/cms/s/0/b6868fec-13b2-11e3-9289-00144feabdc0.html#axzz2lNUNiLQK

Smith, Nina, Valdemar Smith, and Mette Werner (2006) 'Do Women in Top Management Affect Firm Performance? A Panel Study of 2500 Danish Firms', *International Journal of Productivity & Performance Management* 55: 569–93.

Solon, Olivia (2012) 'Testosterone is to Blame for Financial Market Crashes, Says Neuroscientist', *Wired*, 13 July. http://www.wired.co.uk/news/archive/2012-2007/13/testosterone-financial-crisis

Sommer, Iris E., André Aleman, Anke Bouma, and René S. Kahn (2004) 'Do Women Really Have More Bilateral Language Representation Than Men? A Meta-Analysis of Functional Imaging Studies', *Brain* 127: 1845–52.

Sommer, Iris E., André Aleman, Metten Somers, Marco P. Boks, and René S. Kahn (2008) 'Sex Differences in Handedness, Asymmetry of the Planum Temporale and Functional Language Lateralization', *Brain Research* 1206: 76–88.

Stanton, Elizabeth Cady (2010) *Eighty Years and More: Reminiscences 1815–1897* (Charleston, SC: Bibliobazaar, Open Source).

Steele, Claude M. and Joshua Aronson (1995) 'Stereotype Threat and the Intellectual Test Performance of African-Americans', *Journal of Personality and Social Psychology* 69: 797–811.

Steinpreis, Rhea E., Katie A. Anders, and Dawn Ritzke (1999) 'The Impact of Gender on the Review of the Curricula Vitae of Job Applicants and Tenure Candidates: A National Empirical Study', *Sex Roles* 41: 509–28.

Stoetz, Fiona Harris (2001) 'Young Women in France and England, 1050–1300', *Journal of Women's History* 12: 22–46.

Summers, Lawrence H. (1992) 'Investing in All the People', Policy Research Working Paper Series 905 (Washington, DC: World Bank). http://www-wds.worldbank.org/servlet/WDSContentServer/WDSP/IB/1992/05/01/000009265_3961003011714/Rendered/PDF/multi_page.pdf

——— (2005) 'Remarks at NBER Conference on Diversifying the Science & Engineering Workforce', 14 January. http://www.harvard.edu/president/speeches/summers_2005/nber.php

Szalavitz, Maia and Bruce D. Perry (2010) *Born for Love: Why Empathy Is Essential—and Endangered* (New York: William Morrow).

Thomas, David A. (2004) 'Diversity as Strategy', *Harvard Business Review* (September): 98–108.

Tischler, Linda (2004) 'Where Are the Women?' *Fast Company*, February. http://www.fastcompany.com/48593/where-are-women

Toft, Dorte (2012) 'Berlingske Business', blog post 'Danmark som frizone for "Hold kæft, kælling". Fordel?', 22 April. http://bizzen.blogs.business.dk/2012/04/22/danmark-som-frizone-for-hold-kaeft-kaelling-fordel/

Tong, Rosemarie (2007) 'Feminist Thought in Transition: Never a Dull Moment', *Social Science Journal* 44: 23–39.

Torry, Harriet (2013) '30% Female Quota for German Boards Proposed', *The Wall Street Journal*, 18 November. http://online.wsj.com/news/articles/SB10001424052702303531204579205452997816042

Traister, Rebecca (2012) 'How the "War On Women" Quashed Feminist Stereotypes', *The Washington Post*, 11 May. http://articles.washingtonpost.com/2012-2005-11/opinions/35458661_1_anti-feminist-feminist-stereotypes-bella-abzug

Tversky, Amos and Daniel Kahneman (1974) 'Judgment under Uncertainty: Heuristics and Biases', *Science* 185: 1124–31.

UNESCO (2010) *Global Education Digest 2010: Comparing Education Statistics across the World*, (Montreal: UNESCO Institute for Statistics). http://www.uis.unesco.org/Library/Documents/GED_2010_EN.pdf

United Nations (2010) *The World's Women 2010* (New York: United Nations).

—— (2013) 'Governance'. http://www.un.org/en/globalissues/governance/, accessed 8 March 2013.

United Nations Office on Drugs and Crime (2011) Global Study on Homicide. http://www.unodc.org/documents/data-and-analysis/statistics/Homicide/Globa_study_on_homicide_2011_web.pdf

Valian, Virginia (2005) 'Beyond Gender Schemas: Improving the Advancement of Women in Academia', *Hypatia* 20: 198–213.

Vervenioti, Tasoula (2002) 'Charity and Nationalism: The Greek Civil War and the Entrance of Right-Wing Women into Politics', in *Right Wing Women: From Conservatives to Extremists Around the World*, ed. Paola Bacchetta and Margaret Power (New York and London: Routledge), 115–26.

Vorauer, Jacquie and Sandra M. Kumhyr (2001) 'Is This About You or Me? Self-Versus Other-Directed Judgments and Feelings in Response to Intergroup Interaction', *Personality and Social Psychology Bulletin* 27: 706–19.

Wallis, C. (2004) 'The Case for Staying Home: Why More Young Moms are Opting Out of the Rat Race', *Time*, 22 March.

Warming, Kenn (2012) 'For Better or For Worse: Experiences of Men in Caring Occupations', in *Men, Masculinity and the Common Good in an Era of Economic Uncertainty*, ed. Phillip W. Schnarrs and James P. Maurino (Maurino, TN: Men's Studies Press), 48–69.

Weeks v. *Southern Bell Telephone Co.*, 408 F.2d 228 (1969) (5th Circuit Court of Appeals).

West, Martha S. and John W. Curtis (2006) 'AAUP Faculty Gender Equity Indicators 2006', American Association of University Professors. http://www.aaup.org/reports-publications/publications/see-all/aaup-faculty-gender-equity-indicators-2006

Williams, Joan (2000) *Unbending Gender: Why Family and Work Conflict and What to Do About It* (New York: Oxford University Press).

Wittenberg-Cox, Avivah (2008) *Why Women Mean Business: Understanding the Emergence of our Next Economic Revolution* (London: John Wiley & Sons).

Woodzicka, Julie A. and Marianne LaFrance (2001) 'Real Versus Imagined Gender Harassment', *Journal of Social Issues* 57: 15–30.

Working Mother (2011). '100 Best Companies 2011', Executive Summary. http://www.workingmother.com/best-companies/2011-working-mother-100-best-companies.

World Economic Forum (2013) 'The Global Gender Gap Report 2013'. http:/ http://www.weforum.org/reports/global-gender-gap-report-2013/www.weforum.org/reports/global-gender-gap-report-2013

World Health Organization (2011) *Global Status Report on Alcohol and Health*. http://www.who.int/substance_abuse/publications/global_alcohol_report/en/

——(2013) 'Suicide Rates per 100,000 by Country, Year and Sex'. http://www.who.int/mental_health/prevention/suicide_rates/en/, accessed 29 July 2013.

Young, Rebecca M. and Evan Balaba (2006) 'Psychoneuroindoctrinology', *Nature* 443 (12 October): 634.

Zosuls, Kristina M., Diane N. Ruble, Catherine S. Tamis-LeMonda, Patrick E. Shrout, Marc H. Bornstein and Faith K. Greulich (2009) 'The Acquisition of Gender Labels in Infancy: Implications for Sex-Typed Play', *Developmental Psychology* 45: 688–701.

INDEX